Buying a Home
in
Cyprus

A Survival Handbook

by
Anne Hall

SURVIVAL BOOKS • LONDON • ENGLAND

First published 2000 (as Buying a Home in Greece & Cyprus)
Second Edition 2001 (as Buying a Home in Greece & Cyprus)
Third Edition 2005

Survival Books Limited,
26 York Street, London W1U 6PZ, United Kingdom
☎ +44 (0)20-7788 7644, 🖷 +44 (0)870-762 3212
✉ info@survivalbooks.net
💻 www.survivalbooks.net
To order books, please refer to page 299.

British Library Cataloguing in Publication Data.
A CIP record for this book is available
from the British Library.
ISBN 1 901130 64 9

Printed and bound in Finland by WS Bookwell

ACKNOWLEDGEMENTS

My sincere thanks to all those who contributed to the successful publication of the third edition of this book, in particular those who took the time and trouble to read and comment on the draft versions. I would especially like to thank Joanna Styles, friend and fellow Survival Books writer, for her tireless advice, support and encouragement, David Hampshire, Joe and Kerry Laredo (editing, proofreading and dtp) and Jim Watson for his illustrations, cartoons, maps and cover. My special thanks go to all the people in Cyprus who gave me the benefit of their experience and professional expertise, particularly Chris Calogirou, a registered estate agent of long standing in Limassol, his associate in the UK, Andrew Creswell of JAF Marketing, and Areti Charidemou, of Areti Charidemou and Associates, a Limassol-based lawyer. All three patiently answered my questions, checked my material and showed me the kindness for which the Cypriot people are deservedly famous.

TITLES BY SURVIVAL BOOKS

Alien's Guides
Britain; France

The Best Places To Buy A Home
France; Spain

Buying A Home
Abroad; Cyprus; Florida;
France; Greece; Ireland; Italy;
Portugal; South Africa; Spain;
Buying, Selling & Letting
Property (UK)

**Foreigners Abroad: Triumphs
& Disasters**
France; Spain

Lifeline Regional Guides
Costa Blanca; Costa del Sol;
Dordogne/Lot; Normandy;
Poitou-Charentes

Living And Working
Abroad; America;
Australia; Britain; Canada;
The European Union;
The Far East; France; Germany;
The Gulf States & Saudi Arabia;
Holland, Belgium & Luxembourg;
Ireland; Italy; London;
New Zealand; Spain;
Switzerland

Making A Living
France; Spain

Other Titles
Renovating & Maintaining
Your French Home;
Retiring Abroad

Order forms are on page 299.

WHAT READERS & REVIEWERS

When you buy a model plane for your child, a video recorder, or some new computer gizmo, you get with it a leaflet or booklet pleading 'Read Me First', or bearing large friendly letters or bold type saying 'IMPORTANT – follow the instructions carefully'. This book should be similarly supplied to all those entering France with anything more durable than a 5-day return ticket. It is worth reading even if you are just visiting briefly, or if you have lived here for years and feel totally knowledgeable and secure. But if you need to find out how France works then it is indispensable. Native French people probably have a less thorough understanding of how their country functions. – Where it is most essential, the book is most up to the minute.

LIVING FRANCE

Rarely has a 'survival guide' contained such useful advice. This book dispels doubts for first-time travellers, yet is also useful for seasoned globetrotters – In a word, if you're planning to move to the USA or go there for a long-term stay, then buy this book both for general reading and as a ready-reference.

AMERICAN CITIZENS ABROAD

It is everything you always wanted to ask but didn't for fear of the contemptuous put down – The best English-language guide – Its pages are stuffed with practical information on everyday subjects and are designed to complement the traditional guidebook.

SWISS NEWS

A complete revelation to me – I found it both enlightening and interesting, not to mention amusing.

CAROLE CLARK

Let's say it at once. David Hampshire's *Living and Working in France* is the best handbook ever produced for visitors and foreign residents in this country; indeed, my discussion with locals showed that it has much to teach even those born and bred in l'Hexagone. – It is Hampshire's meticulous detail which lifts his work way beyond the range of other books with similar titles. Often you think of a supplementary question and search for the answer in vain. With Hampshire this is rarely the case. – He writes with great clarity (and gives French equivalents of all key terms), a touch of humour and a ready eye for the odd (and often illuminating) fact. – This book is absolutely indispensable.

THE RIVIERA REPORTER

A mine of information – I may have avoided some embarrassments and frights if I had read it prior to my first Swiss encounters – Deserves an honoured place on any newcomer's bookshelf.

ENGLISH TEACHERS ASSOCIATION, SWITZERLAND

HAVE SAID ABOUT SURVIVAL BOOKS

What a great work, wealth of useful information, well-balanced wording and accuracy in details. My compliments!

THOMAS MÜLLER

This handbook has all the practical information one needs to set up home in the UK – The sheer volume of information is almost daunting – Highly recommended for anyone moving to the UK.

AMERICAN CITIZENS ABROAD

A very good book which has answered so many questions and even some I hadn't thought of – I would certainly recommend it.

BRIAN FAIRMAN

We would like to congratulate you on this work: it is really super! We hand it out to our expatriates and they read it with great interest and pleasure.

ICI (SWITZERLAND) AG

Covers just about all the things you want to know on the subject – In answer to the desert island question about the one how-to book on France, this book would be it – Almost 500 pages of solid accurate reading – This book is about enjoyment as much as survival.

THE RECORDER

It's so funny – I love it and definitely need a copy of my own – Thanks very much for having written such a humorous and helpful book.

HEIDI GUILIANI

A must for all foreigners coming to Switzerland.

ANTOINETTE O'DONOGHUE

A comprehensive guide to all things French, written in a highly readable and amusing style, for anyone planning to live, work or retire in France.

THE TIMES

A concise, thorough account of the DOs and DON'Ts for a foreigner in Switzerland – Crammed with useful information and lightened with humorous quips which make the facts more readable.

AMERICAN CITIZENS ABROAD

Covers every conceivable question that may be asked concerning everyday life – I know of no other book that could take the place of this one.

FRANCE IN PRINT

Hats off to *Living and Working in Switzerland*!

RONNIE ALMEIDA

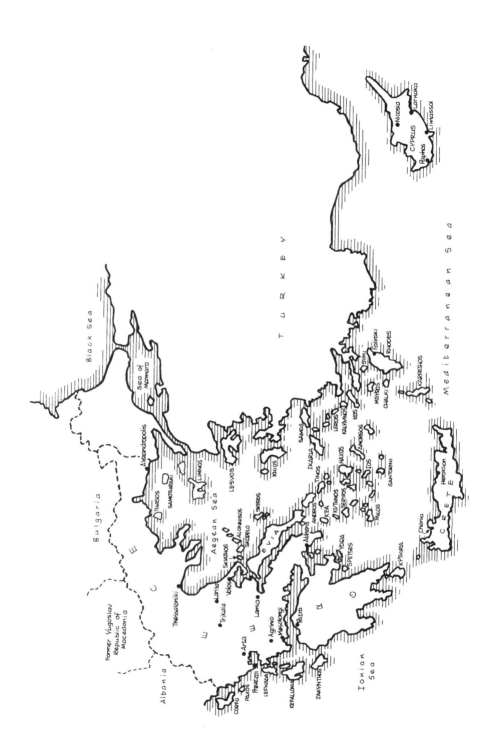

CONTENTS

4. MONEY MATTERS 127

5. THE PURCHASE PROCEDURE 141

6. MOVING HOUSE 155

7. TAXATION 169

11. NORTHERN CYPRUS 247

APPENDICES 263

INDEX 287

ORDER FORMS 299

NOTES 301

IMPORTANT NOTE

Readers should note that the laws and regulations concerning buying property in Cyprus aren't the same as in other countries and are liable to change periodically, especially since the Republic of Cyprus joined the European Union (EU) in May 2004. Cyprus is going through a transition period while adjusting to EU membership and laws are subject to change and revision. I cannot recommend too strongly that you always check with an official and reliable source (not necessarily the same) and take expert legal advice before paying any money or signing any legal documents. However, don't believe everything you're told or have read - even, dare I say it, in this book!

To help you obtain further information and verify data with official sources, useful addresses and references to other sources of information have been included in all chapters and in Appendices A, B and C. Important points have been emphasised throughout the book in bold print, some of which it would be expensive or foolish to disregard. Unless specifically stated, the reference to any company, organisation, product or publication in this book doesn't constitute an endorsement or recommendation.

THE AUTHOR

Anne Hall was born in the UK and began her working life at the BBC in London. Before having her children, she worked chiefly in broadcasting and television production, both for the BBC and for independent production companies. She studied English literature as a mature student at the University of London and began her freelance writing career after a family move to the Costa del Sol, Spain in 2002. She writes for UK publications and English-language publications in Spain. She has also written *Making a Living in Spain* for Survival Books. Anne is married with two children.

AUTHOR'S NOTES

- This book was originally published as *Buying a Home in Greece and Cyprus*.

- Except for Chapter 11, the information in this book applies only to the Republic of Cyprus and not to the self-proclaimed Turkish Republic of Northern Cyprus, occupied and recognised only by Turkey.

- Place names are written using the most common international form, but the Greek equivalent (using the English alphabet) most often used in Cyprus is also given.

- Frequent references are made to the European Union (EU), which comprises 25 countries, and to the European Economic Area (EEA), i.e. the EU countries plus Iceland, Liechtenstein and Norway.

- The currency of Cyprus is the Cypriot pound, abbreviated to CY£, which in May 2005 was roughly equivalent to GB£1.2/US$2.2/€1.7 (check the current rate, e.g. using an online currency converter, such as 🖳 www.xe.com/ucc). Cyprus hopes to have adopted the euro by 2007 or 2008.

- Prices quoted should be taken as estimates only, although they were mostly correct when going to print. Prices include value added tax unless otherwise indicated, although prices in Cyprus are sometimes quoted exclusive of tax.

- His/he/him (etc.) also mean her/she/her (no offence ladies!). This is done simply to make life easier for both the reader and, in particular, the author, and isn't intended to be sexist.

- Warnings and important points are shown in **bold** type.

- All spelling is British English and not American English.

- All times are shown using am (*ante meridiem*) for before noon and pm (*post meridiem*) for after noon. All times are local (see page 237).

- The following symbols are used in this book: ☎ (telephone), 🗐 (fax), 🖳 (internet) and ✉ (email).

- Lists of useful addresses, further information and useful websites are contained in **Appendices A, B** and **C** respectively.

- For those who are unfamiliar with the metric system of weights and measures, conversion tables are included in **Appendix D**.

- Maps of Cyprus are included in **Appendix E** and a map of the eastern Mediterranean is on page 6.

INTRODUCTION

If you're planning to buy a home in Cyprus or even just thinking about it, this is **THE BOOK** for you! Whether you want a villa, a townhouse, an apartment or a village house, a holiday or a permanent home, this book will help make your dreams come true. The purpose of *Buying a Home in Cyprus* is to provide you with the information necessary to help you choose the most favourable location and the most appropriate home to satisfy your individual requirements. Most importantly, it will help you avoid the pitfalls and risks associated with buying a home abroad, as homebuying for most people is one of the largest financial transactions they will undertake during their lifetimes.

You may already own property in your home country; however, buying a home in Cyprus (or in any foreign country) is a different matter altogether. One of the most common mistakes many people make when buying a home abroad is to assume that the laws and purchase procedures are the same as in their home country. Although the legal system in Cyprus bears many similarities to that of the UK, the purchase procedure is not the same! Buying property in Cyprus is generally safe, although if you don't obtain legal advice and follow the rules provided for your protection, a purchase can result in a serious financial loss – as some people have discovered to their cost.

Before buying a home in Cyprus you need to ask yourself exactly why you want to buy a home there? Do you 'simply' want a holiday home, is your primary concern a long-term investment, or do you wish to work or retire there? Where and what can you afford to buy? How will local taxes affect your investment? *Buying a Home in Cyprus* will help you answer these and many other questions. It won't, however, tell you where to live, what to buy, or, having made your decision, whether you will be happy – that part is up to you!

With a copy of *Buying a Home in Cyprus* to hand you will have a wealth of priceless information at your fingertips – information derived from a variety of sources, both official and unofficial from those who know Cyprus well and have long experience in the property market. This book will help reduce the risk of making an expensive mistake that you may regret later and will help you make informed decisions and calculated judgements instead of rash assumptions (forewarned is forearmed!). Most important of all, it should help you save money and repay your investment many times over.

The worldwide recession in the early '90s caused an upheaval in world property markets, during which many so-called 'gilt-edged' property investments went to the wall. However, property remains one of the best long-term investments and it's certainly one of the most pleasurable. Buying a home in Cyprus is a wonderful way to make new friends, broaden your horizons and revitalise your life – and it provides a welcome bolt-hole to recuperate from the stresses and strains of modern life. I trust this book will help you avoid pitfalls and smooth your way to many happy years in your new home, secure in the knowledge that you've made the right decision.

Good luck! **Anne Hall**
May 2005

1.

MAJOR CONSIDERATIONS

Buying a home abroad is not only a major financial commitment, but also a decision that can have a huge influence on other aspects of your life, including your health, security and safety, your family relationships and friendships, your lifestyle, your opinions and your outlook. You must take into consideration any restrictions that might affect your choice of location and type of property, such as whether you will need to learn another language and whether you will be able (or permitted) to find work if you want (or need) to. Think about whether you will be able to adapt to and enjoy the climate, whether it will be possible for you to take your pets with you, and not least, whether you will be able to afford the kind of home (and lifestyle) that you want. In order to ensure that you're making the right move, it's as well to face these and other major considerations before making any irrevocable decisions. This chapter addresses the most serious concerns of anyone planning to buy a home and live in Cyprus, including the climate, economy, cost of property, cost of living, permits and visas, language, health and pets.

IMPORTANT NOTE

With the exception of Chapter 11, this book deals primarily with buying a home in The Republic of Cyprus. When it refers to Cyprus, it's referring to the southern two-thirds of the island, administered by the Greek Cypriot government. In Chapter 11 there's an overview of the property market in what's known as the Turkish Republic of Northern Cyprus (TRNC). This is the northern third of the island, which has a separate, Turkish Cypriot government but is only recognised internationally by Turkey. Chapter 11 also looks briefly at the 'Cyprus Problem' and how the political and legal situation on this divided island may affect you if you decide to buy a home in Northern Cyprus.

WHY CYPRUS?

Cyprus, famous as the legendary birthplace of Aphrodite, the goddess of love, has many attractions, not least its reliable sunshine, blue skies and excellent sandy beaches. It's an island of great beauty with a wide variety of contrasting landscapes, including mountains with vine-clad foothills, citrus and olive groves, and pine and cedar forests. The island has a rich cultural heritage and a wealth of fascinating archaeological sites. Timeless villages are a short drive from modern, cosmopolitan towns. Cyprus is a botanist's dream with an abundance of wild flowers. Almost 2,000 species of plant flourish there, over 100 of which are found nowhere else.

Cyprus (pop. 802,500) is Europe's southernmost point and the Mediterranean's third-largest island after Sardinia and Sicily, being also the most easterly of the Mediterranean islands. It covers 9,251km² (5,781mi²) and stretches 240km (150mi) from west to east and 96km (60mi) from north to south. The island, although politically part of Europe, is geographically nearer the Middle East, with Turkey to the north (a mere 69km/43mi away) and Israel, Lebanon and Syria to the east. Because of its geographical position, the island has been of huge strategic importance to invaders from Europe and Asia throughout its history. Cyprus has been home to Assyrians, Egyptians, Persians, Romans, Byzantines, Crusaders, Lusignans, Venetians, Ottoman Turks and the British – it has been termed the meeting point of the continents of Europe, Asia and Africa – and as a result has developed a unique character and traditions. Its wealth of fascinating remains include Greek and Roman temples and monuments, Byzantine churches and medieval castles, all of which co-exist happily with cosmopolitan hotels, bustling shopping centres and modern housing developments. Watersports, particularly snorkelling and diving, are popular on the coast, and the central area, the Mesaoria plain, is the island's market garden.

Today, Cyprus has a distinctly Hellenic feel, having much more in common with Greece than simply its language. Cyprus benefited hugely from the legacy of its last rulers, the British, who were largely responsible for the island's excellent communications, its legal system and public services, good health system and schools, low crime rate, road system (where traffic drives on the left) and, not least, the English language, which is spoken by some 90 per cent of the population. For Britons, all this gives the island a comforting air of familiarity alongside all the benefits of a Mediterranean location.

Around 60 per cent of foreign homebuyers in Cyprus are British and the island is also popular with Russian and German citizens, although in far smaller numbers. British buyers are usually looking for a holiday home or considering Cyprus as a retirement location. It's extremely popular with British retirees, although since 2001 property agents have noticed a rise in interest from younger people with families who are considering living and working in Cyprus.

Most foreigners, especially the British, are concentrated around Paphos and the west of the island, with smaller numbers preferring Limassol (*Lemesos*), which combines a cosmopolitan town with proximity to the beach. For details of all areas see **Chapter 3**.

Property

Many people buy a holiday home in Cyprus with a view to living there permanently or semi-permanently when they retire. The island has always been a popular location with British buyers, especially retirees, and almost 30,000 of them own homes there, a further 10,000 choosing to rent properties. However, estate agents are now seeing an increased demand from younger people with young families who want to work or start a business. Those who have lived in Cyprus for many years and been used to a steady, if rather unremarkable, property market are beginning to see property supplements appear in newspapers and growing numbers of property magazines for sale. This is a relatively new departure for Cyprus and illustrates the dramatic change in the property market on the island during the last few years.

There are many excellent reasons for buying a home in Cyprus, although it's important not to be under any illusions about what you can expect. The first and most important question you need to ask yourself is **exactly** why you want to buy a home in Cyprus? For example, are you seeking a holiday home or a more permanent home because you want to live and work on the island or perhaps retire there? If you're looking for a second or holiday home, remember that flight times from the UK to Cyprus are far longer than to Spain or France (around four hours), which may affect how often you and your family can enjoy a property.

Perhaps you have plans to work or start a business in Cyprus, which has been made far easier for EU citizens since Cyprus became a member of the Union in May 2004. If this is your long-term plan, you will be faced with a completely different set of criteria than if you were 'simply' buying a holiday home. You should look at the cost of living and the cost of property in the different areas of Cyprus to see what suits you best. If you have school-age children, you should consider what their schooling options will be. You may want a property that's more accessible to main roads and the major towns. Does it have reliable postal services and access to telephone lines? Can it be connected to all the necessary services?

Before buying, you must also ask yourself: Can I really afford to buy a home in Cyprus? What of the future? Is my income secure and protected against inflation and currency fluctuations? Buying a home in Cyprus is cheaper than buying in Spain or France and can be a good, long-term investment. (For an overview of the cost of property in Cyprus and the cost of living see pages 27 and 28 respectively.) The country has recently become a healthier market for investors, having experienced a property boom in anticipation of joining the EU. Cyprus signed its accession treaty in April 2003 and became a full EU member in May 2004. The market stabilised a little at the end of 2004, but a thriving property market seems set to continue in 2005, with new developments springing up all over the island.

Laws relating to property ownership in the Republic of Cyprus have changed since the country joined the EU but there are still certain restrictions on property purchase by non-resident foreigners, although it's thought that by 2009 these will be lifted for all EU citizens. The current situation (early 2005) as it affects foreign buyers is explained in **Chapter 5**, but you should always check the latest regulations and laws with a professional legal adviser.

If you plan to buy property in Cyprus, you should also be aware that the island has been divided since the Turkish invasion in 1974. There's information about this and what's known as the 'Cyprus Problem' in **Chapter 11**.

If you're considering letting your property to offset the mortgage and running costs, you should be aware of the following letting restriction:

 Cypriot law states that property owned by foreigners who aren't resident in Cyprus can be let only long-term to resident Cypriots or EU nationals. In other words, short-term holiday lets are illegal (see Chapter 9). If you want to let your property in Cyprus, you should obtain professional legal advice on your particular situation.

Research

Before deciding to buy a property in Cyprus, it's advisable to do extensive research and read a number of books, like this one, which are especially written for those planning to live or work in Cyprus. The internet is also a valuable research tool and you can find out plenty of useful information from the list of Cyprus websites included in **Appendix C**). It also helps to study specialist property and lifestyle magazines such as *Homes Overseas, International Homes* and *A Place in the Sun* (see **Appendix B**) and visit overseas property exhibitions. You can find out about exhibitions from the magazines mentioned above.

SURVIVAL TIP
Bear in mind that the cost of investing in a few books or magazines (and other research) is tiny comparedwith the expense of making a big mistake. However, don't believe everything you read, but check all important information yourself!

For further information on researching before buying, see page 76.

Advantages & Disadvantages

There are both advantages and disadvantages to buying a home in Cyprus, although for most people the benefits outweigh any drawbacks. Some of the many advantages have been outlined above; here is a summary of the main advantages.

- Guaranteed sunshine and high temperatures for most of the year;
- A very low crime rate;
- Low taxation, especially for retirees;
- An excellent quality of life;
- A particularly low cost of living;
- A slow, relaxed pace of life;
- The friendliness and warmth of the Cypriot people;
- 90 per cent of the Cypriot population speak English.

For Britons, there's the added advantage that Cypriot legal and financial procedures are similar to those in the UK.

Naturally, there are also a few disadvantages, including:

- Unexpected renovation and restoration costs if you buy an old property (and if you don't do your homework);
- The dangers of buying a property with debts and other problems (if you don't take legal advice);
- Restrictions on letting your property (see **Chapter 9**);
- Overcrowding in popular tourist areas during the peak summer season;
- Traffic congestion and pollution in some towns;
- Water shortages in some regions (particularly during the summer);
- The expense and time spent getting to and from Cyprus if you own a home there.

BUYING FOR INVESTMENT

Since the year 2000, property in Cyprus has gradually become a better investment, not just in the popular coastal areas, but increasingly in the main towns too. Property investment doesn't necessarily mean big business investment (although this is happening more and more in

Cyprus) but can be on a personal level for the benefit of you and your family. In a sense, any home you buy (in Cyprus or elsewhere) is an investment, in that it provides you with rent-free accomodation. It may also yield a return in terms of increased value (a capital gain), although that gain may be difficult to realise unless you 'trade down' or move to another area where property is cheaper. There are essentially four main categories of investment property:

- A holiday home, which can provide a return in many different ways. It can provide your family with rent-free accommodation while (hopefully) maintaining its value. It may also produce a capital gain if property values rise faster than inflation (as in recent years). Subject to local restrictions (see **Chapter 9**), it can also generate an income from letting.

- A home for your children or relatives, which may realise a capital gain;

- A business property, which could be anything from a private home with bed and breakfast or guest accommodation, to a shop or office;

- A property purchased purely for investment, which could be a capital investment or provide a regular income, or both. Many people have invested in property to provide an income on their retirement. In Cyprus there are restrictions on letting (see **Buying to Let** below and **Chapter 9**).

A property investment should be considered over the medium to long term: a minimum of five and preferably 10 to 15 years. Bear in mind that property isn't always 'as safe as houses' and investments can be risky over the short to medium term; there may be income tax and capital gains tax to pay (see **Chapter 7**) when you sell a second home and you also need to ensure that you recoup purchase and sale fees.

Buying to Let

Buying to let isn't as straightforward in Cyprus as in most other popular European countries. **If you aren't a resident of Cyprus and you're planning to buy property to let, you should bear in mind that the law works to protect the tourist industry, which means that you aren't permitted to let your property on a short-term basis to holidaymakers.** However, there are ways you can let your property legally and many people do let their properties on a short-term basis to friends and family. Always take professional advice on your particular situation; see **Chapter 9** for more details.

If, after receiving professional advice, you decide to let your property in Cyprus, there are certain financial considerations to be made. The rent should cover the mortgage (if applicable), running costs and void periods (when the property isn't let). **Bear in mind that competition and rental rates vary with the region and town, and an area with high rents and occupancy rates today may not be so fruitful next year.** The situation is changing particularly fast in Cyprus as the government responds to the influx of property buyers by improving the island's infrastructure so that new areas become popular while others may stagnate. Gross rental yields (the annual rent as a percentage of a property's value) are around 8 per cent, depending on the area, and net yields (after expenses have been deducted) are 2 to 3 per cent lower.

Before deciding to invest in a property, you should ask yourself the following questions:

- Can I afford to tie up capital in the medium to long term, i.e. at least five years?
- How likely is the value of the property to rise during this period?
- Can I rely on a regular income from my investment? If so, how easy will it be to generate that income? Will I be able to pay the mortgage if the property is empty and, if so, for how long?
- Am I aware of all the risks involved and how comfortable am I with taking those risks (see above and **Chapter 9**)?
- Do I have enough information to make a rational decision?

See also **Mortgages** on page 136, **Taxation of Property Income** on page 176, **Location** on page 56.

CLIMATE

Hardly surprisingly, the overwhelming attraction of Cyprus (apart from the tax incentives) for most foreigners is its excellent climate, with an average of 340 days' sunshine per year. Most of Cyprus has a climate classed as 'arid Mediterranean' and it's the hottest, driest island in the Mediterranean. There's no rain during the summer months and relatively little falls in May and October. The Troodos mountains are the wettest part of the south of the island and have an average of around 200mm (49in) of rain annually, although from January to March rain falls as snow. In common with many southern European countries, Cyprus periodically suffers from lack of rainfall leading to droughts and water shortages. Frequent weather forecasts are broadcast on TV and radio and published in daily newspapers.

Temperature

Approximate average maximum/minimum temperatures for Cyprus' main towns are shown below in Centigrade and Fahrenheit (in brackets). The sea is generally warm most of the year in Cyprus, which enjoys average temperatures of 19°C (68°F) in winter and 28°C (86°F) in the summer months.

Location	Spring	Summer	Autumn	Winter
Larnaca (*Larnaka*)	32/12 (70/38)	32/12 (90/53)	27/8 (80/47)	21/3 (70/38)
Nicosia (*Lefkosa*)	36/10 (96/50)	40/17 (103/63)	28/6 (82/42)	22/2 (71/34)
Paphos (*Pafos*)	30/12 (86/54)	33/19 (91/65)	26/10 (79/50)	22/5 (71/41)

To make a rough conversion from °C to °F, multiply by two and add 30.

Summer

Summers are generally very hot and last from May to late September, when temperatures average 30°C (90°F) on the coast and 38°C (100°F) inland, except in the Troodos mountains, which become a cool haven. Some parts of the island can be extremely hot and dusty in the months of July and August, despite the sea breezes – especially Nicosia (*Lefkosia*), positioned as it is, away from the coast in the middle of the island.

Winter

Winters in Cyprus can hardly be classed as such (at least not by northern European standards), although in some areas the temperature may drop suddenly. Along with Portugal's southern Algarve coast and Spain's Costa del Sol, Cyprus is one of the warmest areas in Europe in winter, when temperatures rarely fall below 16°C (62°F), with the exception of the Troodos mountains, where snow falls in winter and skiing is popular. The rainy season coincides with the winter months from December to February, with an average of 14 days' rain in January.

Spring & Autumn

As in all southern European countries, spring and autumn are the most pleasant seasons, when it's warm and sunny but rarely too hot.

However, spring and autumn are short compared with northern European seasons and April is the height of spring when the landscape is covered in flowers, before becoming dry and dusty until winter.

ECONOMY

If you're considering buying a property in Cyprus, the financial implications of the purchase are usually one of the major factors that influence your decision. Those implications include the state of not only the Cypriot economy, but also that of your home country (or the country where you earn your income). This (and your assets and job security there) may dictate how much you can afford to spend on a purchase, whether you can maintain your mortgage payments and pay for the upkeep of a property, and how often you can afford to visit Cyprus each year. Your home country's economy is also important if you plan to retire to Cyprus and will be primarily living on a pension, as pension income is rarely guaranteed. If you intend to live and work in Cyprus, and especially if you plan to run a business, the state of the economy will be a major consideration.

The Republic of Cyprus has a generally prosperous economy, with a relatively low rate of inflation (2.1 per cent in 2004) and unemployment (4.8 per cent in 2004), according to government figures. More than 40 per cent of the land on the island is given over to food production. Its main crops are cereals, citrus fruits and the famous Cyprus potatoes. The country's main industries are consumer products, finance and banking, IT, food and drink, hotel and catering and tourism.

Tourism has been the dominant sector in the Cypriot economy since the late '70s. Between the '70s and the '90s, Cyprus experienced an enormous growth in the number of tourists visiting the island, from around 165,000 in 1976 to almost 1.5 million in 1989 and almost 3 million in 2001. The economy relies heavily on the tourist industry and so can be somewhat volatile and affected by fluctuations in other western European economies and world politics.

Cyprus enjoys a strategic position between Europe and the Middle East and was for a long time an attractive location for 'offshore' enterprises. However, offshore taxation benefits in Cyprus changed in 2003 in preparation for the island's accession to the EU and there are no longer any offshore companies in Cyprus. Nevertheless, Cyprus is still an attractive location for foreign investors thanks to its 10 per cent corporate income tax rate, which is the lowest in the EU.

Gross domestic product (GDP) per capita in Cyprus is CY£10,787 (€18,550, GB£12,766), which is 80 per cent of the EU average. Steady economic growth has resulted in increased employment within the services sector (particularly finance, property and business services), which accounts for around three-quarters of the workforce. Strengthening domestic demand pushed GDP growth up to 3.7 per cent at the end of 2004. According to EU figures, foreigners account for 11.7 per cent of the workforce. They're generally employed in the tourist industry, in hotels and restaurants, manufacturing and the retail sector, making up a shortfall in local labour.

Economic policy on the island during the last three or four years has been driven by a need to meet the critieria for entry into the EU. This has had a mixed effect on the economy. Tax reforms in 2003 (see **Chapter 7**) in anticipation of EU entry combined with slightly reduced tourism figures had a negative impact on the country's economy, creating a significant budget deficit. This meant that Cyprus failed to meet the EU's criteria to enter the Exchange Rate Mechanism (ERM), which is a first step towards adopting the euro as its currency. The government has since instigated some tough economic measures and managed to control the deficit to just under 5 per cent of GDP. As a result, the country hopes to be using the euro by 2007 or early 2008.

COST OF PROPERTY

One of the major considerations (or **the** major consideration) for anyone contemplating buying a home in Cyprus is whether they can afford to buy a home there and, if so, what kind of home they can afford and where. Cyprus has a flourishing property market, particularly since it was agreed that the it would join the European Union. At the beginning of 2005 it was beginning to stabilise, but there's still a significant and increasing demand.

Foreign buyers, especially British retirees, have traditionally been attracted to Cyprus because of the relatively low cost of property compared with many other European countries. This is still the case, although prices have risen faster since 2000. On average, prices are around 40 per cent lower than in Spain and around 50 per cent lower than in France. It's still possible to find older village homes and newer properties at relatively reasonable prices.

Property values generally increased in line with inflation up to around 1999. Since 2000, prices have increased faster than inflation and the property market experienced something of a boom in anticipation of the island's EU membership. Prices have seen average increases of around 15 per cent per year since then, although prices in many resort areas and new developments have risen annually by as much as 50 per cent. In early 2002, a detached house in Paphos, a popular area with British buyers, sold for around CY£98,000. In 2005, a similar house would be expected to sell for twice that price, depending on the location. Many experts believe that the market is now stabilising. Although house prices rose around 10 per cent in 2004, the market slowed towards the end of the year and a 5 per cent rise is forecast for 2005.

Despite the recent increases, a slice of the good life in Cyprus doesn't have to cost a fortune, with old village homes available from as little as CY£60,000, modern apartments from around CY£75,000 and fairly large detached villas from around CY£250,000, depending on the location. (Prices in some of the more popular resort areas, especially in Paphos and on the golf resorts, are considerably higher.) If you're seeking a substantial home with a sizeable plot and a swimming pool, you will usually need to spend over CY£350,000 (depending on the area). For details of the popular areas in Cyprus and a guide to the prices of specific types of property, see **Property Prices** on page 94.

If you're planning to buy a property in Cyprus, you should take into account any legal fees and taxes, such as transfer fees, property tax, stamp duty and registration of the mortgage, if you have one (see **Fees** on page 97). These usually amount to around 11 per cent of the purchase price. Don't forget that if and when you sell your property you will need to recover all the above costs.

For many Cypriots, owning land and their own home is high on the list of priorities, so Cypriot home ownership is fairly high. Generally, locals don't buy and sell for profit and consider property less as a financial investment and more of an investment in their family's future. Property is often kept in the family once it has been purchased and some people buy extra land to pass on to their children so that they in turn can build their own property. **You shouldn't expect to make a quick profit when buying property in Cyprus, although more and more agents are now offering what they call 'investment possibilities' because of the increasingly healthy property market.** It's usually wiser to do as the Cypriots do: look upon a property as an investment in your family's future happiness, rather than merely in financial terms.

COST OF LIVING

No doubt you would like to try to estimate how far your Cyprus pounds (currently worth around GB£1.18 and €1.72) will stretch and how much money (if any) you will have left after paying your bills. The cost of living is relatively low in Cyprus, with prices around 25 per cent lower than in most northern European countries. Limassol was recently highlighted as one of the five least expensive cities in Europe. As expected, prices have risen slightly since the country's EU accession, and a survey carried out by the Cyprus Consumers' Association in 2004 showed that prices had risen on average by 1.6 per cent since then.

According to the results of the Cypriot government's Household Budget Survey 2004, average monthly outgoings for a single person are CY£647, for a couple CY£970 and for a couple with two children, CY£1,358. A couple owning their home can live fairly comfortably on a net income of between CY£6,000 and CY£7,000 per year (many pensioners live on less).

It's obviously difficult to calculate an average cost of living, as your expenditure depends on your circumstances and lifestyle. Shopping for expensive consumer goods such as hi-fi equipment, electronic goods, computers and photographic equipment, for example, is generally better value than in many other European countries and North America, with many well known brands available in shops in the main towns. The difference in your food bill, on the other hand, will depend on what you eat and where you lived before coming to Cyprus. Food is cheaper than in most northern European countries and around CY£250 will feed two adults for a month, including (inexpensive) wine, but excluding luxuries like fillet steak, caviar and imported delicacies. Local wines and spirits are good value and eating out is affordable, a meal for two averaging CY£25. It's a good idea to avoid the tourist areas, where prices are higher than average.

The Consumers' Association publishes *The Cyprus Good Food Guide*, which is updated annually and includes information on eating out and restaurants which offer good value. Consumer publications from the UK, US and Ireland are available at the CA's reading library in Nicosia (☎ 22-516 112–4, 🖳 www.cyprusconsumers.org.cy).

PERMITS & VISAS

Before making any plans to buy a home in Cyprus, you must check whether you will need a visa or residence permit and ensure that you will be permitted to use your property when you wish and for whatever purpose you have in mind.

If there's a possibility that you or a family member will wish to live or work permanently in Cyprus, you should enquire whether it will be possible before making any plans to buy a home there. In general, foreigners may buy property in Cyprus (although there are some restrictions), but they aren't allowed to remain in the country for longer than 90 days without obtaining a residence permit. **This includes EU citizens.**

Permit and visa infringements are taken very seriously by the authorities and non-compliance can result in severe penalties, including fines and deportation.

Entry Restrictions

Notwithstanding normal entry requirements (detailed below), Cyprus has certain entry restrictions (some of which are due to the Turkish invasion of the country in 1974). You will be refused admission to the country if you fall into any of the following categories:

- You hold a passport issued by the Turkish Republic of Northern Cyprus.

- You've entered Cyprus via any port or airport in the northern part of the island.

- You hold a passport from the former Republic of Yugoslavia which bears the renewal stamp "Macedonia". (You will be allowed entry if you have a Yugoslav passport without this stamp.)

You may also have problems entering the Republic of Cyprus (and possibly Greece) if you have a northern Cyprus stamp on your passport. This applies to all those entering Cyprus, irrespective of nationality and length of stay. If you plan to go northern Cyprus, it's advisable to get immigration officials there to stamp a separate piece of paper on entry, rather than your passport. This is a commonly accepted procedure. If you want to go on a day trip from the Republic of Cyprus to the northern part of the island, the Turkish Cypriot immigration officials will simply give you a day pass and not stamp your passport. For further details about the division of the country and how it may affect you, see **Chapter 11**.

Visitors

Subject to the entry restrictions outlined above, any citizen of the following countries can enter Cyprus and remain for up to 90 days with their passport or national identity card, provided it includes their photograph: Andorra, Argentina, Australia, Austria, Bulgaria, Belgium, Bolivia, Brazil, Brunei Darussalam, Canada, Chile, Costa Rica, Croatia, Czech Republic, Denmark, Ecuador, El Salvador, Estonia, Finland, France, Germany, Greece, Guatemala, Honduras, Hungary, Iceland, Ireland, Israel, Italy, Japan, Latvia, Liechtenstein, Lithuania, Luxembourg, Malaysia, Malta, Mexico, Monaco, Netherlands, New Zealand, Nicaragua, Norway, Panama, Paraguay, Poland, Portugal,

Republic of Korea (South), Romania, Russia, San Marino, Singapore, Slovakia, Slovenia, Spain, Sweden, Switzerland, United Kingdom, United States of America, Uruguay, Vatican City, Venezuela, Hong-Kong Special Administrative Region (holders of HKSAR passports only) and Macao Special Administrative Region (Macao SAR passports only) provided they're in possession of a valid passport. **A visa is required by nationals of all other countries.**

Full lists of procedures and requirement are available on the website of either the Cyprus Government (⌨ www.cyprus.gov.cy) or the Cyprus Tourism Organisation (⌨ www.cyprustourism.org). If you require a visa, you should contact the nearest Embassy or Consulate of the Republic of Cyprus (listed in **Appendix A**) **before** planning any visit. Visa applications must be submitted in person and include all supporting documentation such as proposed travel arrangements and (if you're visiting for business) an official letter from a company in Cyprus. If you wish to study in Cyprus, you must provide a letter from the school or university confirming details and the duration of your course.

As a foreigner, you're advised always to carry your passport or residence permit (if you have one), which serves as an identity card, a document all local nationals must carry by law. **You can be asked to produce your identification papers at any time by the police and other officials and if you don't have them you can be taken to a police station and questioned.**

Temporary Residence Permits

If you plan to stay longer than 90 days, you must apply for a Temporary Residence Employment (TRE) permit at your nearest Immigration Office (listed below). After five years, you can apply for permanent residence. See also **Working** on page 33.

● **Larnaca** – Larnaca Police Station, Piale Pasia, Larnaca (☎ 24-804 242);

● **Limassol** – Limassol Police Station, Kyrillou Loukareos, Kakos Center, Limassol (☎ 25-805 200);

● **Nicosia** – Nicosia Police Station, Parodos Leoforou, RIC, Nicosia (General Information: ☎ 22-802 334, Registration: ☎ 22-802 348);

● **Paphos** – Paphos Police Station,Ypolohagou N.Papageorgiou, Polykatikia, PA.SY.DI First Floor, 8011 Paphos (☎ 26-806 200).

There are several kinds of TRE permit, including the following:

● **Category A** – Self-employed in agriculture;

● **Category B** – Self-employed in mining;

- **Category C/D** – Self-employed in a trade or profession;
- **Category E** – Offered permanent employment;
- **Category F** – Not working (e.g. retired).

For a Category F permit, you're required to prove that you can support yourself financially, and you won't be allowed to do work of any kind once you have this type of permit. The official wording is: 'Persons who possess and have fully and freely at their disposal a secured annual income, high enough to give them a decent living in Cyprus, without [their] having to engage in any business, trade or profession.'

Make sure that you complete the correct form when applying. If you're in doubt, check with your lawyer or Immigration Office staff.

If you're looking for a job but haven't found one when you need to apply for a TRE permit, the Immigration Department may want to see evidence that you can support yourself financially until you find a job. Each case is considered on its own merits; if you can supply bank statements to prove your financial status, your application will be looked upon more favourably.

A TRE permit should be applied for at least a month before the end of your first 90 days in Cyprus. The following is a guide to the documents required to obtain a TRE permit, but always check with the relevant Immigration Office (see above) for up-to-date requirements:

- Your passport, valid for at least a year;
- Four passport photographs;
- Your birth certificate(s) and, if appropriate, marriage certificate;
- Evidence of income or financial self-sufficency, including bank statements from a bank in Cyprus showing average balance or pension payments, where appropriate. Note that your annual income should be in the region of CY£6,000 per person, plus around CY£3,000 for each dependent person, although there are no set limits and each case is considered on its own merits.
- Evidence of medical insurance cover (if you aren't covered by Cypriot social insurance – see **Social Insurance** on page 186);
- Evidence of residence in the form of a title deed or sale or rental contract;
- A completed application form and CY£25 in cash;
- Copies of all the above documents;
- Separate copies of documents and application forms for all dependants.

If you have a job offer, you should also submit confirmation of this from your prospective employer or a certificate of employment stamped by the Labour Department. The certificate is included with the application form you will be given at the Immigration Department. It states the type and duration of work you've been employed to do.

A lawyer can prepare the required documentation on your behalf (and will charge you around CY£75 for doing so) or you can go several weeks in advance to the Immigration Office for the area where you live, collect the necessary forms and make an appointment for the issue of your permit. Appointments must be made in person, and you must take the completed forms and other documents in person, either on your own or with your lawyer (in which case you don't need an appointment).

Once you've submitted your application, you will be given an Alien's Registration Certificate (Form P74) and your TRE permit (sometimes known as a 'pink slip') will be issued within a maximum of six months. It's valid for not less than five years from the date of issue and is usually automatically renewable on request, although after five years you can apply for permanent residence. If applicable, you may start work while your application is being processed.

Further information about TRE permits and a downloadable application form can be found on the Ministry of Interior's website (🖥 www.moi.gov.cy – go to the bottom right corner of the home page for a link to information in English, including the application form.

WORKING

As Cyprus is now a member of the EU, work permits aren't required for any EU citizen who wants to work or start a business on the island (although certain formalities must be observed – see **EU Citizens** below). As a result, increasing numbers of young EU citizens are looking at the possibility of living and working in Cyprus and bringing up their families there. The Mediterranean climate, the slower pace of life and the low crime rate are all very attractive. Yet, before you make any decisions about moving to Cyprus to work, you should ensure that it will be possible for you or any family members to work in Cyprus and dispassionately examine your motives and credentials. What kind of work can you realistically expect to do there? Don't forget that you will be competing with well qualified Cypriots for jobs.

Although English is widely spoken on the island (by around 90 per cent of the population), you may find that some employment areas are closed to you unless you speak fluent Greek. This naturally depends on which area of employment you choose. Even if your qualifications are acceptable in theory, if you want to practise a profession such as the law, engineering or accountancy, you must pass specialist exams in Greek. Those expatriates who come to work in Cyprus usually find jobs or start businesses in tourism, information technology or the construction industry, where foreign qualifications are more readily accepted.

EU Citizens

Since Cyprus joined the EU in 2004, citizens of the European Economic Area (EEA), which includes all EU countries, are guaranteed freedom to work in Cyprus exactly as they are in all EU countries. As an EU citizen you may enter Cyprus simply with your passport or national identity card and look for work for a period of up to 90 days. **However, if your intention is to remain in the country, either to work or start a business (or study or retire), you should begin the application process for a temporary residence permit (see page 31) as soon as possible**. If you're working for a fixed period in Cyprus for a foreign company, your employer should arrange your application for you.

If you will be working in Cyprus for **less than 90 days** (e.g. in seasonal employment), you must declare the fact to the Immigration Department within eight days of your arrival on form 2DECL.

Non-EU Citizens

Non-EU citizens intending to work in Cyprus require a work permit (as well as a visa – see page 29) **before** arriving in the country. **In order to issue a work permit, the Ministry of Labour must be satisfied that a Cypriot or an EU citizen isn't available to do the job**.

There are two categories of permit: Executive and Non-executive. Executive refers to those who are directors or partners of companies registered with the Registrar of Companies in Cyprus, as well as departmental managers of international companies with offices in Cyprus. Non-executive refers to other managerial, professional, administrative, technical and clerical staff. A work permit, when granted, is usually valid for three months or a year.

Recognition of Qualifications

Cyprus's membership of the EU means that, in theory at least, EU citizens cannot be denied access to a profession in Cyprus if you've been awarded the necessary qualifications in your home country. In addition, if your qualifications are from a UK university they will automatically be recognised in Cyprus, as many Cypriots obtain their professional qualifications from UK universities. If you want to use your professional qualifications in Cyprus, you must apply for recognition to the competent body which regulates your profession. They will examine your application and qualifications and issue a licence so that you may practise your profession in Cyprus. They must inform you of their decision within four months and provide you will a full statement of the reasons for their decision. If there's any doubt or concern about the recognition of your qualifications, the competent body can ask the opinion of the Cyprus Council for the Recognition of Higher Education Qualifications (KYSATS).

The Department of Labour of the Ministry of Labour and Social Insurance is the national reference body which provides information to EU nationals who want to practise a regulated profession in Cyprus. Full information about regulated professions and details of the District Labour Offices are available from the Ministry of Labour and Social Insurance (☎ 22-401 600, 💻 www.mlsi.gov.cy/dol).

Social Insurance

If you're planning to work in Cyprus, you must apply to your local District Labour Office to register for social insurance (see page 186). The locations of all the District Labour Offices can be found on the website of the Ministry of Labour and Social Insurance (💻 www.mlsi.gov.cy/dol – go to the English version and search for 'District Labour Offices').

STARTING A BUSINESS

Many people turn to self-employment or start their own business when they start a new life abroad, although this can be very risky indeed in a foreign country. If you're thinking of doing this in Cyprus, you must do plenty of research into the country and its history, people, culture and of course business environment. In theory, now that Cyprus has joined the EU, other EU citizens can work as a self-employed person or start a business in Cyprus without restriction. For example, EU citizens are now able to start a business without needing a local Cypriot partner and there's no minimum investment required. The exception to this relaxation of regulations is businesses related to financial services, which are subject to strict criteria.

The majority of businesses established by foreigners in Cyprus are linked to the leisure and catering industries, followed by property investment and development. The most common include holiday accommodation, e.g. bed & breakfast, villas, apartments and cottages, catering, e.g. bars, cafés and restaurants, shops, property agencies, translation bureaux, language schools, and holiday and sports centres, e.g. tennis, golf and water sports).

Whichever kind of business plans you have, establish the infrastructure first, including a bank account, accountant and lawyer. The advice of a good local lawyer, who understands the business climate in Cyprus and is experienced in company incorporation, is vital. That way you can always ensure that you're operating within the law and the lawyer will take you through the preparation of a brief financial report so that you can present your proposal to a financial institution. He will also help you apply for a company name and complete all the necessary paperwork for incorporation, for which he will charge between CY£700 and CY£1,000. It's worth paying a lawyer to complete the application on your behalf. **There are severe penalties for anyone who ignores the regulations and legal requirements.**

You can obtain help, advice and business information from a number of organisations in Cyprus, such as the Central Bank of Cyprus (💻 www. central bank.gov.cy), the Cyprus Chamber of Commerce (💻 www.cci. org.cy) and the Employers' and Industrialists' Federation (💻 www.oeb-eif.org).

As with starting a business in any country, it's important to keep your plans small and manageable and work well within your budget, especially in the early days, rather than undertaking some grandiose scheme that's impossible to see through. You should have a contingency plan and sufficient funds to last until you're established (this also applies to employees). As in many countries, most people are self-employed for the lifestyle and freedom it affords (no clocks or bosses!) rather than for the financial rewards (which can be non-existent). Generally speaking, you shouldn't consider running a business in Cyprus in a field in which you don't have previous experience, and it's often wise to work for someone else in the same line of business in order to gain experience, rather than jump in at the deep end.

Most people are far too optimistic about the prospects for a new business and over-estimate income levels (it often takes years to make a profit) and under-estimate costs. You must be realistic or even pessimistic when calculating your income and over-estimate the costs and under-estimate the revenue (then reduce it by 50 per cent!). New projects are rarely, if ever, completed within budget, and you need to ensure that you have sufficient working capital and can survive until a business takes off. Cypriot banks are very conservative and extremely wary of lending to new businesses, especially businesses run by foreigners. If you wish to borrow money to buy property or for a business venture, you should also carefully consider where and in what currency to raise the necessary finance. The majority of businesses established by foreigners in Cyprus are linked to the leisure and catering industries, followed by property investment and development. **In Cyprus certain businesses are termed 'saturated activities' and applications for investment in such businesses are rejected outright.** Check with the Central Bank of Cyprus (see above) for up to date information.

Buying an Existing Business

It's sometimes easier to buy an established business than to start a new one, and it's less of a risk. The paperwork for taking over an existing business is also simpler, although still complex. If you plan to buy a business, always obtain an independent valuation (or two) and employ an accountant to audit the books. **Never sign anything you don't understand completely even if you think you understand it.**

Offshore Companies

Since Cyprus' EU accession in May 2004, there have been no offshore companies in Cyprus. Previously there were some 40,000 registered offshore companies, taking advantage of the tax benefits. All companies must now pay 10 per cent corporation tax on their profits, but this is still the lowest rate in the EU.

RETIREMENT

Retiring to Cyprus is a very popular option, especially for Britons. The combination of the mild climate, the wide use of English, the low crime rate, the low cost of living and tax benefits (see below) is attractive to many retirees. There's also an extensive support network for expatriates moving to the country or those living there for part of the year. UK retirees are particularly well provided for with English-language newspapers (see **Appendix B**), several British societies in the main cities and towns and a UK Citizens' Association (UKCA), which has branches in Larnaca, Limassol and Paphos (☎ 25-344 578, 🖳 www.ukca.com.cy).

Benefits

There are substantial tax benefits for retirees in Cyprus, which imposes very low income tax on pensions and has double-taxation treaties with many countries under which retirees' pensions aren't subject to withholding tax at source, although husbands and wives are taxed separately (see **Chapter 7**).

Some countries, e.g. Canada and the UK, have an agreement with Cyprus that allows state pensions to remain index-linked when pensioners are resident in Cyprus. UK retirees can check their situation with the Inland Revenue's International Centre for Non-Residents (☎ UK 0151-210 2222, 🖥 www.inlandrevenue.gov.uk) or the International Pension Service (☎ UK 0191-218 7777, 🖥 www.dwp.gov.uk).

Once you arrive in Cyprus as a retiree, there are also a number of duty-free privileges, including the duty-free importation of a car (see page 69) and personal effects.

Permits

Retired and non-active EEA nationals don't require a visa before moving to Cyprus, but a Temporary Residence Employment permit Category F (see page 32) is necessary. If you plan to retire to Cyprus, you should apply for this as soon as you can after arrival. (You're allowed to stay in Cyprus without a residence permit for up to 90 days, but the application process can take over a month). Along with your application for a TRE permit, you must provide proof that you have an adequate income or financial resources to live in Cyprus without working. The minimum amount is around CY£6,000 per person, but each case is considered individually by the authorities. **When your application is approved, you won't be allowed to be involved in any form of business or work, whether paid or unpaid and will always have to support yourself while you live in Cyprus.**

LANGUAGE

In the Republic of Cyprus, the official language is Greek and Cypriots write in Standard Modern Greek, which they're taught at school. However, they speak Greek Cypriot, which is a dialect of Greek that reflects the influence of the myriad of nations that have ruled Cyprus over the years. Although it observes the grammar and syntax of the Greek language, it contains certain non-standard words, including some from Ancient Greek, and some words are pronounced in a different way. If many local words and pronunciations are used, it can be difficult for a Standard Modern Greek speaker (e.g. from mainland Greece) to understand. Nevertheless, if you speak Standard Modern Greek well, you will have little difficulty being understood, and Cypriots will happily 'standardise' their Greek so that you can understand them.

The second language of Cyprus is English, as the country was a British colony from 1878 until 1960. Many Greek Cypriots have lived and worked or been educated in the UK, and, in some cases, the US. English is considered a symbol of sophistication and many Cypriots strive to perfect their English. It therefore isn't essential to learn Greek, even if you plan to live and work there.

Unfortunately, because so many Cypriots speak English, many residents (particularly the British) make very little effort to learn more than a few words of Greek and live life in isolation as if they were on an extended holiday. Although you can certainly get by this way (thanks to the language skills of Greek Cypriots) for anyone living, and certainly working, in Cyprus, it's far from ideal. Learning Greek helps you to appreciate the Cypriot way of life and make the most of your time in the country, and opens many doors that remain firmly closed to resident 'tourists'. Even just learning the basic pleasantries in Greek will earn you the respect of Greek Cypriots.

If you're planning to work or start a business, learning Greek shouldn't be seen as an option, but as a necessity. Speaking English and some Greek will tranform both your social life and your business opportunities! There are some business sectors, such as tourism, construction and some areas of information technology, where you won't need to communicate in Greek to do business, but if you're a professional wanting to practise your profession, it's essential to learn the language.

Learning Greek

Greek is a difficult language to learn, not least because it has an entirely different alphabet from other languages, although this can be mastered relatively easily. The alphabet has 24 letters as well as 12 combinations or diphthongs, and if you can master it you will find speaking the language easier as well as being able to understand signs and notices. The key to speaking and understanding Greek is the stress placed on particular letters, which, when put in the wrong place, can change the meaning completely! Greek grammar also has its difficulties, particularly verbs, but it's easy to acquire a rudimentary understanding of how the language works. 'All' that's required is a little hard work and some help and perseverance, particularly if you're only mixing with English-speaking friends and colleagues. You won't just 'pick it up' (only young children are blessed with that privilege), but must make a real effort to learn. Fortunately the Cypriots are extremely tolerant of foreigners' tortured attempts to speak their language and any effort is appreciated, although you may find that they reply in English.

Most people can teach themselves a great deal online and through the use of books, tapes, videos and CDs. The Cypriot government, through the Cyprus Broadcasting Corporation (CyBC) and in collaboration with a Cyprus website (🖳 www.kypros.org), offers an online Greek course. There's a selection of 105 lessons on audio files, online student notes and even an online Greek dictionary. It's completely free and all you need to do is register on the website (🖳 www.cybc.com.cy).

However, even the best students require some help and you can find out about Greek lessons by contacting the Ministry of Education and Culture (☎ 22-512 774), who can tell you about your local Government Institute for Foreign Languages. Greek Language for Foreigners classes are held (usually in the afternoons and evenings) at some of the state schools in Cyprus during term time. Information is available by contacting the school secretary and the cost is very low (between CY£18 and CY£20 per year). Private language schools can be found in the yellow pages under 'Institutes'. Private teachers advertise in local newspapers. Most schools and teachers offer free tests to help you find your appropriate level and a free introductory lesson.

Don't expect to become fluent in a short time unless you have a particular flair for languages or already have a good command of Greek. Unless you desperately need to learn quickly, it's best to arrange your lessons over a long period. However, don't commit yourself to a long course of study, particularly an expensive one, before ensuring that it's the right course for you. Some schools offer combined courses where language study is linked with optional subjects, including Cypriot art and culture, history, and traditions. For more information contact the Cyprus Tourism Organisation or the Cypriot embassy in your home country.

HEALTH

The World Health Organization ranks Cyprus as one of the healthiest countries in the Mediterranean. Since the country's independence from Britain in 1960, the government's main priorities have been health and preventative medicine. Consequently the quality of healthcare in Cyprus is high and life expectancy statistics compare favourably with those of other western countries. Many doctors are trained in the UK, and people living in many Middle Eastern countries choose to visit Cyprus for medical treatment.

Medical and health services are provided through both the public health service and private clinics and hospitals. Public and private medicine operate alongside one another in Cyprus and complement each other. Public General Hospitals as well as private clinics and hospitals are concentrated in the main urban areas, but there are health centres in rural areas, completing a network that meets the medical needs of the whole country.

Cyprus' public health service is funded through the social security payments of those who work on the island, whether Cypriots or foreign residents. The system provides free or low cost healthcare for those who contribute to social security, plus their families and retirees, and emergency treatment for everyone. However, **the full public health service isn't available to foreign visitors, who require private health insurance** (see below) **unless they wish to pay high medical bills.** For information about retirees' entitlements, see page 188.

EU citizens who are visiting Cyprus can receive free outpatient or inpatient treatment with a European Health Card (the old E111), which is issued by the health authority in your home country. **Note, however, that this covers only essential treatment and not routine treatment.** Non-EU visitors must pay for healthcare.

Private Health Insurance

It's essential for visitors to Cyprus to have private health insurance. If you're a resident but aren't paying into the Cypriot public health system via social security payments or an EU pensioner (see below), a requirement of residence is that you have adequate medical cover (see page 188).

Pensioners

Now that Cyprus has joined the EU, pensioners from other EU countries are entitled to use the public health system at reduced cost or free, according to their means (see **EU Citizens** on page 188). **Non-EU pensioners must have private health insurance** (see page 188).

 Health (and health insurance) is an important issue for anyone retiring abroad. Many people are ill-prepared for old age and the possibility of health problems, and foreigners who can no longer care for themselves are often forced to return to their home countries. There are few state residential nursing homes in Cyprus, or hospices for the terminally ill.

Provision for the disabled, such as wheelchair access, must be incorporated in all new public building and tourist facilties, although provision in older buildings and on public transport is below the average for Western Europe.

Doctors & Chemists'

There are many private doctors in Cyprus, and clinics are usually open from 9am to 1pm and from 4 to 7pm, Mondays to Fridays. Doctors charge around CY£10 to CY£12 for a consultation and the cost of most treatment is around half that in northern European countries. Almost all brands of medicines are available in Cyprus and pharmacists are highly qualified (and usually speak English). They can provide medical advice and treatment for minor ailments. Local newspapers list chemists' that are open during the night or at weekends and holidays, along with the names and numbers of doctors who are on call out of hours. There are also area-specific numbers that you can ring out of hours to obtain information about private doctors who are on call and chemists' that are open (or you can ring 192 for information). These are as follows:

Area	Night Chemists'	Doctors on Call
Larnaca	☎ 1404	☎ 1424
Limassol	☎ 1405	☎ 1425
Nicosia	☎ 1402	☎ 1422
Paphos	☎ 1406	☎ 1426

In an emergency, you can call an ambulance, the fire service or the police by dialling ☎ 199 or ☎ 112, where operators speak English.

Health Benefits & Problems

The climate and lifestyle in any country has a noticeable affect on mental health and people who live in hot climates are generally happier and more relaxed than those who live in cold, wet climates (such as northern Europe). The generally mild climate of Cyprus is very therapeutic, especially for sufferers from rheumatism and arthritis and those who are susceptible to bronchitis, colds and pneumonia. The slower pace of life is also beneficial for those who are susceptible to stress (it's difficult to remain uptight while napping in the sun), although it takes some foreigners time to adjust.

On the other hand, Cyprus' climate can cause problems, particularly to expatriates from cooler climes. Common health problems include sunburn and sunstroke, stomach and bowel problems (due to a change of diet and more often, water, but also poor hygiene), and various problems caused by excessive alcohol consumption. Other health problems are caused by the high level of airborne pollen in spring (note that spring comes earlier in Cyprus than in northern European countries), which particularly affects asthma and hay fever sufferers.

The sun in Cyprus is **very** hot, and you should limit your exposure and avoid it altogether during the hottest part of the day, wear protective clothing (including a hat) and use a sun block. Too much sun and too little protection will dry your skin and cause premature ageing, to say nothing of the risks of skin cancer. Care should also be taken to replace the natural oils lost from too many hours in the sun and the elderly should take particular care not to exert themselves during hot weather.

PETS

Should you wish to import a pet or to acquire one locally, there are certain procedures and precautions to be taken.

Importation

Bringing certain pets to Cyprus has been made easier since the country joined the EU. If you're bringing a dog, cat or ferret from another EU country and it meets the criteria for the new European Pet Passport (formerly the PETS certificate), you should be allowed to bring it into Cyprus without quarantine. To qualify for a passport, these pets must be microchipped (a microchip is painlessly inserted in their neck), vaccinated against rabies and undergo a blood test to check that they have sufficient antibodies to fight disease. Once a pet is given the all-clear, there's a wait of six months before your European Pet Passport can be issued and your pet can travel.

Additionally, 24 to 48 hours prior to your departure for Cyprus, you pet must be checked for any parasites by a government-authorised vet and a certificate issued. This certificate, along with your pet's European Pet Passport and copies of the rabies vaccination certificate and the blood test results to prove your pet is protected, are the required documentation to enter Cyprus. You should also be able to prove where your pet started its journey and that it's a domestic pet and not intended for sale. This arrangement is only for animals imported from rabies-free countries and countries where rabies is under control. The DEFRA website (see below) has detailed information, but the arrangement covers most European countries plus Bahrain, Canada and the US. However, the current quarantine law will remain in place for pets coming from Eastern Europe, Africa, Asia and South America.

The cost to pet owners is around GB£200 (for a microchip, rabies vaccination and blood test), plus GB£60 a year for annual booster vaccinations. Shop around and compare fees from a number of veterinary surgeons, but all the above procedures must be carried out by a government authorised vet; otherwise, they're invalid. Only certain routes and carriers are licensed to carry animals and DEFRA has full details.

Particular consideration must be given before exporting a pet from a country with strict quarantine regulations, such as the UK, although all of the above procedures ensure that you will be able to return to the UK with your pet at short notice, provided your pet is checked for parasites 24 to 48 hours before the return journey. Additional information is available from the Department for Environment, Food and Rural Affairs (DEFRA, UK ☎ 020-7904 6000 or 020-7238 6951, 🖳 www.defra.gov.uk/animalh/quarantine).

 Certain breeds of dog aren't allowed to enter the country, irrespective of their country of origin. These are the American Pit Bull Terrier or Pit Bull Terrier; Japanese Tosa or Tosa Inu; Dogo Argentino or Argentinian Mastiff; Fila Brasileiro or Brazilian Mastiff.

Local Regulations & Risks

Once you're in Cyprus, you should be aware that a comprehensive law concerning the control of dogs was passed in 2003. This law places the responsibility for the control of dogs onto the local councils, and failure to comply with their bylaws can result in fines. All dogs must be licenced and microchipped for identification purposes. Licences cost CY£15 for a dog, CY£25 for a bitch (unless spayed, in which case the fee is the same as for a dog) and CY£100 for some 'dangerous' breeds.

Take extra care when walking your dog, as poisoned bait can be found in both rural and urban areas. It's used legally by farmers to control vermin, so be extra vigilant when exercising your dog. Obtain advice from a veterinary surgeon, who can supply you with a special first aid kit in case of emergencies.

2.

THE BEST PLACE TO LIVE

Having decided to buy a home in Cyprus, your first task will be to choose the area in which to buy. **If you're unsure about where to buy, the best decision is usually to rent for a period.** There are disadvatages to renting first, such as the cost and the possibility that property prices may increase and so financially restrict your choice. On balance though, it's usually better to take too long over your decision than not to take long enough and to make the wrong decision.

The secret of successfully buying a home is research, research and more research and, if you plan to live permanently in Cyprus, this is particularly important. You may be fortunate and buy the first property you see without doing any homework and live happily ever after. However, a successful purchase is much more likely if you thoroughly investigate the towns and communities in your chosen area, and compare the range and prices of properties and their relative values. This chapter is designed to help you decide where to buy a home in Cyprus, as location is the most important aspect of buying a home. The chapter also includes useful information on getting to Cyprus (a vital consideration when choosing where to buy) and on getting around once you're there.

GEOGRAPHY

Cyprus has two mountain ranges: the Troodos in the west of the island crowned by Mount Olympus (2,000m/6,600ft), the island's highest peak and snow-covered for much of the winter, and the Kyrenia range, which stretch along the northern part of the island. The Troodos has been extensively reforested in recent years and pine and oak forests now cover the western slopes, which are home to an interesting and unique range of flora and fauna. It's in these mountains that most of Cyprus' rivers emerge in the rainy season and several dams have been constructed in the area.

Cyprus has some 768km (480mi) of extremely varied coastline, ranging from spectacular white cliffs and rocky coves to long sandy beaches. There are two natural harbours, at Famagusta and Limassol, and Larnaca has a man-made port. In the centre of the island is the Mesaoria Plain, home to the capital Nicosia and much of the island's agricultural activity, although farming takes place only in winter and spring, as the plain receives no water outside these seasons.

Apart from Nicosia (pop. 208,900), all the major cities are situated on the coast. Limassol is the second-largest city and the island's biggest port, and Larnaca and Paphos, both important holiday resorts, are the third- and fourth-largest respectively.

Since 1974, the island has been divided into two parts: the pariah 'state' known as the Turkish Republic of Northern Cyprus (covering 37 per cent of the island), occupied and recognised only by Turkey, and the Republic of Cyprus in the south. This chapter deals with popular areas for house buyers in the Republic of Cyprus. Information about the property market in the north of the island and how the political and legal situation in that part of Cyprus may affect homebuyers can be found in **Chapter 11**. The Greek spelling (but using the English alphabet) of the place names is given in brackets where appropriate, as road signs and maps of the island often use the international name and the English transliteration of the Greek name interchangeably (see **Roads & Driving** on page 68).

DISTRICTS

The island of Cyprus has six administrative districts (shown on the map in **Appendix E**). As these divisions existed before the separation of the country following the Turkish invasion of 1974, some of them cross the border between the Republic and northern Cyprus. In this chapter, when the districts of Famagusta, Larnaca and Nicosia are referred to, this means only the parts of those districts in the Republic. For information about the remainder of these districts and the district of Kyrenia, which is wholly in the north, see **Geography & Popular Locations** on page 257. Confusingly, the main city or town in each district has the same name as the district itself; in this book, the name alone always refers to the district, and the capital is referred to as Nicosia city, Paphos town, etc. The Troodos mountains are mainly in Nicosia but the foothills, where most of the villages are situated, are in Limassol, which is the heading under which they're discussed below.

Famagusta (*Ammochostos*)

Famagusta is a divided district, the major part of it being in northern Cyprus (see page 258). However, the small part in the Republic contains three popular locations with foreign buyers.

Agia Napa

The resort of Agia Napa, a once quiet fishing village, is a busy, sophisticated tourist centre, with many luxury hotels and an exciting, if somewhat notorious, nightlife. This area is very popular with young holidaymakers, interested only in eating, drinking and getting a suntan.

If you're looking for quiet and relaxation, this isn't the place to buy a property. It's extremely crowded during July and August, but completely deserted in the winter. The beaches in this area are generally good, particularly Nissi Beach, which is reminiscent of the Caribbean and rated among the best in Cyprus.

Protaras & Paralimni

Nearby are the resort of Protaras and the town of Paralimni. Protaras is a highly developed tourist area, but that doesn't detract from the beauty of its beaches, which are among the country's best and have been awarded the EU Blue Flag. Some of the best snorkelling and diving can be found here.

Larnaca (*Larnaka*)

Larnaca isn't as popular with homebuyers as some of the other areas of Cyprus. This is mainly because its landscape, which is comparatively flat, lacks the beautiful countryside of Limassol or the stunning sea views of Paphos and its environs. However, the area is currently having something of facelift and there's much discussion about removing two of its less attractive features, the oil refinery and cement works, although this hasn't happened yet. As a result, it's increasing in popularity.

Larnaca City

The city of Larnaca (pop. 73,200) is situated in the south-east of the island and is one of the oldest cities in the world, with numerous monuments that bear witness to its colourful history, including several Byzantine churches. Larnaca is the first glimpse of Cyprus for many visitors, as it's home to the island's main international airport (the other international airport is at Paphos). Larnaca is also a popular holiday destination, with modern facilities and good shops. It's one of two major ports in the south of the island and also has a large yacht marina. Nearby are the Hala Sultan Tekke Mosque, a site of Muslim pilgrimage, and the Larnaca Salt Lake, an important migration destination for many birds, including flamingos.

Villages

Just to the north-east of Larnaca, the village of Oroklini, with sea and mountain views, is becoming more popular, as it's only ten minutes from the town centre and has easy access to main roads. To the west of Larnaca, towards Limassol, are the villages of Maroni, which is popular with buyers from northern Europe and Kalavassos, a typical Cypriot village within five minutes drive of Governor's Beach. The nearby resort of Pyla, with good mountain and sea views, is also increasing in popularity.

Limassol (*Lemesos*)

Limassol's 18 miles of coastline are extensively developed and the area is popular with tourists all year round, making it the busiest winter resort in Cyprus.

Limassol City

Limassol, in the south of the island, is Cyprus' second-largest city (pop. 163,900) and is the main port and passenger ferry terminal on the island. It developed as a small settlement in pre-Christian times and for many years was a fishing community. It wasn't until around the tenth century that it became one of the major towns on the island. It's now a thriving business centre as well as a coastal resort. Many large international companies have their offices there and, in the old city, new and old buildings rub shoulders, creating a fascinating architectural mix. The city has a large marina, and there are a number of golf courses nearby.

Both the city and the outskirts of Limassol are popular with foreign buyers. Those who work in the city tend to buy spacious apartments in or near the town, while others prefer the surrounding villages, such as Laneia and Souni (see below). There are extensive fruit (mainly citrus) plantations in the countryside around Limassol, which is also the centre of a thriving wine industry, the fruits of which are enjoyed every September at the annual Wine Festival.

There has been extensive tourist development here over the last few years, but Limassol retains its character and charm, especially the old city with its medieval castle. The city effectively combines old and new and has a vibrant feel. The Limassol carnival in early spring is an important event for the town, as is the wine festival in September.

Eight miles to the east of the town is the ancient city and harbour of Amathus. The archeological remains of Amathus are spread over a wide area and there's some evidence that part of the site is still underwater.

Many package tourists come to beaches to the east of Limassol, where there's a considerable amount of development as there is at nearby Governor's Beach. Prices are continuing to rise in Limassol (around 20 per cent in 2004) and there's a high demand for new properties. Some of villages surrounding Limassol are becoming more and more popular with buyers.

Akrotiri Peninsula

To the west of Limassol on the Akrotiri Peninsula are the famous Lady's Mile beach, one of the best in Cyprus, and the Akrotiri Salt Lake, home to migrating colonies of flamingos in winter. There are also the impressive cliff-top ruins of Kourion, capital of the ancient Hellenic kingdom.

Laneia & Souni

Laneia is a traditional Cypriot village around 15 minutes north of Limassol, which is much favoured by artists of all nationalities and enjoys dramatic mountain views. Many Cypriots have moved from Laneia to the towns, and there are many properties needing restoration there. It's popular with foreign artists in search of a peaceful setting. Many foreigners build houses in the mountain areas surrounding Laneia.

Souni village, between Limassol and Paphos towns, is a simple village without many amenities, but has the advantage of beautiful views overlooking Episkopi Bay and Cyprus's best-known archeological site, Kourion. New properties, including bungalows and houses, are being built close to Souni at reasonable prices.

Other Villages

The traditional village of Lofou, around 18km (10mi) to the north of Limassol and close to Laneia, is a listed village, currently being restored by UNESCO. The villages of Palodia, a short drive to the north of Limassol, and Pyrgos and Moni, both to the north-east, are all increasing in popularity with foreign buyers. In the small villages there are no apartments and very few small or townhouse type properties. There are typical village houses, and many foreigners buy land in the surrounding areas and build large villas with big gardens.

Pissouri

Around 20km (12mi) east of Paphos town are the Pissouri Village development and Pissouri Bay, both of which continue to attract foreign buyers. Their popularity is thanks to excellent views of the bay, sandy beaches and a traditional village square. The main British military bases, known as Sovereign Base Areas (SBAs), are situated in this area and much of the land west of Limassol lies within their boundaries.

Troodos Mountains

Mount Olympus (1,951m/6,400ft) is the highest mountain in Cyprus and not to be confused with the mountain of the same name in Greece. It's part of the Troodos range, which stretches almost the length of southern Cyprus. Some of the most spectacular scenery in Cyprus is to be found here, and there's a winter ski resort at Mount Olympus, less than a hour's drive from the coastal resorts. The Troodos mountains are covered with carefully preserved pine forests and have a network or rather winding, but good quality, roads that link all the main inhabited parts of the mountain range. The Cyprus Tourism Organisation (CTO) organises nature trails and hiking expeditions that allow you to enjoy the trees, flowers (some of which are only found on Cyprus) and, of course, the breathtaking scenery.

There are nine Byzantine monasteries and churches in the mountain villages, which are UNESCO World Heritage listed sites. Platres, on the southern slopes of the mountain range, is the most popular of the hill resorts and has many hotels, which Cypriots flock to in the hot summer months, although outside the summer season it's relatively quiet. Around Platres there are many forest hiking trails. Fikardhou and Lazania are two officially 'preserved' villages nearby which contain houses from the Ottoman period. Other villages popular with foreign visitors and buyers are Omodhos and Kakopetria, but there are plenty more that are worth exploring.

Nicosia (*Lefkosa*)

Although Nicosia is a large district, it's generally of little interest to foreign homebuyers, with the notable exception of parts of the city (see below). The central Masaoria Plain becomes very hot and dusty in the summer, and the short stretch of coast in the Republic (see map in **Appendix E**) is virtually deserted.

Nicosia City

Nicosia is the capital of Cyprus and its largest city (pop. 208,900). It's divided in half by two walls: the 16th century Venetian wall separating the new city from the old, and the 'Green Line' that divides northern and southern Cyprus following the Turkish invasion of 1974.

The city has been the capital of Cyprus since Medieval times and is now the cultural focus of the country. The old city still has its star-shaped Venetian walls, which were built to protect the city and its inhabitants from invaders in the 15th century. Three of the ancient city gates survive: Famagusta, Kyrenia and Paphos Gates.

Despite the division of the city after the Turkish invasion, Nicosia still has a strong business tradition and remains the commercial heart of the island, with the head offices of many major companies located there. A number of the narrow streets in the old city have been pedestrianised, so you can wander at your leisure and enjoy the incongruous mix of crumbling, traditional buildings and familiar UK high street chains, including Marks & Spencer and Woolworths, and the US coffee chain Starbucks. Outside the old city, there's a bustling modern shopping centre and every type of bar and restaurant imaginable and plenty of nightlife. Many Cypriots moved out of Nicosia to the outskirts after the invasion, but they're now beginning to move back in. But, despite its fascinating history and culture, many tourists never get as far as Nicosia, and outside the summer season facilities are limited.

If you want to consider city life in Nicosia, remember that the city's location on the central plain means that it gets considerably hotter and dustier in the summer than the coastal towns and it's considerably colder in the winter. Traffic congestion is also a problem and, as in any city, parking is restricted. Although Nicosia isn't as popular with foreign homeowners, who prefer to be close to the sea, there are some beautiful old stone properties in the old city, as well as more modern properties on the outskirts. Older properties are usually government protected, but sympathetic renovation (see page 118) is usually looked on favourably by the authorities.

Paphos (*Pafos*)

Until relatively recently, Paphos was the remotest and least developed part of the island. However, the building of Paphos airport in 1983 changed the area for ever. The airport, just 10km (6mi) from the town, is the island's second international airport and has been a major factor in the island's ever-expanding tourist industry. There has been extensive development of the area to meet the demands of tourists and foreign homebuyers. As a result, Paphos has some of the most expensive property in Cyprus but is still one of the most unspoilt locations (depending on which area you choose), as it was among the last to be developed and has strict planning regulations which restrict the height of apartments and hotels to just three storeys.

Paphos Town

The town of Paphos (pop. 48,300), situated in the south-west of Cyprus, is famous as the legendary birthplace of Aphrodite and was the capital of the island during Hellenistic and Roman times. Visitors can see the rock which marks the spot where the godess of love is said to have risen from the sea. The area around Paphos contains some of Cyprus' finest archaeological treasures, such as the Temple of Aphrodite and the Tomb of the Kings (underground tombs carved out of the rock and dating back to the fourth century BC). History and legend aside, Paphos is blessed with a dramatic and beautiful coastline, which makes it the most popular area on the island, for both holidaymakers and foreign property buyers, especially retirees.

Paphos actually comprises two separate towns: Kato Paphos, where the harbour, archeological area, luxury hotels and nightlife are situated; and Ktim Paphos, the old town on the hill, which many consider the true centre of Paphos. Ktima is where you can find the best shops and the museums. There's an outdoor market there from Mondays to Saturdays selling food and traditional Cypriot goods. Kato is where the holidaymakers head for to enjoy the numerous harbourside tavernas and souvenir shops. The area between the two parts of Paphos town is being snapped up by developers, as it enjoys wonderful views and cool sea breezes in the summer.

The town itself is something of a slave to tourism, but it has managed to retain its attractiveness and small town feel. There are a few older houses in this area, but few foreigners live in the town itself, most preferring to live on the outskirts in one of the many new luxury developments or in one of the surrounding villages.

The Coast

Around Paphos are countless developments, among the most popular being Kamares Village, around 15 minutes north of Paphos in the village of Tala, and Coral Bay, part of Pegeia village, which is hugely popular with British buyers. Pegeia began life as a village but is now almost classed as a suburb of Paphos with a population of around 6,000 (many of them British) and plenty of shops and tavernas. The hillside is covered with properties of all kinds. Many people live here permanently, but there's also a substantial amount of holiday home ownership. This is important to bear in mind if you're considering buying in the area, as in the summer you may be disturbed by holidaymakers.

Further north along the coast, the Akamas Peninsula is home to the Akamas National Park, noted for its magnificent jagged coastline, pine forests and a host of unique flora and fauna. The beaches here are among the best on the island, and resorts such as nearby Latchi and Polis are far less developed and cheaper than Paphos town but still only 20 minutes away. Both Polis and Latchi boast beautiful beaches and a harbour and are popular with cratsmen who want to practise their trade in naturally beautiful, peaceful surroundings.

Golf Developments

Golf developments are a relatively new phenomenon in Cyprus. The Cypriot government is well aware that golf courses and associated developments attract high quality tourism to the island, and its long-term strategy for golf course development is to have a total of nine golf courses on the island. However, there's considerable opposition from those who are concerned about the use of land, environmental issues and high water consumption. Water is sometimes in short supply on the island, particularly during the summer months.

There are currently three main golf developments, all of them close to Paphos town: the Tsada Golf Club, the first in Cyprus; the Secret Valley Golf Club development, 18km (10mi) from Paphos; and the Aphrodite Hills development.

Aphrodite Hills is an award-winning development that has expanded over 235ha (580 acres) and continues to do so, although considerable efforts have been made to develop it in an environmentally friendly manner. It's set high on the hill above Paphos and is built on two sides of a ravine overlooking the sea. The western plateau contains properties that are used for tourist accomodation and the eastern plateau contains residential properties. There's also a luxury hotel, shops and restaurants. Aphrodite Hills has some of the most expensive and exclusive properties in Cyprus. The prices of apartments, town houses and villas on Aphrodite Hills are also rising faster than on the rest of the island.

The Secret Valley development is close to the supposed birthplace of Aphrodite and is a new course set in a beautiful valley around 18km (13 mi) east of Paphos.

LOCATION

The most important consideration when buying a home is usually its location – or as the old adage goes, the **three** most important points are location, location and location! **This is particularly important if you're buying for investment.** A property in a reasonable condition in a popular area is likely to be a better investment than an exceptional property in a remote location. There's usually no point in buying a 'dream' property in a terrible location.

 The wrong decision regarding location is one of the main causes of disenchantment among foreigners who have purchased property abroad.

Where you buy a property in Cyprus will depend on a range of factors, including your preferences, your financial resources and, not least, whether you plan to work or not. The 'best' area in which to live depends on a range of considerations including the proximity of schools, shops, public transport, bars and restaurants, entertainment and sports facilities, swimming pool and beaches. If you have a job in Cyprus, the location of your home will probably be determined by that of your place of work. However, if you intend to look for employment or start a business, you must live in an area that allows you the maximum scope. Unless you have good reason to believe otherwise, you shouldn't rely on finding employment in a particular area. If, on the other hand, you're looking for a holiday or retirement home, the whole of Cyprus is your oyster. If you're looking for a permanent home, don't be too influenced by where you've spent an enjoyable holiday or two. A town or area that was adequate for a few weeks' holiday may be totally unsuitable for a permanent home, particularly regarding proximity to shops, medical services, and sports and leisure facilities.

If you have little idea about where you wish to live, read as much as you can about the different areas of Cyprus (see **Districts** on page 49 and **Appendix B**) and spend some time looking around your areas of interest. The climate and cost of living in Cyprus are very similar island wide (see **Climate** on page 24 and **Cost of Living** on page 28), but the lifestyle can vary considerably from area to area.

Cyprus is a small country and there are plenty of beautiful areas to choose from, all within reasonably easy travelling distance of the coast, the airports and the large towns and cities. When looking for a home, bear in mind travelling times and costs to airports, your place of work, shops and schools (and the local bar/restaurant). If you buy a remote country property, the distance to local amenities and services could become a problem, particularly if you plan to retire to Cyprus. If you live in a remote rural area, you will need to be much more self-sufficient than if you live in a town and you will need to use the car for most journeys (which will increase your cost of living).

If possible, you should visit an area a number of times over a period of a few weeks, both on weekdays and at weekends, in order to get a feel for it (it's often better to walk than to drive). A property seen on a balmy summer's day after a delicious lunch and a few glasses of Cypriot wine may not be nearly so attractive on a subsequent visit without sunshine and the warm inner glow. If possible, you should also visit an area at different times of the year, e.g. in both summer and winter, as somewhere that's wonderful in summer can be forbidding and inhospitable in winter (or vice versa if you don't like extreme heat).

In any case, you should view a property a number of times before deciding to buy it.

If you're unfamiliar with an area, most experts recommend that you rent for a period before deciding to buy (see **Renting Before Buying** on page 83). This is particularly important if you're planning to buy a permanent or retirement home in an unfamiliar area. Many people change their minds after a period and it isn't unusual for buyers to move once or twice before settling down permanently.

If you will be working in Cyprus, obtain a map of the island so that you can see how the different areas relate to one another. Decide the maximum distance you will consider travelling to work, e.g. by drawing a circle with your work place in the middle. Obtain a large-scale map of the area and mark the places where you've viewed properties, at the same time making a list of the plus and minus points of each one. If you use an estate agent, he will usually drive you around and you can then return later to the properties that you like best at your leisure (provided you've marked them on your map!). If you're looking at properties on your own in the countryside, it's sensible to take a mobile phone with you in case you get lost! Note that agents may be reluctant to give you the keys to visit a property on your own.

There are many points to consider regarding the location of a home, including the following.

Accessibility

Is the proximity to public transport, e.g. an international airport, port or access to a main road important? Don't believe all you're told about the distance or travelling times to the nearest airport, main road, beach or town, but check yourself. Note that travelling times to and from airports in resort areas are always longer in the summer months.

SURVIVAL TIP
Although it isn't so important if you're
buying a permanent home in Cyprus and planning to
stay put, one of the major considerations when buying a
holiday home is communications (e.g. air links)
with your home country.

If you're buying a home with a view to retiring, check the local public transport, as you may not always be able (or wish) to drive. There's little point in choosing an isolated spot or somewhere with a limited public transport system, when in a few years' time you may have to rely on local bus or taxi services to get about (see **Getting Around** on page 66).

You should also consider the terrain of your chosen home, as a location with lots of hills or steps could become an insurmountable problem if you have mobility problems or become disabled.

Amenities

What local health and social services are provided? How far is the nearest hospital with an emergency department? What shopping facilities are provided in the neighbourhood? How far is it to the nearest town with good shopping facilities, e.g. a supermarket? How would you get there if your car was out of action? Many rural villages have few shops or facilities, so they aren't usually a good choice for a retirement home.

Community

Do you wish to live in an area with many other expatriates from your home country or as far away from them as possible? In some parts of Cyprus, it's almost impossible to get away from other foreigners, so if you wish to integrate with the local community, avoid the foreign 'ghettos' and choose an area or development with mainly local inhabitants. Even in small villages, most people will be able to speak some English as it's so widely spoken on the island. However, foreign residents in rural areas who take the time and trouble to integrate into the local community and learn a little of the local language are invariably warmly welcomed.

On the other hand, if you wish to mix only with your compatriots and don't plan to learn any Greek at all, living in a predominantly foreign community may be ideal. However, developments inhabited largely by second homeowners can be like ghost towns for most of the year. In these areas many facilities, businesses and shops are closed outside the main tourist season, and in some areas even local services such as public transport and postal collections may be severely curtailed.

Good neighbours are invaluable, particularly when you're buying a holiday home in a village. If you're buying a permanent home, it's important to check on your prospective neighbours, particularly when buying an apartment. For example, are they noisy, sociable or absent for long periods? Do you think you will get on with them?

Crime

The crime rate is unusually low in Cyprus – around one-sixth of the European average (see **Crime** on page 216) – which makes it a very attractive location, especially if you're retired or have a young family.

Employment

How secure is your job or business? If there's a possibility that you will need to move in a few years' time, you should consider renting or at least buy a property that will be relatively easy to sell and recoup the cost. If you will be working from home, make sure that a property has a telephone line installed (or that you can quickly get one installed) and that you can have access to broadband if required (see **Telephone Services** on page 229). You may also wish to check whether mobile phone reception is possible in the local area. Reception is generally good all over the island, but check with the mobile telephone company and those who regularly use mobile telephones on the island.

Garden

If you're planning to buy a property with a large garden or plot, bear in mind the high cost and amount of work involved in its upkeep. If it's to be a second home, who will look after the garden (and house) when you're away? Do you want to spend your holidays mowing the lawn and cutting back the undergrowth? It's best to choose low-maintenance gardens with little lawn, plenty of paved areas and drought-loving plants. Bear in mind that fruit and olive trees need a lot of work (pruning, watering and harvesting). Do you want a home with a lot of outbuildings? What are you going to do with them? Can you afford to (and will you get permission to) convert them into extra rooms or guest accommodation?

Local Council

There are two types of local authority in Cyprus: municipalities and communities councils. Municipalities account for the local government of around 60 per cent of the island and communities councils cover the rest of the population. Whichever type of council it is, you should try to find out whether it's well run. What are the views of other residents about its performance? If the municipality is efficiently run, you can usually rely on good local social and sports services and other facilities.

Noise

Noise can be a problem in Cyprus, particularly in a busy tourist area, where you should find out what the noise level is like in high season **before** buying. Although you cannot choose your neighbours, you can at least ensure that a property isn't located next to a busy road, industrial plant, commercial area, building site, discotheque, nightclub, bar or restaurant. If you like a quiet life, don't buy an apartment in a block where there are lots of second homes which may be rented out to boisterous holidaymakers, who can be noisy, not just during the busy summer months, but in the mild winter months too. Look out for objectionable neighbouring properties and check whether nearby vacant land has been zoned for commercial activities. In towns, traffic noise, particularly from motorcycles, can continue all night!

Parking

If you're planning to buy in a town or city, is there adequate private or free on-street parking for your family and visitors? Even with the relatively low crime rate in Cyprus, in the cities it can be important to have secure off-street parking.

 Parking can be a problem in towns and in the capital, Nicosia, and private garages or parking spaces may be difficult to find. In out-of-town developments there may be inadequate parking for residents and visitors, particularly in summer, so it's advisable to ensure that you have a private garage or a reserved parking space close to your home.

Traffic congestion is a problem in many towns and resorts, particularly during the high season. Bear in mind also that an apartment or townhouse in a town or community development may be some distance from the nearest road or car park. How do you feel about carrying heavy shopping hundreds of metres to your home and possibly up several flights of stairs? If you're planning to buy an apartment above the ground floor, you may wish to ensure that the building has a lift (that works!).

Property Market

If you're planning to buy a property mainly for investment (see page 22), you should base your decision regarding the location and type of property on the investment potential, rather than your own preferences. Depending on your investment plans, you will need to ensure that it's in a popular area, with good access to facilities and within easy travelling distance of an airport. Letting a property in Cyprus to holidaymakers on a short-term basis is illegal, although you can let your property on a long-term basis to a Cypriot or an EU citizen resident in Cyprus (see **Chapter 9**).

Schools

If you're planning to move permanently to Cyprus, you must consider your children's present and future schooling. What is the quality of local schools? Are there any bilingual or international schools nearby? Expatriate children generally attend one of the many independent international schools, which are in all the major towns and offer high standards of education. Remember that even if your family has no need or plans to use local schools, the value of a home may be influenced by the quality and location of schools.

Sports & Leisure Facilities

What's the range and quality of local leisure, sports, community and cultural facilities? The proximity to many sports facilities in Cyprus, such as beaches, golf courses and the ski resort on Mount Olympus, isn't a problem thanks to the size of the island, and in most areas you're spoilt for choice, with fishing, watersports, hiking, birdwatching and horse riding.

Tourists

Bear in mind that if you live in a popular tourist area, i.e. almost anywhere on Cyprus, apart from perhaps Nicosia, you will be inundated with tourists in the summer. They won't only jam the roads and pack the beaches and shops, but may even occupy your favourite table at your local bar or restaurant. Bear in mind that while a 'front-line' property on the beach sounds attractive and may be ideal for short holidays, it isn't always the best solution for permanent residents. Many beaches are hopelessly crowded in the peak season, streets may be smelly from restaurants and fast food outlets, parking may be impossible, services stretched to breaking point, and the incessant noise may drive you crazy. You may also have to tolerate water shortages, power cuts and sewage problems. Some people prefer to move inland to higher ground, such as the cool Troodos mountains, where it's less humid, you're isolated from the noise and you can enjoy excellent views.

Town, Village or Coast?

Do you wish to be in a town, in a small village or by the sea? In many places in Cyprus you can enjoy the benefits of both the sea and proximity to a town. Bear in mind that if you buy a property in a remote village, it may be peaceful, but you may have to tolerate poor public transport, longer travelling distances to a town with amenities, solitude and remoteness. Even if that's what you're looking for, you may not be able to pop along to the local shop for fresh bread, drop into a bar for a glass of your favourite tipple with the locals, or have a choice of restaurants on your doorstep. On the other hand, in the countryside you will be closer to nature, will have more freedom (e.g. to make as much noise as you wish) and possibly complete privacy. Living in a remote area in the country will suit those looking for peace and quiet who don't want to involve themselves in the 'hustle and bustle' of town life.

However, many people who buy a remote village home find that the peace of the countryside palls after a time and they yearn for the more exciting city life or coastal nightlife. Even if you're sure that won't happen to you, remember that at least in a town or larger village, the weekly market will be just around the corner, the doctor and pharmacy close at hand, and if you need help or run into any problems, your neighbours will be nearby. If you've never lived in the country, it's advisable to rent before buying. While it's cheaper to buy in a remote or unpopular location, it's usually much more difficult to find a buyer when you want to sell.

GETTING THERE

One of the major considerations when buying a holiday or more permanent home abroad is the cost of getting there. Even if you're going to live in Cyprus permanently, you should consider how easy it will be for family and friends to visit you. You should take into account how long the journey time is to and from airports and ports, how frequent flights are at the time(s) of year when you plan to travel and whether direct flights are available? What's the cost of travel from your home country to the area where you're planning to buy a home? Are off-season discounts or inexpensive charter flights available?

Airline Services

Scheduled Flights

Cyprus is served by some 39 international airlines, including Cyprus Airways (the national carrier) and British Airways, Olympic Airways and Helios Airways, along with countless other scheduled airlines which link the country to all corners of the world via Larnaca and Paphos airports. There are no direct flights from the US or Canada, and passengers must fly via London or any other European city that operates direct flights. The local offices of the main airlines are listed below:

- **British Airways**, Esperidon 15, 3rd Floor, Atlantic Building, Strovolos, 2001 Nicosia, PO Box 22359, 1520 Nicosia (☎ 22-799 999, 🖵 www.britishariways.com). Flights from London Heathrow;
- **Cyprus Airways**, Head Office, Alkaiou 21, PO Box 21903, 1514 Nicosia (☎ 22-663 054, 🖵 www.cyprusairways.com); Ticket Office, Leoforos Archiepiskopou Makariou III, 50 Nicosia (☎ 22-751 996). Flights from UK airports (see below) and a variety of continental European and Middle Eastern destinations;
- **First Choice Airways**, c/o Amathus Navigation Co. Ltd, Leoforos Omirou, 17, PO Box 21601, 1511 Nicosia (☎ 22-716 500, 🖵 www.first choice.co.uk). Flights from Birmingham, Cardiff, East Midlands, Glasgow, London Gatwick, London Stansted, Manchester and Newcastle;
- **Helios Airways**, Ria Court 9, 1st Floor, 22 Nietzsche Street, PO Box 43028, Larnaca (☎ 24-815 700, 🖵 www.flyhelios.com). Flights from Birmingham, Dublin, London Luton, London Stansted, Manchester and Birmingham.

Cyprus Airways offers twice-daily flights from London Heathrow to Larnaca from late March to late October and less frequent services (usually twice or three times per week) from other UK airports (Gatwick, Stansted, Birmingham and Manchester). Cyprus Airways'scheduled flights to Paphos during the summer are far less frequent with only one weekly flight from the above UK airports.

Winter scheduled flights are naturally less frequent: generally one daily flight from London Heathrow and a weekly flight from other UK airports. British Airways offers a daily service to and from Larnaca all year round. Helios Airways, which has recently been taken over by the Libra holiday company, operates scheduled flights to London Heathrow and other airports in the UK and Ireland, as well as some charter flights to other UK airports. Prices for scheduled flights have dropped recently and, if you're travelling out of season, they may be even more of a bargain than a charter flight.

Budget Airlines: Now that Cyprus has joined the EU and become part of the 'open skies' agreement, it's thought that more budget airlines will begin to look at the Cyprus market, although it obviously isn't known whether they will consider the routes profitable. One airline which will increase its services to Cyprus from May 2005 is GB Airways, a franchise partner of British Airways. GB Airways (c/o British Airways,

PO Box 22359, 1520 Nicoisa, ☎ 22-761 166, 💻 www.gbairways.com) will fly from London Gatwick to Paphos five times a week and from Manchester to Paphos twice a week.

Charter Flights

In the past, Cypriot law strictly controlled charter flights both in and out of the island, making it difficult to book seats on charter flights unless they were part of a package holiday. This was partly to protect the national airline, Cyprus Airways, and partly to discourage cheap, mass tourism on the island. Although Cyprus has now joined the EU, the government is still keen to promote the island as an upmarket tourist destination, encouraging the growth of luxury hotels and golf course developments. However, the position on flights is beginning to change, and some airlines, such as Helios Airways, are now offering seats only on charter flights from Luton, Birmingham and Manchester in the UK. Nevertheless, you still cannot rely on getting a cheap charter flight in the same way that you can to some other popular European destinations.

Airports

There are two international airports in Cyprus, one in Larnaca and the other in Paphos, although the availability of scheduled flights to and from Paphos is limited. This is primarily a tourist airport used by package holiday companies and, if you're flying to and from Cyprus out of season, you will usually have to use Larnaca airport.

 You may not enter the Republic of Cyprus via any airport or port in the northern, Turkish controlled part of the island, as these have been declared prohibited ports of entry by the Greek Cypriot government.

Ferry Services

There are currently no ferry connections between Cyprus and other countries. There are, however, regular cruises from Cyprus and it's well placed as a gateway to the Eastern Mediterranean. You can travel to Greece and the Greek Islands, Lebanon, Syria and Egypt, but sailings to Israel have been posponed until further notice. The main ports for passenger cruises are Larnaca and Limassol.

GETTING AROUND

Public transport services within Cyprus are generally good and there have been considerable improvements in recent years. There are no railways on the island, but you can get around by hired car, bus or taxi. Buses and taxis offer an efficient and reasonably priced service in most areas. There are inter-urban buses, which link all major towns and operate a daily service, urban buses and rural buses. There's also an extensive taxi service, which runs throughout Cyprus and operates much like a bus service. The Cyprus Tourism Organisation has contact telephone numbers and prices on its website (⌨ www. cyprustourism.org).

Car Hire

Multinational car hire (rental) companies such as Alamo, Avis, Europcar, Hertz, National and Thrifty have offices in most large towns and at the two international airports. If you're visiting in high season, you should reserve a car before arriving. The cost of car hire in Cyprus is reasonable by international standards, although the condition of hire cars often leaves much to be desired. Be particularly wary of bad brakes and, if possible, test drive a car before you hire it. High-season rates start at CY£11 per day for small cars (usually Japanese), including unlimited mileage and most insurance but excluding VAT at 15 per cent, which brings the price up to around CY12.50 per day. You must also pay a collision damage waiver of CY£3 per day. In high season you should book well in advance, although it's worth checking out fly-drive deals, which can reduce the cost of car hire considerably.

Hire cars in Cyprus are fitted with distinctive red plates with numbers prefixed with a 'Z' and police are usually fairly tolerant of foreign motorists. Note that you aren't permitted to cross the Green Line into northern Cyprus in a hired car. To hire a car in Cyprus you must be at least 21, and for certain categories of vehicle the age limit is 25. Drivers must have held a full licence for a minimum of a year and most companies have an upper age limit of 60 or 65. If a credit card isn't used, there's usually a daily cash deposit.

Buses

Inter-urban Buses

There are several bus companies that link the major towns from Mondays to Saturdays (there's no service on Sundays). The three main operators are Lefkosia Interurban Buses Ltd, operating between Nicosia and Limassol (☎ 22-665 814), K. Interurban Buses Ltd, operating between Nicosia and Larnaca and between Limassol and Larnaca (☎ 24-643 492), and Neo Amoroza Buses, operating between Paphos and Polis (☎ 26-936 822).

Urban Buses

Separate bus companies operate services in Ayia Napa, Larnaca, Limassol, Nicosia, Paphos, Paralimni and Polis. Buses run frequently during the day, and in some tourist areas buses run until midnight during the summer.

Rural Buses

Almost all Cyprus' villages are connected to the nearest town by a nationwide rural bus service. Buses are usually limited to once or twice a day and run at suitable times to take villagers to and from work. The inter-urban bus companies (see above) also provide routes to the larger surburban villages.

Taxis

Service Taxis

This is a low-cost, shared taxi service (taxis hold between four and eight passengers) which provides connections between all the major towns in Cyprus. Taxis run every half hour on weekdays and every hour at weekends, but there's no service on public holidays. Service taxis don't run between towns and villages. Passengers can be picked up and dropped anywhere within municipal boundaries. Taxis are operated by Travel and Express/Cyprus Interurban Taxi Co. Ltd and can be booked by telephone. There's a central number (☎ 77-777 474), which will connect you to the relevant local agency; or you can call a local office directly (Larnaca ☎ 24-661 010, Limassol ☎ 25-877 666, Nicosia ☎ 22-730 888, Paphos ☎ 26-923 800).

Urban Taxis

This is a 24-hour service which operates in all the main towns. Taxis can either be hailed on the spot or booked by telephone (Larnaca ☎ 24-828 253, Limassol ☎ 25-305 673, Nicosia ☎ 22-807 149, Paphos ☎ 26-940 279). Make sure the taxi you use has a taximeter, as it's illegal to operate or use a taxi without one. There are separate tariffs for daytime (6am to 8.30pm) and nighttime (8.30pm to 6am), the night tariff being slightly more expensive. There's an initial charge and then a per km fare, with extra charges for waiting and carrying luggage and a small supplement for travel on public holidays.

Rural Taxis

There's also a rural taxi service, but these taxis can only be hired from their base station. The exception to this is when the taxi is hired at an airport or a seaport, where the taxi driver must present his official documentation. Meters aren't installed on these taxis and tariffs depend on the time of day (or night), waiting times and luggage, although costs are very reasonable, starting at just over CY£0.20 per km.

Roads & Driving

The Cypriot road system is good, with well surfaced, toll-free motorways (A roads) connecting the capital, Nicosia, with the coastal towns of Larnaca, Limassol and Paphos. There are also good main roads (B roads), which run parallel to the corresponding motorways and usually closer to the coast, linking Limassol and Nicosia to the Troodos mountains. Off the main routes, minor 'roads' are identified as E and F roads. These are often forest roads are some are unsurfaced and can be mere tracks and rather dangerous, especially in wet weather. There are no roads linking the Republic of Cyprus with northern Cyprus.

Driving is on the left and road signs are in English and Greek. Look out for place names that are sometimes in English and sometimes in a direct translation of the Greek (but using the English alphabet) which can be very confusing – especially as their use isn't consistent throughout the island. Distances are given in kph. The maximum speed limit on motorways is 100kph (62mph) and the lower limit is 65kph (40mph). In built-up areas the limit is 50kph (31mph). On all other roads the limit is 80kph (50mph).

In December 2004, a government minister revealed that the death toll in Cyprus is currently double the EU average and that the country had some of the most careless drivers in Europe. As a result, the Cypriot government "announced a string of deterrent and punitive measures", according to a report in the *Cyprus Mail* in January 2005. Since then, the Cypriot authorities have imposed licence penalty points and fines for driving offences in an effort to improve Cyprus' appalling road safety record. These are given for speeding, dangerous or negligent driving, driving under the influence of alcohol or drugs as well as relatively minor offences, such as using a mobile phone while driving and not wearing a seat belt or (on a motorbike) a helmet (see **Rules of the Road** on page 71). Fines for minor offences incur fines of around CY£50; for more serious offences, fines are determined by the courts. If you're using a foreign driving licence, you cannot incur penalty points but can be fined and even imprisoned!

The Cyprus Automobile Association (CAA, 12 Chrysanthou Mylona Street, 2014 Nicosia, ☎ 22-313 233, 💻 www.cyprusaa.org) can provide maps and information on motoring in Cyprus and offers 24-hour recovery assistance to members.

Importing a Car

There are two factors which affect the import of cars (and other vehicles): whether or not you're importing it from another EU country, and whether or not you're retiring to Cyprus. As there are no regular ferry services to Cyprus from mainland Europe, the cost of getting your car to Cyprus my be prohibitive in any case.

Unless you're a retiree (see below), if you're importing a car from outside the EU . . . don't! You must pay import duty, excise duty and VAT, which can add up to more than the value of the car.

If you're importing a car from another EU country, you're exempt from paying import dutyand VAT on it (assming that you've paid the necessary duty in your home country). You must still pay excise duty, although if you're retiring to Cyprus you can claim this back (see below). You must be able to prove that the car has been imported from another EU member state and that it has been in your possession in your home country for a minimum of six months. You must complete form T2L (available from your vehicle supplier or the customs authorities in your home country or Cyprus) and, in the case of a used vehicle, you must produce the number plates and the vehicle registration documents. Failure to provide the necessary documents will render you liable for import duty. You must declare an imported vehicle to Cypriot customs and pay any duty and taxes due within 24 hours.

If you're retiring to Cyprus, whether or not you're an EU citizen, you can reclaim any excise duty and VAT paid on import. Relief from duty is granted on condition that you're resident in Cyprus and neither you nor any of your family is doing paid work in Cyprus. A husband and wife can import two cars duty- and tax-free, although they must be registered in separate names. You must apply in person to the Relief Section of Customs Headquarters in Nicosia for the Car Tax Concession as soon as you've applied for residence (see page 31). Required documents are as follows:

- Passports for yourself and (if applicable) your spouse;
- Evidence of residence (e.g. sale contract, rental contract, permission to purchase in Cyprus);
- Temporary residence permit or Alien's Registration Certificate;
- Driving licence (either Cypriot or from your home country);
- Evidence of financial independence or that you're receiving an income from abroad;
- Copies of all the above.

Application forms and more information are available from Director of Customs, Customs Headquarters in Nicosia (✉ headquarters@customs. mof.gov.cy). The Cyprus government website (🖳 www.mof.gov. cy/mof/customs) has details of conditions and procedures. **If you're planning to import a car into Cyprus, you should check the latest regulations with the customs authorities**. Further information on importing a car can be obtained from the CAA (see above).

If you want to export (even temporarily) a car registered in Cyprus, you must obtain an export permit from the Ministry of Commerce and Industry.

Driving Licences

The new-style EU driving licences are valid until expiry. Any other type of foreign licence or an international driving permit is valid for six months, and residents must apply for a Cypriot licence before the six-month period has expired. To apply for a Cypriot licence, you should submit the following to the Department of Road Transport in Nicosia (☎ 22-807 139):

- Your existing licence;
- A completed application form with photographs;
- Your identity card or proof of registration with the Immigration Office;
- The fee of CY£35.

Car Insurance

You will need to check with your insurance company that you're correctly insured before arriving in Cyprus, where third party liability insurance is the minimum required by law. Since 2001, Cyprus has been part of a European agreement that vehicles registered in any of the countries party to the agreement are assumed to be insured in their country of origin. If you plan to remain on the island for a long period (or indefinitely), you should insure your car with a local insurance company or through one of the local agents for the large European insurance companies. There are plenty to choose from and you can find them listed in the yellow pages. Costs vary according to cover, but the minimum legal cover costs around CY£80 for an average car.

Rules of the Road

The following general road rules may help you adjust to driving in Cyprus. Don't, however, expect other motorists to adhere to them (many local drivers invent their own 'rules').

- Driving is on the left.

- Alcohol is a major factor in many road accidents and recently the authorities have lowered the permitted levels of blood alcohol concentration, in an effort to reduce the number of accidents. The concentration is now 39mg of alcohol per 100ml of breath and 90mg of alcohol per 100ml or blood.

- All motorists must carry two red warning triangles. First-aid kits and fire extinguishers are recommended, and petrol cans are prohibited.

- There are 'stop' or give way' signs at junctions and no automatic give way to the right (or left) rule. Priority is given to the right at roundabouts.

- The law requires that all cars, minibuses and vans under 3.5 tonnes have seat belts fitted in the front and back seats, and the wearing of seat belts is **compulsory**; this includes passengers in rear seats when seat belts are fitted. Children under five aren't allowed to travel in the front seat of a vehicle under any circumstances and must use a seat belt in the back. Children between five and ten are allowed to travel in the front only if an appropriate child seat belt is fitted. You will be awarded penalty points on your licence or fined for not complying. **If you have an accident and weren't wearing a seat belt, your insurance company can refuse to pay a personal injury claim.**

- Dipped headlights should be used in built-up areas after sunset.

- Horns should be used only in emergencies, particularly in towns at night and close to hospitals, when lights should be flashed to warn other motorists or pedestrians.

- White or yellow lines mark the separation of traffic lanes. A solid single line or two solid lines means no overtaking in either direction.

A solid line on your side of the road means that overtaking is prohibited in your direction. You may overtake only when there's a single broken line in the middle of the road or double lines with a broken line on your side of the road. No overtaking may also be shown by the international road sign of two cars side by side – one red and one black.

- Always check your rear view and wing mirrors carefully before overtaking, as motorists often seem to appear from nowhere and zoom past at high speeds.

- It's illegal to overtake on an inside lane unless traffic is being channelled in a different direction. Motorists must indicate before overtaking and when moving back into an inside lane after overtaking.

- Be particularly wary of moped riders and cyclists. It isn't always easy to see them, particularly when they're hidden by the blind spots of a car or are riding at night without lights. **Follow the example set by other motorists, who, when overtaking mopeds and cyclists, usually give them a wide berth.** If you knock them off their bikes, you may have a difficult time convincing the police that it wasn't your fault; far better to avoid them (and the police).

- Cars mustn't be overloaded, particularly roof racks, and luggage weight shouldn't exceed that recommended in manufacturers' handbooks.

- Parking and waiting are prohibited on double and single yellow lines, although single lines allow loading and unloading. Be careful where you park, particularly in towns and cities. **Never** park across entrances, at bus stops or taxi ranks, in front of fire or ambulance stations or schools or near pedestrian crossings. Always check parking signs carefully, and ask someone if you aren't sure whether parking is permitted.

- Helmets must be worn on motorcycles, although you will see many bare-headed motorcyclists.

- All motorists in Cyprus must be familiar with the local highway code, available from book shops.

3.

YOUR DREAM HOME

Once you've considered possible locations for your dream home in Cyprus, you must decide on the type of property that will best suit your requirements and consider the purchase options and the fees associated with buying. When buying a home anywhere, it isn't advisable to be in too much of a hurry – and Cyprus is no exception. Before looking at properties, it's important to have a good idea of the type of property you want (see page 92) and the price you wish to pay. Have a good look around in your chosen region(s) and obtain an accurate picture of the types of properties available, their relative prices and what you can expect to get for your money. Most importantly make a list of what you want and don't want in a property – if you don't do this, you're likely to be overwhelmed by the number of properties to be viewed.

To reduce the chance of making an expensive error when buying in an unfamiliar region, it's often wise to rent a house for a period (see **Renting Before Buying** on page 83), taking in the worst part of the year (weather-wise). This allows you to become familiar with the region and the weather, and gives you plenty of time to look around for a home at your leisure. Although you should bear in mind that the healthy property market in Cyprus means that prices are rising faster than in previous years, don't rush into anything. There's no shortage of properties for sale on the island, with developers working around the clock to provide more. Whatever kind of property you're looking for, you will have an abundance from which to choose. Wait until you find something you fall head over heels in love with and then think about it for another week or two before rushing headlong to the altar! One of the advantages of buying property in Cyprus is that there's often another 'dream' home around the next corner – and the second or third dream home is often even better than the first. Extensive research is the best way to help you make the right decision.

This chapter is designed to help you decide what sort of home to buy and to help you avoid problems (see below). It also contains information about renting, estate agents, cost of property, fees, buying a resale or a new home, community development properties, buying for investment, inspections and surveys, renovation and restoration, and building your own home.

RESEARCH

The secret of successfully buying a home in Cyprus is research, research and more research. A successful purchase is much more likely if you thoroughly investigate the various areas of the island, the types of property available, prices and relative values, and the procedure for buying property. The more research you do before buying a property in Cyprus the better. Research should (if possible) include advice from those who already own a home there, from whom you can usually obtain invaluable information (often based on their own mistakes). Although it's a common practice, mixing a holiday with property purchase isn't advisable, as most people are inclined to make poor decisions when their mind is fixed on play rather than business.

 Some people make expensive (even catastrophic) errors when buying a home in Cyprus, often because they don't do sufficient research and are simply in too much of a hurry – often setting themselves impossible deadlines such as buying a home during a long weekend or a week's holiday.

There are numerous sources of information about property in Cyprus, including publications such as this one and those listed in **Appendix B**, websites (see **Appendix C**) and exhibitions. Property exhibitions are now common in the UK and Ireland, and are increasingly popular with prospective buyers, who can get a good idea of what's available and make contact with estate agents and developers. The main exhibition organisers in the UK and Ireland are listed in **Appendix B**. You may be charged an admission fee. Outbound Publishing (1 Commercial Road, Eastbourne, East Sussex BN21 3XQ, UK, (☎ 01323-726040, 🖥 www.outboundpublishing.com) publishes *World of Property*, a quarterly publication containing many properties for sale in Cyprus (and other countries), as well as organising exhibitions in the south and north of England.

AVOIDING PROBLEMS

The problems associated with buying property abroad have been highlighted in the last decade or so, during which time the property market in many countries has gone from boom to bust and back again. The Cypriot property market is relatively 'safe' compared with that in other countries popular with foreign buyers, particularly Spain. As Cyprus is a small island, there's a more tightly knit community of estate agents, developers and lawyers, all of whom speak fluent English, and there are fewer 'cowboy' operators, as the market is more highly regulated and estate agents must be licensed and qualified in property law. There are thousands of foreign property owners in Cyprus, the vast majority of whom are happy with their purchases and encountered few or no problems when buying their homes. Nevertheless, the many possible pitfalls in the property purchase procedure mustn't be ignored, and you should seek reliable professional advice before making any major decisions.

Common Mistakes

Common mistakes made by buyers in Cyprus include:

- Buying a house in the wrong area (rent first).
- Buying a home that's difficult to resell.
- Not using professional advice, especially that of a local lawyer (see below).
- Buying a home for renovation and not researching the practicalities and the costs (see **Renovation** page 118).
- Not having a proper survey done (see page 114).
- Not including any necessary conditional clauses in the contract (see page 148).
- Buying a property for a business, e.g. to convert into self-catering accommodation, and being over-optimistic about possible income, consequently taking on too large a mortgage or leaving inadequate funds to live on.
- Making a hasty decision without doing proper research.

 Many people have had their fingers burnt by rushing into property deals without proper care and consideration. It's all too easy to fall in love with the attractions of a home in the sun and to sign a contract without giving it sufficient thought.

If you aren't absolutely certain, don't allow yourself to be rushed into making a decision, e.g. by fears of an imminent price rise or of losing the property to another buyer. Although many people successfully buy holiday or retirement homes in Cyprus, it's vital to do your homework thoroughly first.

Legal Advice

It cannot be emphasised too strongly that anyone planning to buy property in Cyprus must take expert, independent legal advice.

Although Cypriot law is very similar to British law, don't make the mistake of thinking that house-buying procedures are the same as in the UK. Don't assume anything but take expert advice.

The relatively small price – in comparison with the cost of a home – of obtaining legal advice is excellent value, if only for the peace of mind it affords. Trying to cut corners by saving legal costs is foolhardy in the extreme when tens or hundreds of thousands of pounds are at stake.

SURVIVAL TIP
Never sign anything, or pay any money, until you've sought legal advice in your own language, from a lawyer who's experienced in Cypriot property law.

If you aren't prepared to do this, you shouldn't even think about buying a property! Most people who experience problems take no precautions whatsoever when purchasing property and, of those that do take legal advice, many do so only after having already paid a deposit and signed a contract (or when they hit problems). Don't leave your brains behind at the airport. You wouldn't buy and sell property in your home country without legal advice, so don't do it in Cyprus!

Areti Charidemou & Associates

International Law Office based in Limassol, Cyprus
Serving clients worldwide

Legal experts trained in the UK and Greece and fluent in English and Greek

Areas of expertise are property law and conveyancing throughout the Republic of Cyprus, residency and work permits in Cyprus, Offshore companies, local companies, international tax planning, Trusts, Wills.

Areti Charidemou and Associates
21 Vasili Michailidi Street, 3026 Limassol, Cyprus
Postal Address: P.O. Box 54708 CY-3727 Limassol, Cyprus
Tel. +357 25 746103, Fax +357 25 344019
Email: info@aretilawyers.com

The only professionals legally qualified and permitted to give legal advice in Cyprus are lawyers, so don't take legal advice from anyone else. Don't pick a lawyer at random, but engage one who has been highly recommended by someone you can trust. Before engaging him, you should check that he's a member of the Cyprus Bar Association (23 Loukis Akritas Street, Ayios Dhometios, CY-1508 Nicosia, ☎ 22-779 156, 🖥 www.cyprusbarassociation.org), which is 'compulsory'. You can check the member list on the website or telephone the association and give the lawyer's name. All Cypriot lawyers speak English and many deal principally with foreign homebuyers and know and understand the problems you may come up against. **Although it may seem expensive and legal checks on a property may mean you have to wait extra time before buying, you shouldn't attempt a purchase without legal advice.**

Employing Professionals

There are very few expatriate estate agents, builders and surveyors practising in Cyprus, where estate agents, building contractors and surveyors are strictly licensed and it's difficult for expatriates to meet the stringent registration requirements (see **Estate Agents** on page 86 and **Surveyors** on page 114). Although property developers don't require a licence, they can work only with licensed contractors. The authorities regulating these professions regularly check the qualifications of everyone claiming to be a professional. Nevertheless, you should always check the credentials of any professionals you employ, whatever their nationality. All professionals throughout Cyprus speak English and often other languages too.

 It's never advisable to rely solely on advice proffered by those with a financial interest in selling you a property, such as a builder, developer or estate agent, although their advice may be excellent and totally unbiased.

Checks

There are a number of essential checks to be made before you buy a home in Cyprus. These should all be made by your lawyer, but you should be aware of them so that you can ask your lawyer the right questions at the right time.

● Make sure that the vendor is the legal owner of the property and that there are no outstanding debts relating to it, such as a mortgage. This is done via the Lands Office.

- If you're buying a new property or one that's under construction, make sure that the vendor has obtained the agreed Town Planning and Building Permits. If he hasn't, ensure that your lawyer makes this a condition of the sale contract. This will ensure that the vendor is legally authorised to carry out the construction of your property.

- Make sure that your sale contract is deposited with the local Lands Office, especially if the property is part of a new development. A developer may tell you that there are no separate title deeds for your apartment or house. This means that the title deeds cannot be transferred to your name until the whole development is finished, which may be some time. To protect your rights, the sale contract must be worded in such a way that the vendor is legally committed and your property protected until such time as a separate title deed can be issued to you.

- Make sure any co-owners sign the sale contract. There are often co-owners of property and land in Cyprus and they must **all** sign your sale contract to avoid any future disputes.

- Make sure that your sale contract is stamped and registered by the Lands Office.

Problems can be avoided if you use an experienced local lawyer to draft your sale contract.

Buying Off Plan

Buying off plan (i.e. a property that is being built or yet to be built) is probably the most common method of buying in Cyprus (see page 102). It isn't uncommon to have problems when buying a property off plan, but generally there are fewer problems with buying off plan in Cyprus than in many other countries, and there are many satisfied off-plan property buyers (there may be no alternative if you wish to buy a home in a popular area). Nevertheless, it's worth remembering that the process can be more time-consuming and stressful than buying a resale property. To minimise the chance of experiencing problems (or even eliminate it altogether) when buying off plan, you should do the following:

- Use a local lawyer, experienced in this kind of purchase arrangement.

- Make sure that your lawyer drafts a contract between you and the developer which has your interests uppermost. Usually the completion of each agreed stage of construction is certified by an architect or supervising engineer and then the agreed stage payment is handed over. **Never hand over any money in advance.**

- Make sure the property is finished before making a final payment. A finished property is one where the building is complete in every detail (as confirmed by your own lawyer or architect), communal services have been completed, and **all** the infrastructure is in place such as roads, parking areas, external lighting, landscaping, water, sewerage, electricity and telephone services.

- Use an experienced, registered estate agent (see page 86), who must be insured to cover any serious problems that arise with their clients.

If you follow these simple rules, buying off plan can be one of the best ways to acquire your dream home.

Buying Land

Buying land and having a home built on it is an extremely popular option in Cyprus (see **Building Your Own Home** on page 103) but, unless you're living permanently in Cyprus, you should consider the possible problems before doing so. The advantage is that you will eventually have a house built to your own specifications, but the disadvantage is that you won't be on the spot to supervise building work. It's virtually impossible to co-ordinate work and deal with daily problems if you aren't in Cyprus. You can employ an architect and a contractor or a developer to do this for you rather than trying to deal directly with the builder, but this won't necessarily eliminate all the potential problems. There are also certain checks peculiar to buying land that you must make before you commit yourself financially, including the following:

- Make sure that the piece of land you're shown is the piece of land you pay for. Obtain the title deeds and plot references and the position of the plot on the Lands Office plans.

- Cyprus operates a zoning system, which was changed in 2003, and you should check any restrictions and plans for the zone you plan to build in as well as those for any nearby zones. Ensure that your land or nearby land doesn't qualify as an industrial or farming zone.

- Ensure that planning permission has been granted for the use you intend or that obtaining it is a formality. To obtain a permission, your land must be on a public road or have access to one. If it isn't on a public road and the distance to one is more than 600ft, you won't be granted a building permit (see **Building Your Own Home** on page 103).

- Check the permissible building density. This is the amount of the land that you will be allowed to build on and may limit the size of property you can construct.

EU citizens may buy as much land as they like, but non-EU nationals may buy no more than 3 *donums* (just over 4,000m^2 or almost exactly 1 acre) of land and only one house or apartment.

RENTING BEFORE BUYING

If you're uncertain about exactly what sort of home you want (or where you wish to live), it's advisable to rent a furnished property for a period. This reduces the chance of making a costly error, particularly when you're planning to buy in an unfamiliar area, and in a country where you've simply spent a few happy holidays.

SURVIVAL TIP
Renting before buying is even more important
for those planning to live permanently or set up a
business in Cyprus, when it isn't wise to buy a home
until you're sure that the business
will be a success.

If possible, you should rent a similar property to that which you're planning to buy, during the time of year when you plan to occupy it. Renting allows you to become familiar with the weather, the amenities and the local people, to meet other foreigners who have made their homes in Cyprus and share their experiences, and, not least, to discover the cost of living at first hand. If you plan to live in Cyprus permanently or for long periods, you should rent for at least six months and preferably a year. An area that's quiet and relaxing between November and March can become noisy, congested and stressful between April and October, particularly in package holiday regions. Conversely, a place that's attractive in the summer can 'close' in the winter. If you cannot rent for that long, try to visit for two-week periods in each of the four seasons.

Renting not only allows you to find out whether life in Cyprus is really what you want, it also 'buys' you time to find your dream home at your leisure. You may even wish to consider renting a home long term (or even 'permanently') as an alternative to buying, as it saves tying up your capital and can be surprisingly inexpensive in many regions. Some people let their family homes abroad and rent one in Cyprus, in which case it's possible to make a profit!

Standards can vary considerably, from dilapidated, ill-equipped apartments to luxury villas with every modern convenience. Always check whether a property is equipped to the standard you require and whether it has central heating if you're planning to rent in winter.

If you're looking for a rental property for a several months, e.g. three to six months, it's best not to rent unseen, but to rent a holiday apartment for a week or two to allow yourself time to look around for a longer-term rental. Rentals can be found by contacting owners advertising in local newspapers, such as *The Cyprus Mail*, and in the publications listed in **Appendix B** and through estate agents in most areas, many of whom also handle long- and short-term rentals. **A rental contract is necessary when renting any property, whether long or short-term.**

Long-term Rentals

As Cyprus is a popular holiday destination, in and around resort areas rentals are limited to self-catering units rather than residential accommodation. Long -term rentals are easiest to find in the main towns and cities and in some resorts, such as Paphos, where retirees often rent for long periods before buying. Properties can be let furnished or unfurnished. If you rent unfurnished, there are a number of companies (listed in the yellow pages) who will hire appliances to you.

Short-term Rentals

There's no shortage of short-term rental property in Cyprus, but short-term rents are usually high, particularly in popular holiday areas, where many properties are let as self-catering holiday accommodation. You may, however, be able to take advantage of long-term holiday package deals, which many companies offer during the winter (November to Easter), when you can stay in a self-catering apartment or hotel in Cyprus for several months at an extremely reasonable cost while you research your property purchase. Many estate agents in Cyprus also let self-catering properties in resort areas at a considerable reduction during low season. During the summer, you may get a better deal if you offer to rent long term (e.g. two or three months).

Rental Costs

Property rental costs vary considerably with the size (number of-bedrooms) and quality of a property, its age and the facilities provided, and the length of the rental period (see below). However, the most significant factor affecting rents is the location. Average prices for short- and long-term rentals in the main areas of Cyprus are given below.

Short-term Rentals

There are virtually no short-term rental properties in Nicosia. The prices quoted below are **weekly**.

- **Larnaca** – A two-bedroom house can be rented for around CY£275, a four-bedroom villa for between £750 and £1,200 per week.

- **Limassol** – In Limassol city, a two-bedroom apartment costs around CY£375 and a luxury four-bedroom house CY£1,000. In Pissouri Bay and village, a two-bedroom villa costs CY£650 and a three-bedroom villa CY£825.

- **Paphos** – A two-bedroom apartment costs around CY£400, a three-bedroom house CY£550 and a large villa from CY£750.

Long-term Rentals

The prices quoted below are **monthly**.

- **Larnaca** – A one- or two-bedroom apartment costs around CY£250, a townhouse around CY£300 and a larger detached house around CY£500.

- **Limassol** – Prices are slightly higher than in Larnaca, a one- or two-bedroom apartment costing around CY£270, a townhouse around CY£350 and a larger house between CY£500 and CY£600.

- **Nicosia** – Property in the capital is more expensive than in Limassol, a one- or two-bedroom apartment costing around CY£350, a larger apartment or townhouse around CY£400 and a large or detached house around CY£650.

- **Paphos** – Apartments in cost around CY£270, townhouses around CY£350 and larger houses or villas around CY£500.

Home Exchange

An alternative to renting is to exchange your home abroad with one in Cyprus for a period. This way you can experience home living in Cyprus for a relatively small cost and may save yourself the expense of a long-term rental. Although there's always an element of risk involved in exchanging your home with another family, most agencies thoroughly vet clients and have a track record of successful swaps. There are home exchange agencies in most countries, although some don't cover Cyprus. Among those that do are Home Base Holidays, 7 Park Avenue, London N13 5PG, UK (☎ 020-8886 8752, ⌨ www.homebase-hols.com), Home

Exchange.com (⌨ www.homeexchange.com), Homelink International, Linfield House, Gorse Hill Road, Virginia Water, Surrey GU25 4AS, UK (☎ 01344-842642, ⌨ www.homelink.org.uk – click on 'Other Countries' for properties in Cyprus) and Home Swap International (⌨ www.singles homeexchange.com). *The Home Exchange Guide* by M. Simon and T. Baker (Poyeen Publishing) gives comprehensive information and advice about home exchange.

HOUSE HUNTING

There are many ways of finding homes for sale in Cyprus, including the following:

● Newspapers and magazines, including the English-language publications listed in **Appendix B** (*Homes Overseas* magazine in particular carries a large amount of advertisements from estate agents in Cyprus) and property newspapers and magazines published in Cyprus, such as *BuySell*, which is available weekly, and the monthly magazine *Property & Home Cyprus*;

● Property exhibitions (see **Appendix B**);

● The internet, where there are literally thousands of sites dedicated to property in Cyprus. These can be found by entering 'Cyprus property' in a search engine such as Google (⌨ www.google.com) or Altavista (⌨ www.altavista.com). Note that most of the property sites belong to or are linked to an estate agent.

● Visiting an area. Many property owners sell privately to avoid paying an agent's commission, but be wary of this kind of transaction. If you go ahead, make sure you use an experienced local lawyer.

● Estate agents (see below). Most property owners sell through an estate agent.

ESTATE AGENTS

No one is allowed to advertise property (unless it's their own) other than a registered estate agent, and the vast majority of sales are handled by estate agents, particularly those where non-resident foreign buyers are involved. It's common for foreigners in many countries, especially the UK, to use an agent or marketing company in their own country who works in co-operation with Cypriot agents and developers. Many Cypriot agents also advertise abroad, particularly in the publications listed in **Appendix B**, as well as in expatriate magazines and newspapers

CyprusPropertyDreams

Let us show you how to live the dream in Sunny Cyprus

We specialise only in Cyprus where our personal experience is yours for free.

We are neither estate agents nor developers, we simply act as a marketing company.

Each client is treated individually with a tailor made itinerary.

Estate agent staff will meet you to discuss the portfolio of properties they have found for you, assisting you with negotiations and payment terms.

Mortgages can be advised on from a mortgage broker in Cyprus.

Check our web site for lots of information on Cyprus.

Advice is freely provided; just email us your questions.

Our service is completely FREE and without any obligation or pressure at all.

Client testimonials on our web site.

Inspections trips available, ask for details.

We are not contracted to any developer and only connect you with a fully licensed and registered estate agent in Cyprus for your security and protection. Check estate agents' registration number before you use them; all have to be licensed to sell property

If you want the best advice, visit our website
www.livingcyprus.net
or email us on info@livingcyprus.net
or call us on **0845 095 6407** or international **00 357 99 763401**

in Cyprus, and many also have extensive websites. All Cypriot estate agents have staff who speak English and other foreign languages. As Cyprus is a small island, many agents have property listings covering all the popular areas and are knowledgeable about the entire island.

> **SURVIVAL TIP**
> If you pay a deposit to an agent in
> Cyprus, you should ensure it goes into a separate
> bonded account.

Registration

Cypriot estate agents are strictly regulated by law and must be professionally qualified and registered with the Registrar of Estate Agents. Nevertheless, there are some unregistered 'agents' operating on the island. At the end of 2004, a new law was passed which aimed to protect house buyers and control unregistered agents. The CREAA (see below) is closely monitoring those who call themselves estate agents, property consultants or property finders. Unless they're registered, they're operating illegally and you're advised not to use their services. Always check an agent's registration. Ask for the estate agent's registration number and have it checked if you aren't convinced that it's genuine.

Once an agent is registered, he may choose to be a member of the Cyprus Real Estate Agents' Association (CREAA, ☎ 25-367 467, ✉ solo @cytanet.com.cy). Although this isn't compulsory, most bona fide agents are members of CREAA and you're strongly advised to use the services of a CREAA member to protect your interests. Members must have professional indemnity insurance for a minimum of CY£100,000. They must also possess a thorough knowledge of the law regarding immovable property. They must be able to speak Greek, have extensive experience in selling property or be a university graduate in a relevant subject, possess an untarnished criminal and civic record and not be a bankrupt. If you have a dispute with a member, CREAA will intercede on your behalf and, if necessary, appoint a lawyer for you for a nominal fee. You may be afforded extra protection if the agent is a member of an international organisation, such as the International Real Estate Agents' Association (FIABCI).

Fees

There are no government controls on agents' fees in Cyprus, where an agent's commission is usually paid by the vendor (although he will

Calogirou

Nobody knows the Cyprus Property Market
better...

In the Cyprus Property market since 1945...

Office: 6e-6f, 6th floor, Roussos Centre Point,
Pentadromos Square, Limassol, Cyprus.
P.O. Box 50077, Limassol 3600, Cyprus.
Tel: 00-357-25 362 798.
E-mail: omada@spidernet.com.cy
www.bestcyprusproperties.com

Registered Estate Agents #041

obviously 'include' this in the asking price). The commission charged is normally at least 3 per cent of the selling price (plus VAT at 15 per cent) but the usual fee is 5 per cent (plus VAT). Foreign agents or marketing companies located abroad often work with local agents and share the standard commission, so buyers usually pay no more by using them. However, check in advance whether this is the case and how much you're required to pay. When buying, also check whether you need to pay commission or any extras in addition to the sale price (apart from the normal fees and taxes associated with buying a property – see page 97).

Viewing

If possible, you should have an idea about which area you might want to live in, what sort of property you want and your budget before visiting Cyprus. Obtain details of as many properties as possible in your chosen area and price range, and make a shortlist of those you wish to view. Many estate agents have websites so you can check what's on offer from the comfort of your home, although sites won't show all properties for sale or the latest properties on their books. Agents' wesbites have improved considerably in the last few years, and many provide not only information about the properties and the areas but also information about Cyprus, especially for those thinking of relocating there. Nevertheless, you should always double-check information.

Agents vary enormously in their efficiency, enthusiasm and professionalism and the best ones provide an abundance of associated information and guidance. If an agent shows little interest in finding out exactly what you want, you should look elsewhere. There are plenty of experienced agents in Cyprus keen to give you a good service. There are no national property listings in Cyprus and agents jealously guard their list of properties, although many work with overseas agents in areas that are popular with foreign buyers. Cypriot agents who advertise in foreign magazines or who work closely with overseas agents usually provide coloured photographs and a full description, particularly for the more expensive properties. If you're using a foreign agent, confirm (and reconfirm) that a particular property is still for sale and the price, before travelling to Cyprus to view it.

You're usually shown properties personally by agents and won't be given the keys (especially to furnished properties) or be expected to deal with tenants or vendors directly. You should always make an appointment, as agents need to ensure that a property is available for viewing and there's someone available to show you around. If you're on holiday, it's fine to drop in unannounced to have a look at what's on offer, but don't expect an agent to show you properties without an appointment. If you view properties during a holiday, it's better to do so at the start of it so that you can return later to inspect any you particularly like a second or third time.

You should try to view as many properties as possible during the time available, but allow sufficient time to view each property thoroughly, to travel between properties and for breaks for sustenance. Although it's important to see sufficient properties to form an accurate opinion of price and quality, don't see too many properties in one day (around four to six is usually a manageable number), as it's easy to become confused over the merits of each property. If you're shown properties that don't meet your specifications, tell the agent immediately. You can also help an agent narrow the field by telling him exactly what's wrong with the properties you reject. It's advisable to make notes of both the good **and** bad features and take lots of photographs of the properties you like, so that you're able to compare them later at your leisure. It's also advisable to mark each property on a map so that, should you wish to return later on your own, you can find them without getting lost.

The more a property appeals to you, the more you should look for faults and negative points – if you still like it after stressing the negative points, it must have special appeal.

Viewing Trips

When arranging a trip to Cyprus to view potential properties, bear in mind that there's always more to an area than you can possibly see on a single trip. Always allow yourself sufficient time to view and compare properties offered by a number of agents and developers. A long weekend isn't sufficient time to have a good look around, unless you already know exactly what you want to buy and where, or have already narrowed the field to a few properties. You should always make arrangements in advance so that an agent is available to take you to see the properties you're interested in.

Some agents and developers arrange viewing trips with inexpensive accommodation for prospective buyers and sometimes refund the cost if they buy a property. By all means take advantage of such offers, but don't allow yourself to be pressured by that particular company into buying a property that's on its books on a viewing trip. Tell them in advance that you also want to see other properties; if they're unhappy about that, you might be better off investing a little extra in a no-strings attached, independent trip.

Some agents advertise 'free' inspection flights, which you then have to pay for if you don't buy anything. Check the small print and conditions of inspection flights as well as the reputation of the estate agents offering them before you sign up. Reputable estate agents will probably vet you and how serious you are about buying before accepting you on an inspection trip, which is expensive to lay on. Most agents offer after-sales services and will help you to arrange legal advice, insurance, utilities, and interior decorators and builders, and may offer a full management and rental service on behalf of non-resident owners. Note, however, that agents may receive commissions for referrals and therefore you may not receive independent advice.

SURVIVAL TIP
Never allow yourself to be pressurised
into a purchase and always take independent expert
legal advice before committing yourself
to anything.

TYPES OF PROPERTY

Cyprus offers a wealth of different properties, from small holiday apartments or village homes, modern apartments and townhouses to huge villas with plenty of land and just about everything in between. Both new and old properties are available, including some restored and unrestored old village houses, although these are relatively rare; there was a considerable amount of new building on the island in the early '60s and 80 per cent of housing in Cyprus has been built within the past 30 years. There are many new developments, of varying standard, some with golf courses, swimming pools or other sports facilities, such as tennis courts. Over-development and mass-market tourism has changed some coastal areas beyond recognition, although most inland villages are still unspoilt and full of character. You will find older houses with more character in villages and the surrounding areas. Newer properties built in traditional Cypriot style sometimes lack the character that goes with age.

 Since 1st May 2004, when the Republic of Cyprus joined the EU, value added tax (VAT) has been payable on all new properties, except those where the application for planning permission was submitted to the Planning Department before 1st May 2004 (see page 179). As a result, there's considerable demand for property that's exempt from VAT, including old properties.

Traditional Cypriot houses are built from natural materials, especially stone and wood. The purchase and restoration of typical Cypriot village homes is becoming increasingly popular among foreigners, especially those looking for the peace and quiet of a village. However, in the most popular areas of Cyprus, around the towns of Paphos and Limassol, most property consists of apartments, townhouses and villas, many of which are purpose built for the holiday-home market.

Apartments

There are plenty of apartments available in Cyprus, large and small, in the towns and coastal areas. Their quality and size varies enormously from small studio apartments in a town to spacious front-line beach or golf course apartments. Prices range from around CY£45,000 for a small one-bedroom apartment to around CY£300,000 for a three-bedroom apartment on the prestigious Aphrodite Hills golf development. Unless you're in a resort area, try to avoid buying a studio or one-bedroom apartment, as these are notoriously difficult to sell. Apartments with two and three-bedrooms, both in towns and resort areas, are usually more in demand.

It's best to buy in a small block, e.g. one of no more than around five storeys. Although your common service bills will be higher, the management is likely to be more efficient and you should have more privacy in a smaller block.

The advantages of apartments include low maintenance (once you've carried out any necessary work), security (especially if the block has 24-hour security) and the use of communal gardens and pool (and possibly other facilities such as tennis courts). Apartments situated in towns have the added advantage of local facilities and amenities within walking distance. Disadvantages can include noisy neighbours, poorly maintained communities and crowded complexes during holidays.

Village Properties

As property prices begin to rise on the coast and resort areas become more crowded, foreigners are increasingly looking at village properties in their search for a dream house. Property in villages can range from a tiny house which is a complete ruin to a larger house (which may also be a ruin) with a reasonably large plot and sometimes fruit trees or olive groves. Renovation is almost always necessary unless you pay a premium and buy a property that has already been modernised.

Advantages of village properties include lower prices, peace and quiet and the opportunity to live in the 'real' Cyprus. You're likely to be given an extremely warm and friendly welcome from the locals, as Cypriots are well known for the welcome they extend to both visitors and foreign residents. On the other hand, rural properties usually involve extensive maintenance as well as restoration work, utilities may be poor or non-existent, and amenities and facilities are often some distance away; many Cypriot village communities are somewhat depleted as younger generations leave to work in the towns and cities.

Townhouses

Townhouses are generally rows of terraced houses, often set around communal gardens with a pool. They're usually spacious and often have three or four 'floors', including a basement for a garage and storage and sometimes a roof terrace. Townhouses generally have little outside space or garden except for a small patch at the front and back, often paved as a patio. Construction tends to be recent and is generally of reasonable to good quality. Townhouses are very popular in almost all the new developments in Cyprus, partly because they're usually easier than to sell than an apartment but also because they aren't as expensive to buy or to maintain as a villa.

Villas

It's the dream of many foreigners to own a villa in the sun. You don't often find them in towns and cities but there are plenty in coastal areas that are popular with foreigners. Some villas form part of a complex and may share gardens and a pool, each having a small individual plot, while others are set in huge grounds or luxurious developments. Construction quality is usually excellent and villas are always reasonably spacious and have at least two storeys. Prices start at around CY£100,000 for a two-bedroom villa in a less popular area. In a more sought-after area, such as Paphos, you can expect to pay around CY£400,000 for a five-bedroom villa and if you want to buy a large villa on the Aphrodite Hills golf development, prices reach CY£600,000.

PROPERTY PRICES

This section looks at property prices in the five districts of the Republic. All prices are in CY£. For general information on the property market in Cyprus see **Cost of Property** on page 27.

Famagusta (*Ammochostos*)

Property prices in the main areas of interest to foreign buyers rose by around 30 per cent in 2004 but now appear to have stabilised. Average prices in the two principal resorts are shown below.

Location	Apartment	Townhouse	Villa
Agia Napa	60,000 (2-bed)	100,000 (3-bed)	160,000 (4-bed)
Protaras	65,000 (2-bed)	75,000 (3-bed)	100,000 (3-bed)

Larnaca (*Larnaka*)

Prices in general are rising faster than in other districts (around 25 per cent during 2004), and there are some modern and stylish 'city' apartments and penthouses there, with higher than average prices (between CY£150,000 and CY£200,000). Nevertheless, most property is still far cheaper than in most other parts of the island. The table below shows average prices (in CY£) in the Larnaca district.

Location	Apartment	Townhouse	Villa
Larnaca City	50,000 (1/2-bed)	110,000 (2/3-bed)	150,000 (3/4-bed + private pool)
Oroklini	98,000 (2-bed)	115,000 (2/3-bed)	150,000 (3/4-bed + private pool)

Limassol (*Lemesos*)

The table below shows average prices (in CY£) in the Limassol district. It's difficult to be specific about prices in villages in the foothills of the Troodos mountains. They're still relatively cheap, compared with the rest of the island, but many need extensive renovation, which can be expensive (see **Renovation** on page 118). Although there's a growing trend to buy old village houses and renovate them, not many estate agents have village houses on their books. If you're looking for one of these houses, go to the village in question and ask around. There's usually a Village Head, who will give you advice. Bargains can still be found in really remote villages, but these are only for those who like complete peace and quiet.

Location	Apartment	Townhouse	Villa
Limassol City	85,000 (2-bed)	100,000	200,000
East Beach	75,000 (2-bed)	115,000 (3-bed)	145,000
Souni Village	100,000	N/A	200,000 (3-bed)
Laneia	N/A	60,000 (village house)	120,000
Palodia	N/A	130,000	250,000 (3/4-bed)

Nicosia (Lefkosa)

In the old city centre, a two-bedroom semi-detached house costs around CY£50,000, a semi-detached, 3-4-bedroom house around CY£90,000. Some older properties, especially those in the old city are government protected (which means you must obtain permission before carrying out any renovation), and they're significantly cheaper. There are also plenty of purpose-built apartments on the outskirts of the city, ranging from around CY£50,000 for a one-bedroom apartment to around CY£100,000 for a three-bedroom house. The table below shows average prices (in CY£) in the area surrounding Nicosia city.

Location	Apartment	Semi–det. House	Detached House
Nicosia City	60,000 (1/2-bed)	180,000 (3/4-bed)	200,000

Paphos (Pafos)

The table below shows average prices (in CY£) in the Paphos district. Note, however, that the prices of apartments, townhouses and villas on the Aphrodite Hills development are rising faster than on the rest of the island. At the end of 2004, two- and three-bedroom apartments were selling for between CY£200,000 and CY£300,000, townhouses for around CY£400,000 and three-bedroom villas for between CY£500,000 and CY£600,000.

Location	Apartment	Townhouse	Villa
Paphos Town	75,000 (2-bed)	120,000 (3-bed)	300,00 (3/4-bed)
Pissouri	90,000	115,000 (2-bed)	250,000 (4-bed)
Kamares Village	135,000	190,000	240,000 (3/4-bed)

| Coral Bay | 60,000 | 150,000 | 250,000 (3/4-bed) |
| Pegeia | 78,000 (2-bed) | 150,000 | 300,000 (3/4-bed) |

FEES

A variety of fees are payable when you buy a property in Cyprus, although these are among the lowest in western Europe and usually total around 10 per cent of the purchase price. They're detailed below.

Legal Fees

If you use a lawyer (which is **highly** recommended – see page 78), his services will cost you around CY£1,000, depending on the value of the property and the complexity of the sale. Services include the search with the Lands Office, checking of planning and building permits, checks that the land is suitable for building (if relevant), drawing up of contracts, stamping and registering the contracts, and applying for permission to purchase from the Council of Ministers.

Surveyor's Fees

The Cyprus Scientific and Technical Chamber (ETEK, (22-877 644), with which any surveyor you use should be a registered can give you a guide to charges as well as a list of surveyors registered with them. Average charges are around CY£300, but this naturally depends on the value of your property and the complexity of the report you require.

Stamp Duty

Stamp duty is levied on property purchase contracts at the rates shown below and is at 0.15 per cent is payable within 30 days of signing a contract:

Property Value (CY£)	Tax Rate (%)	Cumulative Tax (CY£)
Up to 100,000	0.15	150
Over 100,000	0.2	

For example, on a property priced at CY£130,000, you will pay CY£210 (CY£150 on the first CY£100,000 plus CY£60 on the remainder).

Application to the Council of Ministers

At least until 2009, the transfer of property to a non-Cypriot requires permission from the Council of Ministers, which costs around CY£150 if you apply for it yourself. This is done by taking all the relevant paperwork to your nearest District Administration Office; these are as follows:

- **Famagusta** – 22 United Nations Street, 6304 Larnaca (☎ 24-801 002, ✉ dao.famagusta@cytanet.com.cy);

- **Larnaca** – 19–21 Constantinos Paleologos Street, PO Box 140103, 6301 Larnaca (☎ 24-801 818, ✉ dao.larnaca@cytanet.com.cy);

- **Limassol** – Gregoris Afxentiou Square (Anexartisias), PO Box 56062, 304 Limassol (☎ 25-806 400, ✉ dao.limassol@cytanet.com.cy);

- **Nicosia** – 2 Alkeos Street, Engomi, 1458 Nicosia (☎ 22-804 122, ✉ nicosia.dao@nicda.gov.cy);

- **Paphos** – 5 Nikodemos Mylonas Street, 8100 Paphos (☎ 26-801 101, ✉ d.o.paphos@cytanet.com.cy).

Your lawyer can make the application on your behalf, and this service is often included in the standard charge for legal fees, so you would save nothing by doing it yourself. Check with your lawyer.

Note that the 'application' is very much a formality, especially since Cyprus joined the European Union, and any bona fide application is usually approved automatically. It's thought that the procedure will eventually be abolished for EU nationals.

Mortgage Fees

If you have a mortgage, you must pay a registration fee of 1 per cent of the amount borrowed. (See also **Mortgages & Loans** on page 136).

Value Added Tax

Since 1st May 2004, when the Republic of Cyprus joined the EU, value added tax (VAT) has been payable on all new properties, except those where the application for planning permission was submitted to the Planning Department before 1st May 2004. The good news is that first-time buyers pay VAT at only 5 per cent. All other buyers pay the standard rate of 15 per cent. VAT regulations haven't been finalised since the country's EU accession, so always check with your lawyer before committing yourself. See also **Value Added Tax** on page 179.

Selling Agent's Fee

This is paid by the vendor in Cyprus and is normally a minimum of 3 per cent, although most agents charge 5 per cent.

Transfer Fee

A property transfer fee is payable when your lawyer goes to the Lands Office to transfer ownership of the property in your name, which can be a long time after purchase (see **Transfer of Immovable Property** on page 151). The fee depends on the value of the property and whether it's purchased in one or more than one name.

For the first CY£50,000 of a property's value, you pay 3 per cent of the purchase price; between CY£50,000 and £100,000, the rate is 5 per cent; and over CY£100,000 the rate is 8 per cent.

If a property is purchased in a single name, the purchaser pays the whole fee. For example, on a property valued at CY£130,000 you will pay CY£6,400, as shown below:

| | Single Name | | |
Value (CY£)	Rate (%)	Amount (CY£)	Cumulative Fee (CY£)
Up to £50,000	3	1,500	1,500
50,000 – 100,000	5	2,500	4,000
100,000 – 130,000	8	2,400	6,400

If the property is purchased in joint names (e.g. husband and wife), the purchase value is divided between the two and each is assessed separately. So, for a property worth CY£130,000, as in the above example, each purchaser is assessed on a value of CY£65,000 and pays only CY£2,250, making a total of CY£4,500 – a saving of CY£1,900 against purchasing in a single name – as shown below:

| | Joint Names | | |
50% of Value (CY£)	Rate (%)	Amount (CY£)	Cumulative Fee (CY£)
Up to £50,000	3	1,500	1,500
50,000 – 65,000	5	750	2,250

Immovable Property Tax

Immovable property tax (IPT) is an annual tax payable by all property owners in Cyprus, irrespective of their residence status (see page 178). If you buy a property for which there's no separate title deed (e.g. a house in a new development), you may have to pay IPT (to the developer), although you can usually reclaim it from the Inland Revenue when your title deed is issued.

The registered owner of the whole plot (the developer) must pay IPT and will charge you the relevant portion of what he has paid. However, provided the estimated value of your property on 1st January 1980 (*sic*) is below CY£100,000, which is almost always the case, you can reclaim the tax, as the first CY£100,000 of a property's value are exempt. In case you're buying a palace, the tax rates are shown below:

Value (CY£) on 1/1/1980	Tax Rate (%)	Cumulative Tax (CY£)
Up to 100,000	0	0
100,000 – 250,000	0.25	375
250,000 – 500,000	0.35	1,250
Over 500,000	0.4	

Make sure you obtain a receipt for any IPT paid, as you must produce this when reclaiming tax.

Utility Fees

If you buy a new property, you will usually need to pay for electricity and water connections, and the installation of meters. (There's no natural gas in Cyprus but bottled gas is cheap and easy to use.) You should ask the builder or developer to provide the cost of connection to services in writing. In resale properties you will probably have to pay for the cost of new contracts, particularly water (see **Utilities** on page 237).

Running Costs

In addition to the fees associated with buying a property, you should take into account the running costs. These may include annual immovable property tax (see above); municipal rates, which depend on the location and the size of property; water, electricity and sewerage charges; maintenance fees for a community development (see page 110); property income tax and the Cyprus Tourism Organisation charge on expected rental income (see page 200) if you let the property; a fiscal representative or tax consultant's fees; garden and pool maintenance (for a private villa); household insurance (see page 189); and a caretaker's or management fees if you leave a home empty. Annual running costs usually average around 3 to 4 per cent of the cost of a property.

BUYING A RESALE PROPERTY

The most popular ways of acquiring a property in Cyprus are buying off plan (see page 102) and building your own home (see page 103); buying a resale property isn't as common as in many other European countries, although buying an older property in a village with a view to renovation is increasingly popular (see page 118). However, modern resale properties are available all over the island and often represent good value, particularly in resort areas. With a resale property you can see exactly what you will get for your money and save the cost of installing water and electricity meters and telephone lines, or the cost of extending these services to a property.

Much of the development on the island has taken place over the last 30 years, so if you buy a resale property in a development, it may be only a few years old. If you're thinking of doing this, ask the neighbours about any problems, planned developments and anything else that may affect your enjoyment of the property. Most residents are usually happy to tell you – unless of course they're trying to sell you their own property! You should also consider having a survey carried out (see page 114) on a resale property, particularly a detached house, as major problems can be found even in properties less than five years old. Be wary of buying a property designed for tourist accommodation, as these are sometimes built with inferior materials and workmanship – cavity walls and good insulation are essential if a property is to be used as a permanent home.

Owners often advertise properties in the local and expatriate press (see **Appendix B**) or by simply putting a 'for sale' sign in a window. Note that, although you can save money by buying direct from an owner, particularly when he's forced to sell, you should **always** employ a lawyer to carry out the necessary checks (see page 142). If you're unsure of the value of a property, you should obtain a professional valuation.

BUYING A NEW HOME

New properties are widely available in Cyprus, and include coastal and urban apartments and townhouses, golf and marina development properties, and a wide range of individually designed villas. Developers and builders are working around the clock to provide new housing, and many estate agents report that clients who come to them looking for a resale home end up buying a new property.

However, many new properties are part of purpose-built developments, some of which are planned as holiday homes and may not be attractive as permanent homes. If you're buying an apartment or house that's part of a development, check whether your neighbours will be mainly locals or foreigners. Some people don't wish to live in a community consisting mainly of their fellow countrymen (or other foreigners) and this may also deter buyers when you wish to sell. On the other hand, some foreigners don't want to live in a Cypriot community, particularly if they don't speak the language.

Modern homes have good resale potential and are considered a good investment by local buyers. It's often cheaper to buy a new home than an old property requiring modernisation or renovation, as the price is fixed, unlike the cost of renovation, which can soar way beyond original estimates. New properties are covered by a warranty against structural defects. On the other hand, new homes may be smaller than older properties and rarely come with a large plot.

The quality of construction of new property in Cyprus is generally good. Building practices tend to be based on materials and design from the Middle East, combined with British standards. More expensive properties use a high proportion of imported fixtures and fittings, and many building materials may also be imported. The quality of a building and the materials used will be reflected in the price, so when comparing prices ensure that you're comparing similar quality. Cheaper properties aren't usually the best built, although there are exceptions. If you want a permanent rather than a holiday home, you're better off opting for high quality construction and materials.

New homes usually contain a high level of 'luxury' features, such as a fully-fitted kitchen (possibly with all appliances fitted; a utility room; large bathrooms (possibly en suite to all-bedrooms); double-glazing on all windows; stone wood-burning fireplace; stone, ceramic or marble floors in kitchens and bathrooms, and terracotta-tiled floors in other rooms; tiled verandas, terraces and patios. Luxury properties that are part of a large development also have a wide range of communal facilities such as a swimming pool (or several), tennis courts and landscaped gardens.

Some new properties are sold directly by property developers or builders, and some are also marketed by estate agents. New developments may have a sales office and/or a show house or apartment on site.

BUYING OFF PLAN

This is probably the most common method of buying property in Cyprus. The island's property market is experiencing a period of high demand and there isn't sufficient housing stock to meet that demand, so developers are busy constructing new properties. Indeed, if you want a new property, you may have little alternative to buying off plan.

Many people are wary of buying off plan because of well publicised problems in other countries, such as Spain, and there are certain precautions to be taken (see page 81), although the process is relatively safe in Cyprus.

When a property is purchased off plan, payment is made in stages as building work progresses. **Note that it's important to ensure that each stage is completed satisfactorily before making payments.** If you're unable to do this yourself, you must engage an independent representative, e.g. an architect or supervising engineer, to do so on your behalf. You should also engage a local lawyer, experienced in off-plan purchases. He will ensure that there's an agreement between you and the developer or builder which protects your interests and ensures that your stage payments are only made once work has been completed to your architect's satisfaction.

When buying a property off plan, you can usually choose the colour of your bathroom suites, wall and floor tiles, carpets, internal walls, external wall plaster, doors and timber finish. You may also be able to alter the interior room layout, although this may increase the price. Note that you should make any changes or additions to a property, such as including a more luxurious kitchen, a chimney or an additional shower room, at the design stage, as these will cost much more to install later. Options may include a Jacuzzi, barbecue, swimming pool, sauna/steam bath, landscaping, garage or car port, central heating and air-conditioning.

BUILDING YOUR OWN HOME

Buying a plot and building a new home to your own specifications is popular in Cyprus, especially among Cypriots who, with an eye on the future, often buy enough land for their children to eventually build their own houses too. You can have an individual architect-designed house built to your own design and specifications or to a standard design provided by a builder. There are many excellent builders in Cyprus, and building your own home allows you not only to design your home, but to ensure that the quality of materials and workmanship are first class. Note, however, that building a home isn't a good idea if you aren't already living permanently in Cyprus and it certainly isn't recommended for the timid. **Red tape and local business practices can make building your own home a nightmare, and it can be fraught with problems.**

Finding an Architect

Your first step should be to employ a registered architect, even before you begin your search for a piece of land, as he can help you search for a suitable plot, advise you about local laws and practices and inform you about local amenities, views and planning zones. After you've found a suitable plot, he will make designs, drawings and plans for you, obtain building permits and necessary permissions (see **Planning Permission** on page 106) and work with you throughout the building of your home. He should check each stage of the building process (which should be detailed in a contract) and sign it off before each agreed stage payment is made.

Architects are a regulated profession in Cyprus, so you should ensure that the architect you appoint is a member of the Cyprus Scientific and Technical Chamber (ETEK), based in Nicosia (☎ 22-877 644), as well as obtaining recommendations from people you trust. A building design can be carried out only by a registered architect. Many people choose an architect based on what they've seen of his previous work on other houses. Make sure he's experienced and understands your requirements fully. Go and see as many of his previous projects as possible and find out exactly how he likes to work. Often younger architects are more up to date with developments and new ideas, but you will have to balance that against the experience of an older architect. Architects' fees, which usually include applications for planning permission, etc. are usually around 6 per cent of the total building costs. Check exactly what's included.

Finding a Plot

In addition to that of an architect, seek the advice of a registered estate agent, many of whom offer plots for sale along with other types of property. If you're interested in buying a plot in a particular village, visit the area and ask local residents; or you may need to approach the Village Head to find out if land is available. Whichever way you find your land, make sure that the ensuing transaction is dealt with by a local lawyer. Plots cost anything from around CY£25,000 to CY£1 million, depending on the area, the size of the plot and the zone that it's situated in. Advertisements will usually tell you what kind of land it is (e.g. agricultural, residential, business, etc.), the area (in m²) of the plot and what percentage of it you can build on, and whether there's road access and services. BuySell, an agency with offices all over Cyprus, publishes a weekly magazine called *BuySell Cyprus Real Estate*, which features several thousand properties for sale, including plots. It costs CY£0.50 and can be found in most newsagents.

Buying a Plot

You should take the same care when buying land as you would when buying a home. Always employ the services of a local lawyer and an architect **before** you decide to buy a plot, as it may be unsuitable for building, e.g. too steep or requiring prohibitively expensive foundations. Your architect should also check that there aren't any restrictions such as high-tension electricity lines, water pipes or rights of way that may prohibit or limit building plans. You should check that the boundaries marked are correct, as title deeds can be vague regarding measurements. Check that the plot you're shown by the vendor is the plot that's actually for sale. Your lawyer will do this and check planning zones to ensure that it has been approved for building and that the plot is large enough and suitable for the house you plan to build. You will only be allowed to build on a certain percentage of the land and this should always be made clear by the vendor, and confirmed by your lawyer.

Before buying land for building, check whether you will be permitted to build the type of house you want to, what the restrictions are on the height and number of floors, and whether building is restricted in any way because of the position of the plot. It should have been approved for road access (without which building isn't possible – see **Planning Permission** on page 106) and it's important to find out whether electricity and water services can be provided and at what cost. Don't rely on the word of an agent, builder or developer, but ensure that your lawyer and architect check all these things for themselves.

Purchase Contract

If you're buying from an independent vendor, your lawyer must check all the above before drawing up the contract and, if necessary, put in any conditional clauses before you sign the contract. **Ensure that the purchase contract is dependent on obtaining the necessary planning permission. If planning permission is flawed, you may need to pay extra to improve the local infrastructure or the property may even have to be demolished!**

If the plot is part of a development, all permissions and permits should have already been obtained by the developer or builder. The contract must state that the plan has been approved and give the date and authority. Some builders and developers offer package deals that include the land and the cost of building a home. However, it isn't always wise to buy the plot from the builder who's going to build your home and you should shop around and compare separate land and building costs. **If you decide to buy a package deal from a builder, you must insist on separate contracts for the land and the building and obtain the title deed for the land before signing a building contract.**

Design

The architect will then draw up rough designs in consultation with you. You should take your time at this stage and give as much input as you can, as once you reach the building stage it may be too late (or too expensive) to make any significant changes. Once the rough designs are approved by you, the architect will produce detailed architectural drawings. These should include overall ground plans and any separate sections of importance. A good architect will ensure that he has taken into account external factors such the position of the building in relation to the sun and wind, any existing buildings, trees, etc., environmental considerations and restrictions and, last but not least, your budget.

Planning Permission

Permission is required for any kind of building, extension, addition or renovation. A number of government departments must give their approval and you will need a number of different permissions. Your architect must apply for these on your behalf, especially as the initial application must be supported by detailed plans and specifications. Once your architect has his designs ready, he will submit them to the local Town Planning Department and you're likely to have a wait of around three to six months before a Town Planning Licence (also called Town Planning Permission) is issued. The architect also engages a civil engineer to make a stability study of the plot. Make use of this waiting time to research where you can find the kind of building materials you need, including floor coverings, tiles and other decorative items. When your architect has the licence and the (satisfactory) result of the stability study, he can submit the plans to the District Administration Office to obtain a Building Licence (or Building Permit). Once you have this, you and your architect can invite tenders from several different building contractors.

An architect should be able to recommend a number of reliable builders, but you should also do your own research, as one of the most important considerations when building a new home is the reputation (and financial standing) of the builder. You should also be wary of an architect with his 'own' builder (or a builder with his own architect), as it's the architect's job to ensure that the builder does his work according to the plans and specifications. It may be difficult for the architect to insist on certain of your requirements if he's too friendly with the builder. Inspect other homes a builder has built and check with the owners about problems they might have had and whether they're satisfied. If you want a house built exactly to your specifications, you will need to supervise it every step of the way or employ an architect and a project manager (especially if you aren't living in Cyprus) to do so for you. Without close supervision it's highly likely that your instructions **won't** be followed. **All building work must be carried out by a registered contractor. It's illegal to use an unregistered builder in Cyprus.**

Building Contract

Before you accept a builder's quotation, you should check whether it includes taxes (which it should) and whether the quotation is an estimate or a fixed price, as an estimated price can escalate wildly due to changes made during building work or simply (claimed) increases in material costs or other 'unforeseen circumstances'. **It's vital to have a contract checked by a lawyer, or an alternative drawn up which protects your interests. Building contracts are often heavily biased in the builder's favour and give clients very few rights.** Sometimes a lawyer can simply amend a building contract, but he may have to re-write it. The contract should include the following:

- A detailed description of the building and a list of the materials to be used (with references to the architect's plans);
- The exact location of the building on the plot;
- The building and payment schedule, which must be in stages according to progress;
- A penalty clause for late completion;
- The retention of a percentage, e.g. 2 to 5 per cent, of the building costs as a 'guarantee' against defects;
- Reference to how disputes will be settled.

It may be difficult or impossible to get the builder to accept a penalty clause for late completion, as buildings are rarely completed on time. It should also be spelt out in the contract **exactly** what 'complete' means, as it's often open to local interpretation.

Ensure that the contract includes all costs, including the architect's fees (unless contracted separately), landscaping (if applicable), planning and building licences (unless included in the architect's fees), and the connection of utilities (water, electricity, etc.) to the house, not just to the building site. The only extra is usually the cost of electricity and water meters.

Warranty

Cypriot law requires a builder to guarantee his work against structural defects. An architect is also responsible for defects due to poor supervision, incorrect instructions given to the builder, or problems caused by poor foundations, e.g. subsidence. Note that it isn't uncommon to have problems during construction, particularly regarding material defects. If you experience problems, you must usually be extremely patient and persistent in order to obtain satisfaction. You should have a completed building checked by a structural surveyor and a report drawn up (see page 114); if there are any defects, he should determine who was responsible for them.

Completion

Once the work is completed, your architect should submit the drawings of the property (as built) to the relevant authorities and will receive a completion certificate (also known as the final certificate of approval) if everything is approved. You then deposit the completion certificate at the District Land Office so that your ownership of the house as well as the land is legally registered.

DEVELOPMENTS

Purpose-built developments, which may include apartments, townhouses and villas, are the main form of new building in Cyprus and most popular areas are seeing an increase in developments. Some are small with a limited number of properties, while others are huge complexes, almost towns in their own right. Property available on developments is varied and caters for different needs and price ranges; many contain a mixture of apartments, townhouses and individual villas. Facilities and amenities also vary greatly: some have sports facilities including swimming pools, tennis courts and golf courses, others have shopping facilities and some have bars and restaurants. (Golf homes are popular, as no one can build in front of you and spoil your view and you can consider the golf course as your lawn and garden. They also usually include discounts on green fees, 'free' golf membership and access to other facilities.)

Some developments (particularly those with a large number of retirees) have permanent resident populations while others turn into ghost towns outside the high season. Many developments are populated mainly by foreigners, usually British, especially around Paphos. Most developments have landscaped gardens and some also offer high security. At the other extreme, cheaper, older developments may consist of numerous cramped studio apartments with few, if any, amenities. Some developments are planned as holiday homes and aren't attractive as permanent homes.

Advantages of buying in a development may include pleasant, well maintained surroundings, 'free' access to a range of leisure and sports facilities, good security (if the development has private security) and a ready-made foreign community often with a good social scene. Disadvantages may include poor or expensive maintenance (you may have little or no control over maintenance costs if they've been agreed by a committee), lack of privacy or noisy neighbours, limited or oversubscribed facilities, and restrictive rules and regulations; some may find a predominantly expatriate atmosphere claustrophobic.

Management

Unlike the situation in Spain, it isn't a legal requirement for owners in a community development to set up a management committee, although there's commonly some kind of management structure to make decisions regarding the maintenance of common elements of a development, such as patios, gardens, roads, and leisure and sports facilities. In many developments, the developer pays all costs for the first year. In some cases, the developer himself then manages the complex; in others, owners collectively set up a management company and form a committee to engage contractors to maintain the development. Either way, the costs of maintenance are shared among the owners, who must agree a set of rules. These may therefore differ from development to development.

Before buying, check whether there's an owners' committee and what you will be committing yourself to if you buy a property on a particular development. For example, if you're buying a holiday home that will be vacant for long periods (particularly in winter), don't buy in an apartment block where heating and/or hot water charges are shared, or you will be paying towards other owners' bills.

Costs

If a committee of owners has been formed and the property purchased is within a complex or development with common areas, you usually sign a general agreement when you take possession of the property. A charge will be made to cover your share of cleaning, repairing, and maintaining common elements such as exterior lighting, landscaping and gardening, paths and parking areas, and a swimming pool, tennis court, etc. This is usually calculated per square metre for each property and must be paid annually at the beginning of every year.

Checks

Before buying a property in a development, it's always wise to ask current owners about the management and maintenance of the development. For example:

- Do they like living there?
- What are the fees and restrictions?
- How noisy are other residents, are the recreational facilities easy to access?
- Would they buy there again (why or why not)?
- Is the development well managed?

If you're planning to buy a property on a development, it's important to ensure that there aren't any outstanding major problems. If there are, you could be liable to contribute towards the cost of repairs, which could run into many thousands of pounds.

TIMESHARE & PART-OWNERSHIP SCHEMES

If you're looking for a holiday home abroad, you may wish to investigate a scheme that provides sole occupancy of a property for a number of weeks each year rather than buying a property outright, although this isn't as popular in Cyprus as in some other European countries. Schemes available include timeshare and part-ownership arrangements, which are described below. **Don't rush into any of these schemes without fully researching the market and before you're absolutely clear what you want and what you can realistically expect to get for your money.**

Timesharing

Also known as holiday ownership, vacation ownership, co-ownership or holidays for life, timesharing is a popular form of part-ownership, although there aren't many timeshare resorts in Cyprus compared with, for example, Spain (a large new complex is currently under construction, to be completed in 2007). The best timeshare developments are on a par with luxury hotels and offer a wide range of facilities, including bars, restaurants, entertainment, shops, swimming pools, tennis courts, health clubs, and other leisure and sports facilities.

Timeshare has earned a poor reputation in some countries, although things have improved in recent years since the introduction of new EU regulations to protect buyers, including a requirement that buyers have secure occupancy rights and that their money is properly protected prior to the completion of a new property. Timeshare companies are required to disclose information about the vendor and the property and to allow prospective buyers a ten-day 'cooling off period', during which they may cancel a sales agreement they've signed without penalty. A guarantee must be provided by the timeshare company that a property is as advertised and, where applicable, the contract must be in the language of the EU country where the buyer is resident or the language of the buyer's choice. You cannot sign away any of your rights irrespective of what's written in the contract; if a new contract isn't in accordance with the new law, it's null and void.

The reason for its unpopularity in Cyprus is partly the poor reputation that timeshare has attracted and its association with fraud, crime and harassment techniques from timeshare salesmen. In 2002, there were reports in the local English language newspaper, *The Cyprus Mail*, of an increase in timeshare selling in Cyprus and timeshare operatives touting for business in the Paphos area, a spot that's popular with British tourists. The Cyprus Tourism Organisation (CTO) has traditionally been against timeshare in Cyprus because of its unsavoury image, but since EU entry in 2004, it has begun to consider some new ground rules so that reputable timeshare can be successfully included within the island's tourism industry.

The Organisation for Timeshare in Europe (OTE, 🖥 www.ote-info.com), which strives to improve the reputation of timeshare and encourage reputable timeshare practices, is working with the Cyprus Tourism Organisation to improve the reputation of timeshare in Cyprus. When Cyprus became an EU member, it had to bring its legislation on timeshare into line with the rest of Europe and timeshare properties had to be licensed as if they were hotel accommodation. It's advisable to check that a timeshare development belongs to the (OTE) whose members must abide by a strict code of ethics. The OTE can give you more information about timeshare and has details of resorts all over the world, including Cyprus.

Further information about timesharing can also be obtained from the Timeshare Council (☎ UK 020-7821 8845) and the Timeshare Helpline (☎ UK 020-8296 0900). The Timeshare Consumers Association (Hodsock, Worksop, Notts, S81 0TF, UK, ☎ 01909-591100, 🖳 www.time share.org.uk) publishes a useful booklet entitled *Timeshare: Guide to Buying, Owning and Selling*. The UK's Department of Trade and Industry publishes *The Timeshare Guide*, which is available free. You can order it by telephone or download the text (☎ UK 0870-150 2550, 🖳 www.dti. gov.uk/publications).

If you don't wish to holiday in the same place each year, you should choose a timeshare development that's a member of an international organisation such as Resort Condominium International (RCI, ☎ UK 0870-609 0141, 🖳 www.rci.com) or Interval International (☎ UK 0870-744 4222, 🖳 www.intervalworld.com), which allow you (usually for an additional fee) to exchange your timeshare with one in another area or country.

Remember that, in general, timeshares are often difficult or impossible to sell at any price and, if you need to sell, you're highly unlikely to get your money back. If you want to buy a timeshare, it's best to buy a resale privately from an existing owner or a timeshare resale broker, when they sell for a fraction of their original cost. When buying privately, you can usually drive a hard bargain and may even get a timeshare 'free' simply by assuming the current owner's maintenance contract.

Part-ownership

Part-ownership involves a group of people (e.g. friends or relatives) buying a property together or purchasing shares in a company that acquires the property. Part-ownership allows you to acquire a share in a property that you wouldn't be able to afford to buy outright. The District Administration in Cyprus (which gives permission to purchase on behalf of the Council of Ministers) doesn't generally give permission for more than four joint owners, although many people consider this to be the optimum number.

Part-ownership can be a good choice for a family seeking a holiday home for a few weeks or months a year and has the added advantage that (because of the lower cost) a mortgage may be unnecessary. Note that it's usually cheaper to buy a property privately with family or friends than from an agent or developer who offers this sort of scheme, in which case you may pay well above the market value for a share of a property (check the market value of a property to establish whether it's good value). Part-ownership is much better value than a timeshare and needn't cost much more.

One of the best ways to get into part-ownership, if you can afford it, is to buy a property yourself and offer shares to others. This overcomes the problem of getting together a consortium of would-be owners and trying to agree on a purchase in advance, which is difficult unless they're close friends or family members. Each part-owner receives a number of shares depending on how much he has paid, entitling him to so many weeks occupancy a year. If a part-owner wishes to sell his shares he must usually give first refusal to the other part-owners, although if they don't wish to buy them and a new part-owner cannot be found, the property will need to be sold.

Part-ownership schemes are available in Cyprus, although, like timeshare, they aren't as common as in other areas of Europe. As with any property purchase, always take legal advice and ensure that a legal contract or agreement is drawn up between a group of buyers and (if applicable) the developer of the property. **A water-tight contract must be drawn up by an experienced lawyer to protect the part-owners' interests.** Even if co-ownership is between family or friends, you must always do this and ensure that there's provision to transfer ownership to another friend or family member if required. A separate agreement should be drawn up covering the maintenance of the property, repairs, renovations, insurance, taxes and utilities bills. Each owner will normally pay utilities charges for his period of occupancy.

SWIMMING POOLS

Foreigners who buy property in Cyprus often choose to install a swimming pool, if they don't buy a home that includes one. There are many swimming pool installation companies in Cyprus or you can buy and install one yourself. Above ground pools are the cheapest, but they're unsightly and are advisable only as a stop-gap or for those who really cannot afford anything better. A better option is a in-ground pool with a liner. A liner pool measuring 8 x 4 metres costs around CY£9,000 fully installed, including filtration and heating. A tiled pool of 8 x 4 metres costs from CY£9,000 to CY£14,000. **You need planning permission to install a pool and should apply a few months in advance.** Pools require regular maintenance and cleaning. If you have a holiday home, you will need to employ someone to maintain your pool (you may be able to get a local family to look after it in return for being able to use it).

INSPECTIONS & SURVEYS

When you've found a property that you like, whether it's an old or a 'new' building, you should make a close inspection of its condition. Obviously this will depend on whether it's an old house in need of complete restoration, a property that has been partly or totally modernised, or a modern home. One of the problems with a property that has been restored is that you don't know how well the job has been done, particularly if the owner did it himself. If work has been carried out by local builders, you should ask to see the bills.

Some simple checks you can do yourself include testing the electrical system, plumbing, mains water, hot water boiler and central heating. Don't take someone's word that these are functional, but check them for yourself. If a property doesn't have electricity or mains water, check the nearest connection point and the cost of extending the service to the property, as it can be **very** expensive in remote rural areas. If a property has a well or septic tank, you should have them tested.

An old property may show visible signs of damage and decay, such as bulging or cracked walls, rising damp, missing roof slates (you can check with binoculars) and rotten woodwork. Common problems include rusting water pipes and leaky plumbing, inadequate sewage disposal, poor wiring, humidity and rising damp, uneven flooring or no concrete base, collapsing facades, subsidence, and cracked internal and external walls. Some of these problems are even evident in developments less than five years old. Some areas are liable to flooding, storms and subsidence, and it's advisable to check an old property after heavy rainfall, when any leaks should come to light. If you find or suspect problems, you should have a property checked by a builder or have a full structural survey carried out by a surveyor. You may also wish to have a property checked for termites and other infestations.

A Cypriot buyer wouldn't make an offer on an old property before at least having it checked by a builder, who will also be able to tell you whether the price is too high, given any work that needs to be done. It's unusual to have a full survey on a property in Cyprus, particularly a property built in the last 10 or 20 years. A structural survey is usually necessary only if the building is old or suspected of being unsound. However, if you're buying a detached property or a village house, especially one built on the side of a hill, it's **always** advisable to have a survey carried out. Generally, if you would have a survey done on a similar property in your home country, you should have one done in Cyprus.

You could ask the vendor to have a survey done at his expense, which, provided it gives the property a clean bill of health, will help him sell it even if you decide not to buy. However, this isn't usual and a vendor may refuse or insist that you carry out a survey at your expense. People don't have surveys as a matter of course in Cyprus and you may find you encounter a negative attitude if you insist that it's the vendor's responsibility. You can make a satisfactory survey a condition of a contract. If a vendor refuses to allow you to do a survey before signing a contract, take legal advice, but be wary, it may be that you should look elsewhere. All Cypriot lenders require a survey before approving a loan, but this is essentially simply a valuation to ensure that a property is worth the purchase price.

Your lawyer can recommend a registered local surveyor, who should be a member of the Cyprus Scientific and Technical Chamber (ETEK), based in Nicosia (☎ 22-877 644). Surveying is a regulated profession in Cyprus and many surveyors speak excellent English. A local surveyor will have extensive knowledge of local properties and building methods.

Always discuss with the surveyor exactly what will be included, and most importantly, what will be excluded (you may need to pay extra to include certain checks and tests). A survey can be limited to a few items or even a single system only, such as the wiring or plumbing in an old house. You should receive a written report on the condition of a property, including anything that could become a problem in the future. A full structural survey should include the condition of all buildings (particularly the foundations, roofs, walls and woodwork), plumbing, electricity and heating systems, and anything else you want inspected such as a swimming pool and its equipment, e.g. filter system or heating.

Inspection Checklist

Below is a list of items you should check when inspecting a property. Note, however, that this is no substitute for an inspection or survey by a professional, or for legal checks by a lawyer.

Title

- Make sure that a property corresponds with the description in the title deeds.
- Check the number of rooms and the area of the property, any terraces and the plot. If there are added rooms (e.g. an extension), terraces, a

garage or a swimming pool that aren't mentioned in the property description, the owner should provide proof that planning permission was obtained. Additions or alterations to a property may require new title deeds for the entire property. If so, enquire whether the current owner will obtain the updated deeds before you buy or pay the costs if they're obtained on completion.

Plot

These checks are particularly important for rural plots.

- Identify the boundaries of the plot. This may require the services of a land surveyor on unfenced rural properties.
- Check that there are no disputes over boundaries, e.g. with neighbours.
- Check the rights of way over the plot.
- Check for streams and underground springs and whether any neighbours have rights of access to water on your land.
- Check the building regulations and zones of any adjoining plots. Don't assume an empty plot is part of a garden or wasteland; it could have planning permission for a large villa or apartment block and potentially ruin your views and privacy.
- Check that there's the required road access (see page 106).

Orientation

- Check the orientation of the property and how much sun it receives, particularly in winter, when north-facing properties can be cold, damp and dark.

Exterior

- Check for cracks and damp patches on walls.
- On older properties check that the walls are vertical and not bulging.
- Check that all the roof tiles are in place and that there's no sagging. Plants growing on a roof are an indication that it isn't well maintained.

Interior

- Check for damp patches throughout a property, including inside cupboards and wardrobes.

- Check for cracks and damp patches on walls.
- Check that the floor is level and that wall and floor tiles are in good condition.
- Check the condition of doors and windows and whether they close properly.
- Check the woodwork for rot and signs of wood-boring insects, such as woodworm and termites (termites are difficult to detect unless damage is extensive).

Furniture & Fittings

- Check what is included in the sale.
- Check that any appliances included in the sale are in good working order.

Space

- Check that there's sufficient for your needs, particularly if you plan to live permanently in the property).
- If it's an apartment, enquire whether there's the possibility of obtaining additional storage space within the building.

Parking

- Check that there's sufficient parking space for your family and visitors.
- If necessary, check whether there's the possibility of buying or renting a garage or parking space nearby.

Utilities

- Check the water supply. If the property's water is provided by wells, make sure that there's sufficient for your needs.
- Check that the water heating system is functional.
- Enquire about heating/cooling units in the house and the annual costs.
- Check the reliability of the electricity supply.
- If there's no electricity supply, find out whether you can connect to the mains supply or whether you can install alternative means (e.g. solar panels).

- Find out whether a property has a septic tank and have it checked.
- Be very wary of utilities shared between several plots or properties. This may cause disputes at a later date.

Garden

- Check whether the garden will need extensive maintenance and, if so, how much a gardener will cost (if you cannot do it yourself).
- On rural land, find out whether the trees require maintenance, e.g. olive and fruit trees, and investigate what you can do with the crops after the harvest.

Swimming Pool

- Check that the pool and equipment (especially the pump) is in good working order.
- Look for cracks in the pool structure and check the condition of the paving around the pool.
- Enquire how much the pool costs to maintain a year.
- If a property doesn't have a swimming pool, check that there's room to build one and that the terrain is suitable.

RENOVATION & RESTORATION

If you want a property with abundant charm and character, you will obviously have to choose an old property. Many foreigners are tempted by the romantic notion of restoring an old village home in traditional Cypriot style and there's still a significant amount of older property on the island in desperate need of restoration to its former glory. You can find them not just in mountain villages, but also in some areas of Limassol and Nicosia. The Cypriot government is aware that part of the country's history is slowly crumbling and, since 1985, it has been encouraging the restoration of certain buildings with a package of substantial financial incentives, which are detailed below. However, before you go ahead with this type of project, it's worth considering some of the possible problem areas and whether it's practical and financially viable for you.

Many foreign buyers look at the very low price tag on an old property and believe they're getting a wonderful bargain, without fully investigating the renovation costs. The price naturally reflects the fact that you will have to spend a considerable amount on the property before it's anywhere near habitable. Many very old village homes in

Cyprus lack basic services such as electricity, a reliable water supply and sanitation. **The price of most restored properties doesn't reflect the cost and amount of work that went into them and many people who have restored a 'ruin' would never do it again and advise others against it.** You may be better off buying a new or recently built property, as the cost of restoring an old property can be astronomical. An extra few extra thousand pounds spent on a purchase may represent better value than spending the money on renovation work.

SURVIVAL TIP
Before buying a property that needs
renovation or restoration, it's vital to obtain accurate
estimates of the work involved from one or more reliable
local builders. You should budget for costs to be up to
100 per cent higher than quoted, as it isn't unusual
for the costs to escalate wildly from
original estimates.

Bear in mind that, if you buy and restore a property with the intention of selling it for a profit, you must take into account not only the initial price and the restoration costs, but also the fees and taxes included in the purchase and possibly capital gains tax. It's often difficult to sell an old renovated property at a higher than average market price, irrespective of its added value.

In general, Cypriots don't care for old homes and much prefer modern apartments and villas with all mod cons, so it may be more difficult to sell an old property, even if it has been fully renovated. This is an important point to remember if you need to sell an old home quickly in an area that isn't popular with foreign buyers. **If you're buying for investment, you're usually better off buying a new home.**

If your heart is set on a property that needs restoration or renovation, obtain a **detailed** estimate of the costs **before** signing a contract. Take a long, hard look at the practicalities and get plenty of expert advice from architects, builders and surveyors. You should **always** engage the services of an experienced local architect for this kind of project (see **Finding an Architect** on page 104). He can advise you throughout the renovation and restoration process and, if necessary, will guide you through the process of applying for financial assistance (see below).

Cost

The cost of restoration depends on the type of work involved and the materials used. Electrical work, masonry work and plumbing is usually costed by the square metre. As a rough guide you should expect the cost of totally renovating an old 'habitable' building to be at least equal to its purchase price and possibly much more. How much money you spend depends on your purpose and the depth of your pockets. If you're restoring a property for investment, it's easy to spend much more than you could ever hope to recoup when you sell it. On the other hand, if you're restoring it as a labour of love with a view to its being your holiday or permanent home, there's theoretically no limit to what you can spend.

Architectural Heritage Properties

The Cypriot government affords certain properties the status of architectural heritage and issues preservation orders on them. If you can restore what would otherwise have been lost to the history of Cyprus, the property is treated accordingly. Any restoration or alteration work on these buildings requires special permission in addition to the usual planning permission (see page 121), and the property must be registered as an architectural heritage property with the Town Planning Department. If you undertake to restore this kind of property, it will be strictly controlled and regularly inspected, although you will also be given a considerable amount of guidance.

Financial Incentives

In order to encourage the restoration of certain listing buildings, the government introduced a package of incentives in 1985. Currently the main benefits to those who restore according to the regulations are as follows:

● A cash grant of 40 per cent of restoration costs or CY£25,000, whichever is lower. Keep receipts, as these costs must be verified.

● Tax reductions, which can include exemption from tax on restoration costs, the refund of property registration fees and exemption from property tax;

● Access to low interest loans to help you with restoration costs. This depends on your income.

● In cases of abandoned listed properties in danger of collapse, an additional local authority subsidy.

The government's Town Planning Department has supported several hundred projects. If you want to take advantage of these incentives, ask a local architect for advice. Your application for renovation will be considered only if your architect presents proper plans and specifications, which must be approved by the Town Planning Department, and renovation will be approved only if it will maintain the property according to the character of the village or area.

Checks

It's vital to check a property for any obvious faults, particularly an old property. Most importantly, a building must have sound walls; if it doesn't, it may be cheaper to erect a new building! Almost any other problem can be fixed or overcome (at a price). A sound roof that doesn't leak is desirable, as is ensuring that a building is waterproof. These are the most important priorities if funds are scarce. Don't believe a vendor or agent who tells you that a roof or anything else can easily be repaired, but obtain expert advice from a local builder. Sound roof timbers are also important as they can be expensive to replace. Old buildings often need a damp-proof course, timber treatment, new windows and doors, a new roof or extensive repairs, a modern kitchen and bathroom, re-wiring and central heating.

Electricity and mains water should already be connected but they often aren't in older, more remote properties. They can be expensive to extend to a property in a remote area. If a house doesn't have electricity or mains water, it's important to check the cost of extending these services to it. Many rural properties get their water from a spring or well, which is usually fine, but you should check the reliability of the water supply – wells can and do run dry! You should also check that the supply available will be adequate for your needs. If you're seeking a waterside property, you should check the frequency of floods and, if commonplace, ensure that a building has been designed with floods in mind, e.g. with electrical installations above flood level and solid tiled floors.

Planning Permission

Planning permission is required for any kind of renovation or restoration work (see page 106). If yours is an architectural heritage property (see page 120), special permissions are also required. It's advisable to employ a local architect who has plenty of experience in restoration projects to apply for the necessary permits and licences on your behalf.

Finding a Builder

Finding a builder who specialises in traditional restoration isn't always easy in Cyprus. Over the last 30 to 40 years, there has been a glut of modern building on the island and builders with traditional building skills are becoming harder to find. This is something that your architect should be able to help you with, especially if he specialises in restoration projects. Generally, you should obtain recommendations and references from previous clients and, most importantly, make sure you see the results of some of their similar projects.

Quotations

You must obtain detailed and **realistic** written quotations from at least two builders, preferably more. You or your architect should detail exactly what's required and the quality of the materials to be used. This is especially important if you're doing a restoration that's to be sympathetic to the original. For example, in some villages, only a certain type stone can be used, and it may be difficult to obtain. Make sure that your quotation contains everything that you want done and that you fully understand every part of it. You should fix a date for start and completion of the work and, if the architect advises it and the builder agrees, include a penalty for failing to finish on time.

Supervision

If you aren't going to be around to supervise the work yourself, it's imperative that you hire the services of an architect or contractor to do so on your behalf. Although this will add to your costs, it's undoubtedly money well spent. Be extremely careful whom you employ if you have work done in your absence, and ensure that your instructions are accurate in every detail. Always make sure that you understand exactly what has been agreed and, if necessary, get it in writing (with drawings). Even if you're on the spot, don't give instructions and then go away and expect things to happen. You must be on site as regularly as possible to ensure that work is carried out to your specifications.

SELLING YOUR HOME

Although this book is primarily concerned with buying a home in Cyprus, you may wish to sell your home at some time in the future (or you may wish to sell a home in order to buy another). Before offering your Cypriot home for sale, it's advisable to investigate the state of the property market. For example, unless you're forced to sell, it definitely isn't advisable during a property slump when prices are depressed. It may be wiser to let your home long term and wait until the market has recovered. It's also unwise to sell in the early years after purchase, when you will probably make a loss unless it was an absolute bargain or prices have rocketed. If you need to sell a property before buying a new one, this must be included as a conditional clause (see page 148) in the contract for a new home.

Having decided to sell, your first decision will be whether to sell it yourself (or try) or use the services of an estate agent. Although the majority of properties are sold through estate agents, a large number of people sell their own homes.

Using an Agent

Most owners prefer to use the services of one or more estate agents, either in Cyprus or in their home country, e.g. when selling a second home. The majority of estate agents in Cyprus are well qualified and reputable and it may pay dividends and save you time to use an expert to sell your home for you. Make sure he's properly registered and a member of CREAA (see **Estate Agents** on page 86). If you purchased the property through an agent, it's often advisable to use the same agent when selling, as he will already be familiar with your property and may still have the details on file. If you own a property in an area popular with foreign buyers, it may be worthwhile using an overseas agent or advertising in foreign newspapers and magazines, such as the English-language publications listed in **Appendix B**.

Agents' Contracts

Before he can offer a property for sale, an estate agent must have a signed authorisation from the owner in the form of an exclusive or non-exclusive contract. An exclusive contract gives a single agent the exclusive right to sell a property, while a non-exclusive contract allows you to deal with any number of agents and to negotiate directly with private individuals. Most people find that it's better to place a property with a number of agents under non-exclusive contracts. Most reputable agents in Cyprus won't insist on an exclusive contract but, if you sign a contract without reserving the right to find your own buyer, you must pay the agent's commission even if you sell your home yourself! Check the contract (exclusive contracts tend to be binding) and make sure you understand what you're signing.

Agents' Fees

The agent's commission is usually paid by the vendor. Fees normally vary from around 3 to 5 per cent, depending on the price of a property.

Your contract should state the agent's commission, what it includes, and most importantly, who must pay it.

Selling Your Home Yourself

While certainly not for everyone, selling your own home is a viable option for many people and is particularly recommended when you're selling an attractive home at a **realistic** price in a favourable market. It may allow you to offer it at a more appealing price, which could be an important factor if you're seeking a quick sale. If you aren't in a hurry, you can ask the 'full' price and save yourself an agent's commission. How you market your home will depend on the type of property, the price, and the country or area from where you expect your buyer to come.

Marketing

Marketing is the key to selling your home. Do some research into the best newspapers and magazines for advertising your property (see **Appendix B**), and place an advertisement in those that look most promising. It's wise to add the words 'no agents' at the end of your advertisement, or most of the calls you receive will be from agents keen to sell your home for you! Unless you're in a hurry to sell, set yourself a realistic time limit for success, after which you can try an agent. The most important thing to remember when selling a home yourself, is that you will need to provide a contract or engage a lawyer to do this for you.

Price

It's important to bear in mind that (like everything) property has a market price and the best way of ensuring a quick sale (or any sale) is to ask a realistic price. Cyprus has been experiencing a strong market since around 2000 and an increasing number of potential buyers are looking at the island as a possible location to live, work or retire. Cyprus hasn't (yet?) experienced the slump of many other popular holiday home markets, but if you want to sell your Cypriot home, make sure you take professional advice about a realistic price. Don't get carried away and ask for absurd price just because the market is healthy.

If your home is fairly standard for the area, you can find out its value by comparing the prices of other homes on the market or those that have recently been sold. Most agents will provide a free appraisal of a home's value in the hope that you will sell it through them. However, don't believe everything they tell you, as they may over-price it simply to encourage you. You should be prepared to drop the price slightly (e.g. 5

or 10 per cent) and should set it accordingly, but shouldn't grossly over-price a home as it will deter buyers. On the other hand, don't reject an offer out of hand unless it's ridiculously low, as you may be able to get a prospective buyer to raise his offer.

When selling a second home in Cyprus, you may wish to include the furnishings (plus major appliances) in the sale, which is common practice in resort areas when selling a relatively inexpensive second home with modest furnishings. In this case you should add an appropriate amount to the price to cover the value of the furnishings.

Presentation

The secret to selling a home quickly lies in its presentation (assuming that it's well priced). First impressions (both exterior and interior) are vital when marketing a property and it's important to present it in its best light and make it as attractive as possible to potential buyers. It may pay to invest in new interior decoration, exterior paint or landscaping. A few plants and flowers can do wonders. Note that when decorating a home for resale, it's important to be conservative and not to do anything radical (such as install a red or black bathroom suite, or paint the walls purple). White is a good neutral colour for walls, woodwork and porcelain.

It may also pay you to do some modernisation, such as installing a new kitchen or bathroom, as these are of vital importance (particularly kitchens) when selling a home. Note, however, that although modernisation may be necessary to sell an old home, you shouldn't overdo it, as it's easy to spend more than you could ever hope to recoup on the sale price. If you're using an agent, you can ask him what you should do (or need to do) to help sell your home. If a home is in poor repair, this must be reflected in the asking price; if major work is needed that you cannot afford, you should obtain a quotation (or two) and offer to knock this off the price.

Capital Gains Tax

Capital gains tax (CGT) is imposed at the rate of 20 per cent on gains from selling a residential property in Cyprus, even if it's a principal home. This includes gains from the disposal of shares in companies that own property. There are, however, certain exemptions from CGT, which include the first CY£50,000 of the value of a residential property and total exemption on transfers arising from a death or gifts made from parent to child or between spouses (see page 178).

4.

MONEY MATTERS

One of the most important aspects of buying a home in Cyprus and living there (even for relatively brief periods) is finance, which includes transferring and changing money, opening a bank account and obtaining a mortgage (taxes are dealt with in **Chapter 7**). If you're planning to invest in a property or a business in Cyprus financed with imported funds, it's important to consider both the present and possible future exchange rates (even a small change in the exchange rate can increase the price of a home dramatically). On the other hand, if you live and work in Cyprus and are paid in Cypriot pounds, this may affect your financial commitments abroad.

 If your income is received in a currency other than Cypriot pounds, it can be exposed to risks beyond your control when you live in Cyprus, particularly regarding inflation and exchange rate fluctuations.

Although the Cypriots generally prefer to pay cash rather than use credit or charge cards, it's wise to have at least one credit card when visiting or living in Cyprus (Visa and MasterCard are the most widely accepted). Even if you don't like credit cards and shun any form of credit, they do have their uses: for example, no-deposit car rentals, no pre-paying hotel bills (plus guaranteed bookings), obtaining cash 24 hours a day, shopping by phone or via the internet, greater safety and security than cash and, above all, convenience. Note, however, that not all Cypriot businesses accept credit cards.

SURVIVAL TIP
If you plan to live in Cyprus for long periods,
you must ensure that your income is (and will remain)
sufficient to live on, bearing in mind devaluations, rises
in the cost of living, and unforeseen expenses such as
medical bills or anything else that may
reduce your income.

Although the cost of living is lower than in many other EU countries (see page 28), foreigners, particularly retirees, shouldn't under-estimate how much money they will need to live comfortably. Economists predicted that prices would rise significantly as a result of the country's EU entry in 2004, but there was only a slight increase in the year following accession. If you're planning to live there permanently, it's wise to seek expert financial advice, as it may provide the opportunity to reduce your tax bill. This chapter includes information about Cypriot currency, importing and exporting money, banking and mortgages.

CYPRIOT CURRENCY

Following the Republic of Cyprus' EU accession on 1st May 2004, it's thought that southern Cyprus will adopt the euro (€) in late 2007 or early 2008. At present, however, Cypriot currency is the Cyprus pound (CY£), which is divided into 100 cents. Although it isn't traded internationally, it's a strong, stable currency, reflecting the economy on the island. Coins are minted in values of 1, 2, 5, 10, 20, and 50 cents and banknotes printed in denominations of CY£1, CY£5, CY£10 and CY£20. Sums in cents are normally written CY£0.50, etc. It's wise to obtain some local currency banknotes and coins before arriving in the country and to familiarise yourself with them. You should have some local currency in cash when you arrive, although you should avoid carrying a lot of cash. This will save you having to queue to change money on arrival at an airport (where exchange rates are usually poor).

IMPORTING & EXPORTING MONEY

EU membership means that all previous exchange control restrictions have been lifted, and there are now no restrictions on importing or exporting funds in any currency, although you must declare large amounts (see **Declaration** below). You no longer have to prove that property is to be purchased with foreign currency. The Central Bank of Cyprus, which is the supervisory authority for all banks operating in the Republic of Cyprus, introduced the Capital Movement Law in 2003, which aimed to harmonise Cyprus legislation with that of the EU's Free Movement of Capital laws. Certain amendments to banking law are currently under review, following the country's EU accession. Always check with your financial adviser or the Central Bank in Cyprus about the latest regulations.

Declaration

The Capital Movement Law (see above) specifies that cash in any currency or gold up to the value of CY£7,300 may be freely imported or exported into Cyprus. The Central Bank of Cyprus operates strict anti-money laundering regulations and so any sums higher than that (especially those in cash) must be declared to Customs and Excise at the port of entry. All banks are required to obtain full identification from account customers, be familiar with customers' normal account movements, and report any amounts deposited in excess of US$100,000 (around CY£45,000), especially if they're in cash. Transfers of capital are tax free, but any worldwide income is liable to be taxed (see **Chapter 7**).

International Bank Transfers

If you plan to import money to Cyprus for the purposes of buying property or setting up a business, there are a number of ways it can be done, all of which are detailed below. When transferring money to Cyprus, research the best exchange rate and the lowest costs. Banks are sometimes willing to negotiate on fees and exchange rates when you're transferring a large amount of money. If you intend to send a large amount of money abroad for a business transaction such as buying a property, you should ensure that you receive the commercial rate of exchange rather than the tourist rate. Keep well informed about exchange rate fluctuations, so that you're able to negotiate effectively with a bank.

 Don't be optimistic about the exchange rate, which can change at short notice and mean that your property purchase can cost you a considerable amount more than you planned.

When transferring or sending money to (or from) Cyprus, you should familiarise yourself with the alternatives and shop around to get the best deal. Before you decide on the best method of transferring funds, check the charges and how soon your money will be available to use. You will be charged by the bank in Cyprus and the bank in your home country. Compare your bank's rate with that of at least one foreign exchange broker who specialises in sending money abroad (particularly large sums). Some of these companies allow you to fix or guarantee the exchange rate for an agreed period, or set upper limits on the rate that you're prepared to accept, although you must pay for these facilities. The leading companies include Currencies Direct (☎ UK 020-7813 0332, 🖳 www.currenciesdirect.com), Foreign Currency Direct (☎ UK 01494-725353, 🖳 www.currencies.co.uk) and Moneycorp (☎ UK 020-7808 0500, 🖳 www.moneycorp.com).

SWIFT Transfers

All commercial banks in Cyprus are members of the Society for Worldwide Interbank Financial Telecommunication (SWIFT) and this is probably the fastest and most efficient method of transferring money to and from Cyprus. The bank that initiates the transfer will charge you a fee and, although a transfer theoretically takes as little as two or three hours, it may be several working days before you actually gain access to your money.

Transferring funds within Europe has been made simpler with the introduction of the International Bank Account Number (IBAN), which standardises the procedure and identifies an account held at any bank anywhere in the world. Despite its name, the IBAN is not a separate bank account number but precedes your own account number and contains the country code under the IBAN system, certain check digits and the bank branch reference number.

Telegraphic Transfers

One of the quickest (it takes around ten minutes) and safest methods of transferring cash is via a telegraphic transfer, e.g. Moneygram, which also has an E-Moneygram service, allowing you to transfer via the internet (☎ UK 0800-666 3947, 💻 www.moneygram.com) and Western Union (☎ Cyprus 22-710 400, 💻 www.westernunion.com). However, this method is one of the most expensive, e.g. commission of 7 to 10 per cent of the amount sent!

Bank Drafts & Personal Cheques

For UK citizens, a bank draft or a personal cheque drawn on a UK bank account is acceptable for credit into an account in Cyprus. Check with your bank in Cyprus to see how long it will take to clear a bank draft or cheque. **Clearance of personal cheques can take a long time (currently 22 working days).** Some banks may offer a shorter clearance service than others to established customers.

Bank Mandate

This is a standing instruction to allow the bank to transfer funds to a specific account at a later date. You should set this up well in advance so that when you need to use the service, procedures can be set in motion smoothly and effectively. Once it's set up, this is usually a very efficient way of transferring money to Cyprus from abroad.

Obtaining Cash

While cheques and credit cards are commonly accepted in major cities and tourist areas, in remote rural areas cash is the most common and sometimes the only form of payment acceptable. Many foreigners living in Cyprus (particularly retirees) keep the bulk of their money in a foreign account (perhaps an offshore bank) and draw on it with a cash card locally using an automatic teller machine (ATM). Banks in the main towns and the capital, Nicosia, have foreign exchange departments where you can buy and sell foreign currencies, cash travellers' cheques, and obtain a cash advance on credit and charge cards. This is an ideal solution for holidaymakers and holiday-homeowners, although homeowners will still need a local bank account to pay their bills.

When using a credit or debit card, there's usually a daily limit and a withdrawal charge, and you need a personal identification number (PIN). Some credit card companies don't offer the best exchange rate on withdrawals. Most banks charge around 2 per cent commission with a minimum charge of CY£2.50, so it's expensive to change small amounts. There are also private *bureaux de change* in Cyprus, with longer business hours than banks, particularly at weekends. Most offer competitive exchange rates and low or no commission (but always check). They're easier to deal with than banks, and if you're changing a lot of money you can also usually negotiate a better exchange rate. However, the best exchange rates may still be found at a bank, even taking into consideration commission charges. Never use unofficial moneychangers, who are likely to short change you. The official exchange rates for most European and major international currencies are listed in banks and daily newspapers. **Always shop around for the best exchange rate and the lowest commission**.

There isn't a lot of difference in the cost of buying Cypriot currency using cash, travellers' cheques or a credit or debit card. However, many people carry only cash when visiting Cyprus, which is asking for trouble, particularly if you have no way of obtaining more cash locally, e.g. with a credit card or travellers' cheques. **One thing to bear in mind when travelling anywhere is not to rely on only one source of funds**.

Travellers' Cheques

If you're visiting Cyprus, it's safer to carry travellers' cheques than cash, although these are becoming less common and aren't as easy to redeem as in some other countries, e.g. the US. For example, they aren't usually accepted by businesses, except some hotels, restaurants and shops, all of which usually offer a poor exchange rate. It's best to buy travellers' cheques in pounds sterling for Cyprus. You can buy them from any Cypriot bank, usually for a service charge of 1 per cent. In Cyprus, Thomas Cook travellers' cheques can be cashed commission-free at any branch of the Bank of Cyprus. Banks usually offer a better exchange rate for travellers' cheques than for banknotes.

Always keep a separate record of cheque numbers and note where and when they were cashed. American Express provides a free, three-hour replacement service for lost or stolen travellers' cheques at all their offices worldwide, provided that you know the serial numbers of the lost cheques. Without the serial numbers, replacement can take three days or longer. Most companies provide toll-free numbers for reporting lost or stolen travellers' cheques in Cyprus.

BANKS

Cyprus' banking system is modelled on the British system, with banking practices, services and methods of management and control closely resembling those in the UK. The Central Bank of Cyprus regulates, supervises and monitors the country's banking system. There are currently 14 domestic banks operating in Cyprus: 11 of them are commercial banks and three are specialised financial institutions (see below). In addition, there are around 30 international banking centres on the island. The main domestic and foreign banks are the Alpha Bank Ltd, Bank of Cyprus, Co-operative Central Bank Ltd, Cyprus Popular Bank, Emporiki Bank (Cyprus Ltd), Hellenic Bank, National Bank of Greece (Cyprus) Ltd, Société Générale (Cyprus Ltd) and Universal Bank Ltd. Two other banks operate as branches of foreign banks: Arab Bank plc and National Bank of Greece SA.

The three specialised financial institutions are the Cyprus Development Bank Ltd, the Housing Finance Corporation and Mortgage Bank of Cyprus Ltd. They provide medium- and long-term finance to different sectors. The Cyprus Development Bank Ltd deals with investment banking operations and provides consulting services to companies. The Housing Finance Corporation provides long-term housing loans mainly to low and middle-income families, and the Mortgage Bank of Cyprus Ltd specialises in granting medium and long-term loans for the development of the tourism and manufacturing industries.

In addition to the domestic banks, international banking units (IBUs) are authorised to operate in the country by the Central Bank of Cyprus. However, they're required to deal primarily with non-residents and in currencies other than the Cypriot pound. From 1st January 2001, IBUs were permitted to grant medium- and long-term loans in foreign currencies to residents.

Obtain recommendations and as much information as you can about all the banks before you commit yourself. During the last few years, banks in Cyprus have extended their services beyond traditional banking and now offer such services as insurance, leasing, hire purchase finance, investment and consulting. They've also taken advantage of new technologies and offer customers telephone and internet banking services. All Cypriot banking staff speak English and banks are modern, efficient and well equipped. Commercial banks in Cyprus have correspondents in the major cities throughout the world and transactions can be carried out in all major currencies. Most offer comprehensive services to both personal and business and investment customers, so it's worth researching your options fully.

Further information on Cyprus' banking system can be found on the website of the Central Bank (🖳 www.centralbank.gov.cy) and from the Association of Cyprus Commercial Banks (ACCB), which has a list of members and their services on its website (🖳 www.accb.com.cy).

Opening Hours

Banking hours are usually from 8.15am to 1pm Mondays to Fridays and from 3.15 to 4.45pm on Monday afternoons only. Some branches in tourist areas offer an afternoon service on Tuesdays to Fridays from 3.30 or 4 until 6.30pm. International banks are open from 8.30am to 5.30pm. Banking facilities are available at the island's two international airports (Larnaca and Paphos) up to 24 hours a day. Banks are closed at weekends and on public holidays.

Opening an Account

You can open a bank account in Cyprus whether you're a resident or a non-resident. It's advisable to open a bank account in person rather than by correspondence from abroad. You can open a bank account before arriving in the country via an overseas branch of any Cypriot bank (or a foreign bank operating in Cyprus), but your signature must be ratified before the account can be opened. The Bank of Cyprus has branches abroad; in the UK they're in London, Birmingham and Manchester. Obtain details from as many Cypriot banks as you can as early as possible so that you have plenty of time to compare their services. **Before choosing a bank, you should compare the fees charged for personal accounts, overdrafts, international money transfers and other services.** Ask your friends, neighbours or colleagues for their recommendations and go along to the bank of your choice and introduce yourself. You must be over 18 and provide proof of identity, e.g. a passport and your local address. Note that various types of bank account can be opened, including current accounts and foreign currency accounts).

It isn't wise to close your bank accounts in your home country when you're living permanently in Cyprus, unless you're absolutely certain that you won't need them in future. Even when you're resident in Cyprus, it's cheaper to keep some money in an account in a country that you visit regularly than to pay commission to convert foreign currency. Many foreigners living in Cyprus maintain at least two accounts, a foreign bank account for their international transactions and a local account for day-to-day business.

Offshore Banking

If you have a sum of money to invest or wish to protect your inheritance from the tax man, it may be worthwhile looking into the accounts and services (such as pensions and trusts) provided by offshore banking centres in 'tax havens' such as the Channel Islands (Guernsey and Jersey), Gibraltar and the Isle of Man (around 50 locations worldwide are officially classified as tax havens). A large number of American, British and other European banks and financial institutions provide offshore banking facilities in one or more locations. Most institutions offer high-interest deposit accounts for long-term savings and investment portfolios, in which funds can be deposited in any major currency. Many people living abroad keep a local account for everyday business and maintain an offshore account for international transactions and investment purposes. Money can be deposited in a variety of currencies, many accounts offer a debit card (e.g. MasterCard or Visa), which can be used to obtain cash via ATMs throughout the world, and most offshore banks also offer telephone banking (usually seven days a week) and internet banking.

SURVIVAL TIP
Most financial experts advise investors
not to invest their life savings in an offshore tax haven
until they know what their long-term plans are.

Offshore banking isn't 'tax-free' (i.e. you can no longer hide from the taxman by depositing your money in an offshore bank). You must declare your worldwide income to the relevant tax authority (i.e. in Cyprus if you're resident there, in another country if you aren't), and a recent EU directive, which comes into force on 1st July 2005, allows governments to exchange personal banking information in an attempt to track down tax evaders, although those of Austria, Belgium and Luxembourg have so far been granted an exemption from this requirement.

Accounts have minimum deposits levels which usually range from GB£500 to GB£10,000 ($750 to $15,000), with some as high as GB£100,000 ($150,000). In addition to large minimum balances, accounts may also have stringent terms and conditions, such as restrictions on withdrawals or high early withdrawal penalties. You can deposit funds on call (instant access) or for a fixed period, e.g. from 90 days to one year (usually for larger sums). Interest is usually paid monthly or annually. Monthly interest payments are slightly lower than annual payments, although they have the advantage of providing a regular income. There are usually no charges provided a specified minimum balance is maintained, but some banks (e.g. those in Andorra, Guernsey, the Isle of Man, Jersey, Liechtenstein, Monaco, San Marino and Switzerland) impose a 15 per cent withholding tax on interest earnings, which is due to be increased to 20 per cent in 2008 and to 35 per cent in 2011.

The new EU measures mean that offshore banking is no longer an effective method of (legally) reducing your tax bill, and you may be better advised to investigate other investment options, such as offshore tursts or insurance bonds.

When selecting any financial institution, your first priority should be for the safety of your money. In some offshore banking centres all bank deposits are guaranteed up to a maximum amount under a deposit protection scheme (the Isle of Man, Guernsey and Jersey all have such schemes). Unless you're planning to bank with a major international bank (which is only likely to fold the day after the end of the world!), you should always check the credit rating of a financial institution before depositing any money, particularly if it doesn't provide deposit insurance. All banks have a credit rating (the highest is 'AAA') and a bank with a high rating will be happy to tell you (but get it in writing). You can also check the rating of an international bank or financial organisation with Moody's Investor Service. You should be wary of institutions offering higher than average interest rates, as if it looks too good to be true it probably will be. Further information about offshore banking can be found via the internet (e.g. 🖳 www.ifap.org.uk, 🖳 www.lowtax.net, 🖳 www.money facts.co.uk and 🖳 www.worldoffshorebanks.com). The magazine *Investment International*, which you can also read online (🖳 www. investmentinternational.com), has a wealth of easy to understand information about offshore accounts.

MORTGAGES & LOANS

Mortgages and loans for the purchase of property are far easier to obtain in Cyprus than they used to be. All commercial banks in Cyprus now offer mortages for property or land purchase and, in general, they offer a similar type of service. All mortgages are of the repayment type, and loans can be granted in either Cypriot pounds or any foreign currency. Most financial experts advise clients to obtain a mortgage from a large reputable bank, rather than a small one. **Irrespective of how you finance your purchase, you should always obtain professional advice.**

To obtain a mortgage from a local bank in Cyprus, you must usually provide proof of your monthly income and outgoings such as existing mortgage payments, rent and other loans or commitments. The amount you can borrow will depend on various factors such as your income, trade or profession, whether you're an employee (you will need to produce payslips, an employer's reference and personal bank statements) or self-employed (you will need to produce audited accounts for at least one year's business and personal bank statements), and whether you're married, and if so, whether your partner works. **Note that there are no non-status or self-certification mortgages available in Cyprus and lenders won't take into account any proposed rental income on the property.**

Mortgages are available only on a repayment basis and the minimum amount you can borrow is CY£20,000. There's no maximum loan amount, but it's usually between 60 and 70 per cent of the official valuation of an independent valuer, employed by the lender. Bear in mind that mortgages in Cyprus are generally for a shorter period than in the UK and US, and therefore your repayments may be much higher than you expect. If your loan is in Cypriot pounds, the repayment period can be up to 25 years. **However, the maximum repayment period for mortgages in foreign currencies made to non-residents is ten years.** Interest rates on loans depend on the bank concerned, but will usually be between 2 and 2.75 per cent above the London Inter Bank Offered Rate (LIBOR). This is the rate at which banks lend money to each other. It changes daily and a LIBOR-linked mortgage will normally be adjusted every three months. The base rate of the Central Bank of Cyprus at the beginning of 2005 was 5.25 per cent.

Taking out a mortgage inevitably involves costs. There's an arrangement fee of approximately 1 per cent, depending on the bank. Lenders usually require a life insurance policy and building insurance for a property's full value. If there's no separate title deed for the property because it's part of a development (see page 108), the bank will ask for a guarantee to be issued by the developer, which will cost you 1.8 per cent of the amount loaned.

Mortgage arrangements in Cyprus are usually made by the lawyer in charge of the conveyancing and completion of a sale. They don't usually charge for this service, although they may receive a commission from the lender. The advantage of this system is that a lawyer can better co-ordinate the drawing up of the purchase contract and accompanying paperwork with the loan approval; the disadvantage is that you may not get the most suitable or favourable mortgage, as lawyers don't necessarily know the loan market or have an interest in obtaining the best terms for you. You are, of course, free to choose your own lender.

The property that you're purchasing will be used as collateral for the loan. i.e. the lender takes a first charge on the property, which is declared at the Lands Office on the transfer of the property. If you're buying a property off plan or building your own house, a bank usually advances the mortgage to the builder or developer in stages in line with the agreed stage payments.

SURVIVAL TIP
If you need to obtain a mortgage to buy
a home in Cyprus, shop around and compare interest
rates, terms and fees from a number of banks and
financial institutions – not just in Cyprus but
also your home country.

Re-mortgaging

If you have equity in an existing property, either in Cyprus or your home country, it may be more cost effective to re-mortgage (or take out a second mortgage) on that property than to take out a new mortgage for a second home in Cyprus. It involves less paperwork, and therefore lower legal fees, and a plan can be tailored to meet your individual requirements. Depending on your equity in your existing property and the cost of your Cypriot property, this may enable you to pay cash for a second home.

Foreign Currency Loans

It's possible to obtain a foreign currency mortgage, as opposed to one in Cypriot pounds, e.g. in pounds sterling, euros or US dollars. You may benefit from interest rate changes, but you should be extremely wary about taking out a foreign currency mortgage, as interest rate gains can be wiped out overnight by currency swings and devaluations. **It's generally recognised that you should take out a mortgage in the currency in which you're paid or in the currency of the country where a property is situated.** If the foreign currency in which you have your mortgage is heavily devalued, you will have the consolation of knowing that the value of your Cypriot property will ('theoretically') have increased by the same percentage when converted back into Cypriot pounds. When choosing between a Cypriot pound and a foreign currency loan, take into account all costs, fees, interest rates and possible currency fluctuations. If you have a foreign currency mortgage, you must usually pay commission charges each time you transfer foreign currency into Cypriot pounds or remit money to Cyprus.

Payment Problems & Changing Lenders

If you're unable to meet your mortgage payments, lenders are usually willing to help your readjust your payments. However, it's important to contact your lender as soon as you start having problems; other banks won't consider bailing you out if you're in debt. Different lenders respond to payment problems in different ways, but they always prefer it if you approach them before you get into serious difficulties. Remember that your lender has an interest in helping you sort out any problems and so minimising any losses to himself. If you have short-term problems with repayments, your lender may agree to reduce or even suspend payments for a short period, although these will eventually have to be repaid once your finances are in better shape. If it's a long-term problem, the lender will look for the cheapest way out and may want to repossess the house so that he can sell it to recover the loan. In Cyprus, however, it takes a number of years for repossession cases to reach the courts and during that time the lender cannot foreclose on the loan.

Banks and lenders in Cyprus all offer very similar terms, so there isn't usually much to be gained from changing lenders.

5.

THE PURCHASE PROCEDURE

This chapter details the purchase procedure (or conveyancing) for buying a home in Cyprus. Foreign buyers, especially those from the UK, often assume that because legal and financial systems are based on the same principles as those in the UK, house-buying procedures will be the same. **Cyprus land law and UK land law and the associated procedures aren't the same. It's wise to employ the services of a recommended local lawyer even before you find a property and always before paying any money.** This way you can familiarise yourself with procedures and seek general advice to bear in mind while you're house-hunting. See also **Avoiding Problems** on page 77.

Despite the fact that the Republic of Cyprus is now a member of the European Union (EU), **there are still certain restrictions on property purchase by non-resident foreigners**, although it's thought that by 2009 these will be lifted for all EU citizens. This means that an important part of the conveyancing procedure in Cyprus is your application to the Council of Ministers for permission to purchase a property. This can be applied for directly at your local District Administration Office (see **Appendix A**) or via your lawyer. It should be stressed that, in all bona fide cases, this is very much a formality and is almost always granted, especially for EU citizens.

HOLDING DEPOSIT

In many cases, the vendor will ask for a holding deposit. This is usual in the case of a new property; in the case of a resale, you may pay a deposit only on signing the sale contract (see **Payment** below). A deposit reserves your property and it should be paid directly to the vendor; it isn't kept in a separate (bonded) account until the transaction is completed as in some other countries. Although the payment of a holding deposit is normal procedure in Cyprus, however, you should always take advice from your lawyer before handing over any money. He will advise you to keep the amount to a minimum (usually around CY£1,000) and will draw up a simple document of receipt stating that the deposit paid is subject to satisfactory searches (see **Lawyer's Checks** below). In general, you will lose your deposit only if you withdraw from a sale without a satisfactory reason (i.e. simply 'change your mind').

LAWYER'S CHECKS

Once the sale price has been agreed or a holding deposit paid, your lawyer will begin to draw up the sale contract (see page 147) and make the following checks, which usually takes around a month:

- Verifying with the Lands Office that the vendor has legal authority to sell the property and that there are no debts attached to the property;

- Ensuring that, in the case of several owners, they all agree to the sale and sign the sale contract.

- Checking the ownership of any trees on your land (which may be owned by people other than the registered property owner);

- Establishing the exact boundaries of the plot. This is done automatically by the Lands Office, but you can wait up to a year, so it's preferable to arrange for a private surveyor to do so and to have your lawyer send his report to the Lands Office.

- Verifying that there are separate title deeds for your property or plot. This is very important when you buy a property in a new development (see **Buying Off Plan** on page 102). It may be difficult to get these from a developer and provision must be made in the contract in case the developer or vendor fails to supply them. Your sale contract must be deposited with the Lands Office to protect your rights and put a charge on the property.

- Making sure that, in the case of a property under construction, all the required planning and building permits have been obtained;

- Checking that, in the case of land purchase, you have proper access to your property. You won't be granted planning permission unless you have access to a public road. This must be confirmed before you can apply for planning permission. The regulations state that the distance to a public road must be less than 600ft. If the distance is less than 600ft but you don't have right of access, you must apply for it to the Lands Office, which is a lengthy procedure.

- Verifying planning zones and regulations with the Lands Office. Zoning areas were changed in 2003 and you're permitted to build only on land zoned for building. Your lawyer should also check the zoning of nearby land to ensure that your plot isn't close to an industrial or agricultural zone, which may affect your enjoyment of the property.

- Checking the legal building density (how many square metres of land you can build on) and that the intended use, height and number of floors of any planned buildings are permitted.

- Making sure that the proposed building isn't within a seashore protection zone, which usually extends approximately 300ft from the sea and where no building is permitted.

- Checking whether there are any ancient monuments close to where your plot is, and consulting the Inspector of Antiquities. Ancient monument areas are usually marked 'A.M.' on Lands Office plans (known as the 'Lands and Surveys').

- Verifying that utilities can be connected to the property. Usually electricity can be brought to any part of Cyprus, although it may be expensive if the property is in a remote area. Your lawyer should also ensure that it's easy for the property to be connected to a water supply, including drinking water.

 A lawyer's checks don't cover such things as motorways or major roads being built near your home or any other construction which may affect your enjoyment of the property, and you should check these yourself with the local Town Planning Department.

Many estate agents will carry out the above checks for you and pass the information on to your lawyer. However, it's still advisable to have your lawyer double check. The cost of conveyancing for a property in Cyprus lawyers fees are around CY£1,000, depending on the price, size and how complicated the conveyancing procedure is. Before hiring a lawyer, compare the fees charged by a number of practices and obtain quotations in writing. Always check what's included in the fee and whether it's 'full and binding' or just an estimate (a low basic rate may be supplemented by much more expensive 'extras'). You must employ a lawyer to check the contract (see below) before signing it to ensure that it's correct and includes everything needed, particularly regarding any necessary conditional clauses (see page 148).

FINAL CHECK

When you sign the sale contract, you agree to accept the property in the condition it's in at that time, so **it's essential to check that the property is still in the same condition as when you last saw it, and that it hasn't fallen down or been damaged in any way.**

In Cyprus there's usually a clause in the contract which states that the property must be in the same condition as it was when it was originally inspected by the buyer. Nevertheless, even if you took photographs, it's almost impossible to prove what condition it was in, so it's imperative to check before signing the sale contract.

Your check should include fixtures and fittings and anything that's included in the contract or purchased separately, e.g. carpets, light fittings, curtains or kitchen appliances. Check that these are still present and in good working order. You should also ensure that expensive items (such as kitchen apparatus) haven't been substituted by inferior (possibly second-hand) items.

If you find that anything is missing, damaged or not in working order, you should make a note and insist on an appropriate reduction in the amount to be paid. In such cases it's normal for the lawyer to delay the signing of the sale contract until the matter is settled, although an appropriate amount could be withheld from the vendor's proceeds to pay for repairs or replacements.

> ### SURVIVAL TIP
> **You should refuse to go through with a purchase if you aren't completely satisfied with everything, as it will be difficult or impossible to obtain redress later.**

If it isn't possible to complete the sale, you should consult your lawyer about your rights and the return of your deposit and any other funds already paid.

PAYMENT

If your property is a resale and you can move straight in, you will make whatever payment you've agreed with the vendor at this point. This may be full payment (less any holding deposit paid) or it may be a 'deposit' of as little as 10 per cent of the sale price, in which case the balance is usually payable within a month. If your property is under construction, you make the appropriate stage payment according to the sale contract (normally 30 per cent of the total cost).

The amount due (after the deposit and any mortgages are subtracted), including all fees and taxes (see page 97) except the transfer fee, which isn't payable until you obtain the title deed (see page 151), must be paid by banker's draft or bank transfer. Payments can be made in any currency from any country and are usually made by telegraphic transfer into the client account held by the buyer's lawyer. However, transfers can take a long time and can even get 'lost', and it may be preferable to pay by banker's draft, which means that you will have the payment in your possession (a bank cannot lose it!) and it allows you to withhold payment if there's a last minute problem that cannot be resolved.

When the vendor and buyer are of the same foreign nationality, they can agree that the balance is paid in any currency, and payment can also be made abroad, although signing of the contract may be held up until confirmation of payment is received. However, the sale contract must state the sale price in Cypriot pounds and Cypriot taxes must be paid in Cyprus based on the exchange rate current on the date the contract was signed. At the time of signing, both the vendor and the buyer declare that payment has been made in the agreed foreign currency. In this case the payment should be held by an independent lawyer or solicitor in the vendor's and buyer's home country.

Buying Off Plan

In Cyprus, there are over 300 developers within a relatively small area and the majority are reputable. Nevertheless, you should take certain precautions when buying an uncompleted property off plan, i.e. a property still to be built or which is partly built only. You may find that a developer offers you his own sale contract. This is common, and legitimate, but **you must always have it checked by a lawyer**. A developer's or builder's contract will obviously be drafted with his interests in mind, but your lawyer will check it with your interests in mind and amend it if necessary.

Payment is made in stages. Stage payments vary but you're usually expected to pay CY£1,000 on agreement as a holding deposit and, within a month of that agreement, 30 per cent of the total value of the property, followed by another 30 per cent half way between agreement and completion and finally, on completion, the balance. Sometimes the last two payments are made according to the progress of the work, and the timing and amount of all stage payments are negotiable.

The sale contract for an off-plan property should contain the following:

- The timetable for the property's completion;
- Stage payment dates;
- The completion date and (possibly) penalties for non-completion;
- Guarantees for building work;
- A copy of the plans and drawings.

The completion of each stage should be certified in writing by the supervising engineer or architect before payments are made. Note that it's important to ensure that payments are made on time, or you could forfeit all previous payments and the property could be sold to another buyer. Although developers are generally patient about payments, they will be entitled to terminate the agreement. See also **Avoiding Problems** on page 77, which particularly applies to buying off plan or buying an unfinished property.

SINGLE OR JOINT NAMES

Property can be registered in single, joint or several names. It's preferable to register a property in joint names because of the increased relief from transfer fees (see page 99) and, if the property isn't a private residence, the fact that each person is exempt from the first CY£10,000 of CGT when it's sold (see page 178). There's no inheritance tax in Cyprus, so there's little advantage in registering a property in the names of your children.

SALE CONTRACT

When you're satisfied with the outcome of all checks and all necessary payments have been made, you can sign a sale contract with the vendor. Many Cypriots don't use a written contract for the transfer of immovable property. It's legal to do without one and you may simply register the transfer at the Lands Office, provided there's a separate title deed for the property. However, as a foreigner (and obligatorily when there's no separate title deed for a property), **you're strongly recommended to sign a written sale contract and deposit it at the Lands Office, thereby placing a legal charge on the property, which means that the property cannot be sold to anyone else before you receive the title deeds, which may be months or even years later (see Transfer of Immoval Property on page 151).**

 The sale contract must be deposited with the Lands Office within two months of signing. If you don't do this, the seller can change his mind and you will have little recourse!

If you're buying a property on a development, the developer may have the title deeds to the whole development and it will be a long process to get hold of the title deeds for your particular property. It's therefore particularly important for the sale contract to be deposited at the Lands Office until your title deed is issued.

SURVIVAL TIP

Deposition of the sale contract is the
right of the buyer and non-registration doesn't affect
the validity of the contract, but it's vitally important if
you want to protect your interests until you receive
your title deeds.

Your lawyer will deposit the contract on your behalf but these are the procedures and requirements:

- The contract must be deposited at the Lands Office in the district where the property is situated.

- The original is required for checking but will be returned to you and a copy retained by the Lands Office. Both the original and the copy must be stamped by the Lands Office.

- Form N34, stating both the vendor's and the purchaser's names, must accompany the contract.

- Any mortgages on the property must be declared (so that the lender can claim the property if you default on payment!).

- You must pay a fee of CY£1.

You should then go to the local tax office (the Internal Revenue Department) and pay the stamp duty (see page 97).

Conditional Clauses

Whether for new or for resale properties, sale contracts usually contain a number of conditional clauses that must be met to ensure the validity of the contract. Conditions usually apply to events out of control of either the vendor or buyer, although almost anything that the buyer agrees with the vendor can be included. If accessories, such as carpets, curtains or furniture, are included in the purchase price, you normally have a separate, simple agreement drawn up listing all the items. Any fixtures and fittings present in a property when you view it (and agree to buy it) should still be there when you take possession, unless otherwise stated in the contract (see also **Final Check** on page 144). There are many possible conditional clauses concerning a range of subjects, but the following are the most important:

- Being able to obtain a mortgage, although you should always obtain agreement from a lender before signing a contract;

- Being able to obtain planning permission for construction or renovation work;
- Being able to sell another property;
- That you obtain a satisfactory building survey or inspection (note that you're responsible for organising this – see **Inspections & Surveys** on page 114);
- That permission is granted by the Council of Ministers, if appropriate (see **Application to the Council of Ministers** below). Usually the contract allows for the sale of the property or a reapplication in the event of initial refusal.

You should discuss with your lawyer whether any of the above (or other) conditional clauses are necessary. Matters such as building permits and dependence on another sale should always be included, but take advice on other conditional clauses. **All conditional clauses must be approved by the vendor, and too many may make it impossible to conclude a sale!** For example, a conditional clause that there should be no plans to construct anything (e.g. roads) nearby which would adversely affect your enjoyment or use of a property is unlikely to be accepted.

If any of the conditions aren't met, the contract can be suspended or declared null and void, and the deposit returned. However, if you fail to go through with a purchase and aren't covered by a clause in the contract, you will forfeit your deposit or could even be compelled to go through with the purchase.

Mortgage

If you've arranged a mortgage (see page 136), you must declare it and register it at the Lands Office at the same time as you deposit the signed sale contract. You lawyer will advise you about this and collect all the required paperwork. He will need to complete a Contract and Declaration of Mortgage (N271) in triplicate and prove that all relevant duties and taxes, including utility bills if appropriate, have been paid (see page 100). Most importantly, the title deed of the property under mortgage will have to be supplied to ensure that there are no other charges on the property. If the property has no separate title (e.g. a property on a new development), the developer must give the bank a guarantee; the cost of this is 1.8 per cent of the loan and you must pay it.

Moving In

If you're buying a completed property, once you've signed the sale contract and paid all the required fees, you're entitled to the keys and you may take possession of your property, even if you don't yet have the title deed (see below).

COUNCIL OF MINISTERS APPLICATION

An EU national resident in Cyprus can buy as much land or property as he likes without restriction and without needing permission. Anyone else must apply to the Council of Ministers for 'permission' to buy a property or land and is restricted as follows:

- **EU Nationals** – EU nationals not resident in Cyprus can buy as much land as they like but property purchase is restricted to one house or apartment. This restriction, and the requirement to obtain permission, are likely to be lifted by 2009, but both currently apply.

- **Non- EU Nationals** – All non-EU nationals may buy no more than 3 *donums* (just over 4,000m^2 or almost exactly 1 acre) of land and only one house or apartment.

Anyone other than resident EU nationals must therefore apply, in person or via a lawyer, for permission to buy land or property to the District Administration Office in the area where the property is situated (see **Appendix B** for a list of offices). Along with an application form, you will need to supply the following:

- Your personal details, including your financial status;
- Details of the property;
- Details of the present owner, the sale contract and the terms of payment;
- A copy of your passport.

The authorities then consider your application, a procedure which may take around six months, but you can take possession of the property while you're waiting for permission (!). **It's highly unlikely that your request will be refused, and your contract will still be valid if it is, but you should ensure that your lawyer includes provision for such an event in the contract (see Conditional Clauses on page 148).** Note that Council of Ministers' permission to buy a property is granted for personal use only, not for letting or commercial purposes.

BUYING THROUGH A COMPANY

Properties in Cyprus can be purchased through a company, but the procedure is the same as buying as a private person and there's little or no benefit. You (or the company) will still have to pay all the taxes associated with buying property. When you sell the shares in the company, you're exempt from transfer fees, but not capital gains tax. Before buying property through a company, it's essential to obtain expert legal advice and weigh up the long-term advantages and disadvantages.

TRANSFER OF IMMOVABLE PROPERTY

Once your lawyer has been informed that the new title deed has been issued, he applies to transfer the property legally from the vendor's name to yours. **Note that this can be months or even years after purchase (in the case of an off-plan purchase, it can be as much as five years later!)** The documents required include the following:

- A Declaration of Transfer form (N270). The title deeds of the property or land must be attached to this form.

- A copy of your permission to purchase from the Council of Ministers;

- The sale contract;

- A completion certificate (also known as the final certificate of approval) if you've bought off plan or had building work done. You must have this in order to apply to the Lands Office for the issue of a separate title deed in the case of a property on a development (see page 108). **Ownership cannot be transferred until there are separate title deeds.**

- Receipts for the payment of all fees, charges and taxes, including immovable property tax, capital gains tax (paid by the vendor), sewerage charges, and municipal rates as appropriate.

Your lawyer will collect all the necessary receipts and documents for you and attach them to the application for transfer of immovable property.

Signing

When the new deed (also called the certificate of registration) has been drawn up, all parties (or those acting for them) must go to the Lands Office to sign it. You must produce identification, which can be an identity card or a passport. It's normal for you to be present when the deed is read, signed and witnessed, although foreign buyers (and sellers) often give someone a power of attorney to represent them, which can be arranged by your lawyer at a small charge. If a couple buys a property in joint names, the wife can give the husband power of attorney (or vice versa). **Bear in mind that a power of attorney can be a dangerous document to sign.**

© Lanitis Development

© Cyprus Tourism Organisation

© Lanitis Development

© Lanitis Development

© Lanitis Development

6.

MOVING HOUSE

This chapter contains information about moving house, immigration and customs, registration and finding help. It also contains checklists of tasks to be completed before or soon after arrival in Cyprus.

SHIPPING YOUR BELONGINGS

It usually takes only a few weeks to have your belongings shipped to Cyprus from within Europe. From anywhere else the time varies considerably, e.g. around four weeks from the east coast of America, six weeks from the west coast or from the Far East, and around eight weeks from Australasia.

Customs clearance is no longer necessary when shipping your household effects between European Union (EU) countries. However, when shipping your effects from a non-EU country to Cyprus, you should enquire about customs formalities in advance. If you fail to follow the correct procedure, you could encounter problems and delays, and may be erroneously charged duty or fined. The relevant forms to be completed by non-EU citizens depend on whether your Cypriot home will be your main residence or a second home. Removal companies usually take care of the paperwork and ensure that the correct documents are provided and properly completed (see **Customs** on page 160).

It's advisable to use a major shipping company with a good reputation. For international moves it's best to use a company that's a member of a recognised assocation in your home country, such as the British International Freight Association (BIFA, 🖥 www.bifa.org) in the UK, or a member of either the International Federation of Furniture Removers (FIDI, 🖥 www.fidi.com) or the Overseas Moving Network International (OMNI, 🖥 www.omnimoving.com), with experience in Cyprus. OMNI has extensive country and customs information on its website and allows you to check OMNI members in particular countries. Both FIDI and OMNI subscribe to an advance payment scheme providing a guarantee, whereby, if a member company fails to fulfil its commitments to a client, the removal is completed at the agreed cost by another member or your money is refunded. Some removal companies have subsidiaries or affiliates in Cyprus, which may be more convenient if you encounter problems or need to make an insurance claim. If you engage a shipping company in Cyprus, it's wise to avoid small unregistered companies.

You should obtain at least three written quotations before choosing a company, as rates vary considerably. Removal companies should send a representative to provide a detailed quotation. Most companies will pack your belongings and provide packing cases and special containers, although this is naturally more expensive than packing them yourself.

Ask a company how they pack fragile and valuable items, and whether the cost of packing cases, materials and insurance (see below) is included in a quotation.

If you're doing your own packing, most companies will provide packing crates and boxes. You should ideally make a simple floor plan of your new home with rooms numbered and mark corresponding numbers on furniture and boxes as they're packed, so that the removal company will know where everything is to go and you can leave them to it.

Shipments are charged by volume, e.g. the square metre (m²) in Europe and the square foot in the US. You should expect to pay from UK£2,500 (CY£2,000) to UK£4,750 (CY£4,000) to move the contents of a three- to four-bedroom house within western Europe, e.g. from London to Cyprus. If you're flexible about the delivery date, shipping companies will usually quote a lower fee based on a 'part load', where the cost is shared with other deliveries. This can result in savings of 50 per cent or more compared with a 'special' delivery but may involve delays.

> **SURVIVAL TIP**
> Whether you have an individual or
> shared delivery, obtain the maximum transit period in
> writing, or you may have to wait months
> for delivery!

Be sure to fully insure your belongings during removal with a well established insurance company. **If you insure through the shipping company's own insurance, it's often difficult to claim for any damages.** It's a good idea to cover yourself through an independent company. Insurance premiums are usually 1 to 2 per cent of the declared value of your goods, depending on the type of cover chosen. It's wise to make a photographic or video record of valuables for insurance purposes. Most insurance policies cover for 'all risks' on a replacement value basis. Note, however, that china, glass and other breakables can usually be included in an all-risks policy only when they're packed by the removal company. Insurance usually covers total loss or loss of a particular crate only, rather than individual items (unless they were packed by the shipping company).

If there are any breakages or damaged items, they must be noted and listed before you sign the delivery bill (although it's obviously impossible to check everything on delivery). If you need to make a claim, be sure to read the small print, as some companies require clients to make a claim within a few days, although seven is usual. **Always send a claim by registered post.** Some insurance companies apply an excess (deductible) of around 1 per cent of the total shipment value when assessing claims.

This means that if your shipment is valued at CY£25,000 and you make a claim for less than CY£250, you won't receive anything.

If you're unable to ship your belongings directly to Cyprus, most shipping companies will put them into storage and some offer a limited free storage period prior to shipment (e.g. 14 days).

SURVIVAL TIP
If you need to put your household
effects into storage, it's advisable to have them fully
insured while they're there.

Make a complete list of everything to be moved and give a copy to the removal company. Don't include anything illegal (e.g. guns, bombs, drugs or pornography), as customs checks can be rigorous and penalties severe. Give the shipping company **detailed** instructions about how to find your Cypriot address from the nearest main road or port and a telephone number where you can be contacted. If your Cypriot home has poor or impossible access for a large truck, you must inform the shipping company as soon as possible (the ground must also be firm enough to support a heavy vehicle).

After considering the shipping costs, you may decide to ship only selected items of furniture and personal effects, and buy new furniture in Cyprus. Due to the distance to and position of Cyprus, it isn't as easy to transport your belongings personally as it is to some other European destinations. If you're moving permanently to Cyprus, take the opportunity to sell, give away or throw out at least half of your possessions. It will cut down your removal bill, clear your mind, and make life simpler, plus you will have the fun of buying new furniture that really suits your new house. Bear in mind that everything that can go wrong often does – especially when moving to a foreign country – so allow plenty of time.

PRE-DEPARTURE HEALTH CHECK

There are no immunisation requirements for Cyprus but, if you're planning to take up residence in Cyprus, even for only part of the year, it's wise to have a health check before your departure, particularly if you have a record of poor health or are elderly. If you're already taking regular medication, you should note that the brand names of medicines vary from country to country, and you should ask your doctor for the generic name. If you wish to match medication prescribed abroad, you will need a current prescription with the medication's trade name, the manufacturer's name, the chemical name and the dosage. Most medicines have an equivalent in other countries, although particular brands may be difficult or impossible to obtain abroad.

It's possible to have medication sent from another country and usually no import duty or value added tax is payable. If you're visiting a holiday home in Cyprus for a limited period, you should take sufficient medication with you to cover your stay, although in an emergency a local doctor will write a prescription that can be taken to a local pharmacy. You should also take some of your favourite non-prescription medicines, e.g. cold and flu remedies and creams, as they may be difficult or impossible to obtain locally or may be much more expensive. If applicable, also take a spare pair of spectacles or contact lenses, dentures and a hearing aid.

Domestic tap water is safe to drink, but you should be wary of drinking from public fountains, as not all of them provide drinking water (some have signs). Many people prefer the taste of bottled water, particularly in periods of drought when the quality of tap water sometimes deteriorates.

IMMIGRATION

On arrival in Cyprus, your first task will be to negotiate immigration. Fortunately this presents few problems for most people, particularly European Union (EU) nationals since Cyprus' accession to the EU on 1st May 2004. The country is in something of a transitional period but EU national passports are no longer being stamped on entry into the Republic of Cyprus. Cyprus isn't yet a member of the Schengen Agreement (which states that immigration checks and passport controls take place when you first arrive in a member country, after which you can travel freely between member countries without further checks), which means that these checks and controls apply even if you're arriving from another 'Schengen' country. However, during its EU accession negotiations, the Republic, along with the ten other new member states, accepted the Schengen principles, and it's now simply a matter of the government's rubber-stamping the agreement.

Citizens of the EU, Switzerland, Iceland, Liechtenstein and Norway can all enter the Republic of Cyprus with their passport or national identity card, provided it includes their photograph. Anyone who isn't a national of these countries requires a visa, which should be obtained before arriving in Cyprus. Cyprus allows nationals of most countries to stay for up to 90 days on a tourist visa, but nationals of some countries require a visa for any type of visit (see **Permits & Visas** on page 29).

Cyprus also has some special restrictions on entry, owing to the division of the country following the Turkish invasion in 1974 (see page 30).

If you're a non-EU national coming to Cyprus to work, study or live, you may be asked to show documentary evidence, such as an offer of employment or confirmation letter from your intended place of study. Immigration officials may also ask non-EU visitors to produce a return ticket and proof of accommodation, health insurance and financial resources, e.g. cash, travellers' cheques and credit cards. **The onus is on visitors to show that they're genuine and that they don't intend to breach the Republic of Cyprus' immigration laws.** Immigration officials aren't required to prove that you will breach the immigration laws and can refuse you entry on the grounds of suspicion only.

CUSTOMS

The Single European Act, which came into effect on 1st January 1993 and has applied to Cyprus since its EU accession in May 2004, created a single trading market and changed the rules regarding customs for EU nationals. There are no longer any restrictions on the import or export of Cypriot or foreign banknotes or securities, although if you enter or leave Cyprus with more than CY£7,300 in cash in any currency or gold you must declare it to Cypriot customs.

The shipment of personal (household) effects to Cyprus from another EU country is no longer subject to customs formalities. EU nationals planning to take up permanent or temporary residence in Cyprus are permitted to import their furniture and personal effects, bicycles, motorcycles and private motor vehicles free of duty or taxes, provided they were purchased tax-paid within the EU or have been owned for at least six months. Non-EU nationals planning to take up permanent or temporary residence in Cyprus are permitted to import their furniture and personal effects free of duty or taxes, provided they've owned them for at least six months.

You must be able to prove that you've lived outside Cyprus for a continuous period for 12 months before your arrival and show proof of your intention to settle permanently in Cyprus; you can provide details of your employment in your home country or a sale or rental contract for your home. You must also give details of any intended employment in Cyprus or any other document which shows you will be taking up residence in the country. A detailed inventory of items being imported (even if some are to be imported at a later date), showing their estimated value in Cyprior pounds and the make and serial numbers of all electrical appliances, is advisable (although it's unlikely that anyone will check your belongings) and the shipping company should have a photocopy of your passport.

If you're importing a car which is a used vehicle, you will need to show its registration document, certificate of insurance or a receipt of purchase (see **Importing a Car** on page 69).

If you're taking up residence in Cyprus, whether you're an EU citizen or not, you must complete a form for the transfer of normal residence and present it to any Customs Station or Customs Headquarters, Corner M. Karaoli and Gr. Afxentiou, 1096 Nicosia (☎ 22-601 668, ✉ head quarters@customs.mof.gov.cy). If you require further information about Cypriot customs regulations, contact the Director of Customs at the above address. Information about duty-free allowances can be found on page 228 and information on importing and exporting pets on page 43.

Visitors

Visitors (i.e. those staying in Cyprus for less than 90 days) aren't subject to duty or VAT on the belongings they bring with them. Goods may be imported without formality, provided their nature and quantity doesn't imply any commercial aim. Customs officials can still stop anyone for a spot check, e.g. to check for drugs or illegal immigrants. This applies to the import of private cars, camping vehicles (including trailers or caravans), motorcycles, aircraft, boats and personal effects. All means of transport and personal effects imported duty-free mustn't be sold or given away in Cyprus and must be exported when a visitor leaves Cyprus. Foreign-registered vehicles mustn't be lent or rented to anyone while in Cyprus.

Prohibited & Restricted Goods

Certain goods are subject to special regulations in Cyprus and in some cases their import and export is prohibited or restricted. This particularly applies to the following:

● Narcotic drugs and other 'mind-altering substances'. **Cyprus has a 'zero tolerance' policy towards the import, possession and use of drugs. If found guilty of any drug related offence, you could face a large fine or long prison sentence.**

● Agricultural products or propagating stock, such as fruit, vegetables, cut flowers, nuts, seeds, bulbs and cuttings;

● Guns, ammunition and explosives;

- Flick knives or daggers;
- Pornography in any form;
- Goods bearing a forged trade mark or false trade description;
- Pirated or counterfeit goods (e.g. films, DVDs or computer programmes);
- Live animals or birds (see **Pets** on page 43);
- Animal products (e.g. uncooked meat, fish and dairy products);
- Antiquities (which may not be exported).

If you're unsure whether any goods you're importing fall into the above categories, you should check with Cypriot customs (see above).

EMBASSY REGISTRATION

Nationals of some countries are recommended to register with their local embassy or consulate after taking up residence in Cyprus (see **Appendix A**). Registration isn't usually compulsory, although most embassies like to keep a record of their country's citizens resident in Cyprus. Britons you should go to the British High Commission, Alexander Pallis Street, 1106 Nicosia (☎ 22-861 110, ✉ infobhc@ cylink.com.cy). Office hours are 7.30am to 2pm on Mondays, Wednesdays, Thursdays and Fridays. On Tuesdays the office is open from 7.30am to 1pm and from 2 to 5.30pm.

FINDING HELP

One of the major problems facing new arrivals in Cyprus is how and where to obtain help with day-to-day problems, such as banking, obtaining insurance and registering with utility companies. **This book was written in response to this need.** However, in addition to the comprehensive information provided here, you will also need detailed **local** information. How successful you are at finding local help depends on your employer, the town or area where you live (e.g. residents of resort areas are far better served than those living in rural areas), your nationality, and your sex (women are usually better catered for than men through women's clubs).

Cyprus is better served than most destinations thanks to its large retired expatriate population and the fact that the majority of Cypriots speak good English. There's a considerable amount of information available both in Greek and in English, and any government and official information is always available in both languages. Websites are almost always available in English as well as Greek, particularly those of government, semi-government and local government organisations.

You may find that your friends and colleagues can offer advice based on their own experiences and mistakes. **But take care!** Although they mean well, you're likely to receive as much false and conflicting information as helpful advice (it may not be wrong but often won't apply to your particular situation).

A wealth of useful information is available in resort towns (especially Paphos), where foreigners are well-served by English-speaking clubs and expatriate organisations. Cyprus has a UK Citizens' Association, whose stated object is to 'promote and advance the interests of British expatriate citizens in or connected with Cyprus'. It has offices in Larnaca, Limassol and Paphos and offers a wealth of useful information to members, as well as providing much-needed social contact. The association produces a detailed handbook which covers every aspect of living in Cyprus. Its headquarters is at 39 Thermopylon Street/PO Box 56682, 3309 Limassol (☎ 25-344 578, 💻 www.ukca.com.cy).

Most consulates provide their nationals with local information including details of lawyers, translators, doctors, dentists, schools, and social and expatriate organisations. Other useful contacts can be found through the many expatriate publications (see **Appendix B**).

CHECKLISTS

If you're moving permanently to Cyprus, there are many things to be considered and a 'million' people to inform. Even if you plan to spend just a few months a year in Cyprus, it may still be necessary to inform a number of individuals and organisations in your home country. The checklists below are designed to make the task easier and help prevent an ulcer or a nervous breakdown (provided of course you don't leave everything to the last minute). Not all points are applicable to non-residents or to those who spend only a few weeks or months each year in Cyprus.

Before Arrival

The following are tasks that should be completed (if possible) before your arrival in Cyprus:

- Check that your family's passports are valid.
- Obtain a visa, if necessary, for all your family members. Obviously this **must** be done before arrival in Cyprus.

- Arrange health, dental and optical check-ups for your family before leaving your home country. Obtain a copy of health records and a statement from your private health insurance company stating your present level of cover.

- Arrange health and travel insurance for your family. This is essential if you aren't already covered by an international health insurance policy and won't be covered by Cypriot social security.

- Arrange inoculations and shipment for any pets that you're taking with you.

- Visit Cyprus to compare schools and to arranging schooling for your children (if applicable).

- Open a bank account in Cyprus and transfer funds. Give the details to any companies that you plan to pay by direct debit or standing order (e.g. utility and property management companies).

- If you don't already have one, obtain an international credit card or two, which will prove useful in Cyprus.

- If you live in rented accommodation, give your landlord notice (check your contract).

- Arrange shipment of your furniture and belongings by booking a shipping company well in advance.

- Arrange to sell or dispose of anything you aren't taking with you (e.g. house, car and furniture). If you're selling a home or business, obtain expert legal advice, as you may be able to save tax with some careful tax planning. Note that you may need to pay capital gains tax on any profits from the sale of second and subsequent homes.

- If you're planning to export a car to Cyprus, collect the relevant paperwork.

- Check whether you're entitled to a rebate on any insurance you have (e.g. road tax or car insurance) and obtain a letter from your car insurance company stating your no-claims record.

- Claim any rebate on your tax and social security or other pension contributions to which you're entitled. If you're leaving a country permanently and have been a member of a company or state pension scheme, you may be entitled to a refund or may be able to continue payments to qualify for a full (or larger) pension when you retire. Contact your company personnel office, local tax office or pension company for information.

- Terminate any outstanding loan, lease or hire purchase contracts and pay all bills (allow plenty of time, as some companies are slow to respond).

- Return any library books and anything else borrowed or hired.
- Obtain as many credit references as possible (e.g. from banks, mortgage companies, credit card companies, credit agencies, and companies with which you've had accounts) and references from professionals such as lawyers and accountants. These will help you establish a credit rating in Cyprus.
- Collect any documents necessary to obtain a residence permit and obtain numerous passport-size photographs (students should take at least a dozen).
- Take all your family's official documents with you. These may include:
  - Birth certificates;
  - Driving licences;
  - Marriage certificate, divorce papers or death certificate (if a widow or widower);
  - Educational diplomas and professional certificates;
  - Employment references and curricula vitae;
  - School records and student ID cards;
  - Medical and dental records;
  - Bank account and credit card details;
  - Insurance policies (plus no-claims records);
  - Receipts for any valuables.
- Inform the following:
  - Your employer (e.g. give notice or arrange leave of absence) or clients if you're self-employed;
  - Your local town hall or municipality (you may be entitled to a refund of your local property or income taxes);
  - The police, if it was necessary to register with them in your home country (or present country of residence);
  - Your electricity, gas, water and telephone companies (contact companies well in advance, particularly if you need to get a deposit refunded);
  - Your insurance companies (e.g. health, car, home contents and private pension);
  - Your bank, post office (if you have a post office account), stockbroker and other financial institutions, credit card, charge card and hire purchase companies, lawyer and accountant, and local businesses where you have accounts;

- Your family doctor, dentist and other health practitioners (health records should be transferred to your new doctor and dentist in Cyprus, if applicable);

- Your children's schools (try to give a term's notice and obtain a copy of any relevant school reports or records);

- All regular correspondents, publications to which you subscribe, social and sports clubs you belong to, and friends and relatives. Give them your new address and telephone number and arrange to have your post redirected by the post office or a friend. Give close friends, relatives and business associates a telephone number where you can be contacted in Cyprus.

● If you have a driving licence or car, give the local vehicle registration office your new address in Cyprus and (if applicable) return your car's registration plates.

● Obtain some Cypriot pounds, as this will save you time on arrival and you may receive a better exchange rate.

If you will be living in Cyprus for an extended period (but not permanently), you may wish to give someone 'power of attorney' over your financial affairs in your home country so that they can act for you in your absence. This can be for a fixed period or open-ended and can be for a specific purpose only.

SURVIVAL TIP
You should take expert legal advice
before giving someone power of attorney over
any of your financial affairs.

Finally, allow plenty of time to get to the airport, register your luggage, and clear security and immigration.

After Arrival

The following tasks should be completed after arrival in Cyprus (if not done before):

● Have your visa cancelled and your passport stamped, as applicable.

● If you've taken a vehicle to Cyprus, register it in Cyprus.

● If you haven't brought a vehicle with you, rent one or buy one locally (it's practically impossible to get around in rural areas without a car).

- Arrange whatever insurance is necessary, such as health, car, household and third party liability.
- Contact offices and organisations to obtain local information.
- Make courtesy calls on your neighbours within a few weeks of your arrival. This is particularly important in small villages and rural areas if you want to be accepted and become part of the local community.
- Apply for a residence permit at your local Immigration Office immediately if your intention is to stay more than 90 days or live permanently in Cyprus.
- Apply for a social insurance at the nearest office.
- Apply for a Cypriot driving licence (if necessary).
- Find a local doctor and dentist.
- Arrange schooling for your children (if applicable).

7.

TAXATION

An important consideration when buying a home in Cyprus, whether you're a resident or non-resident, is taxation, which includes income tax, immovable property tax, capital gains tax, inheritance tax and value added tax. (For information about taxes that apply to the sale and purchase of property, see **Fees** on page 97). If you live permanently in Cyprus, you will have to pay Cypriot income tax on your worldwide earnings. However, the good news is that tax rates are some of the lowest in Europe, especially for those who choose to retire there. Cyprus also has double-taxation treaties with many countries, which are designed to ensure that income that has already been taxed in one country isn't taxed again in another (see page 173). Other advantages of living in Cyprus are that there are no inheritance, gift or wealth taxes.

Cyprus has traditionally been considered a favourable tax location, if not exactly a tax haven. In the '70s, in an effort to attract 'offshore' companies to the island, the government introduced a package of tax incentives which ensured its success as a European financial centre. However, once it was agreed that Cyprus should join the European Union, its tax legislation had to come into line with EU requirements and comply with OECD initiatives against harmful tax practices. Consequently on 1st January 2003, the tax system in Cyprus underwent some major reforms, some of which temporarily weakened the country's economy. The main changes in the tax legislation since 1st January 2003 are as follows:

- Any person resident in Cyprus for more than 183 days per tax year (1st January to 31st December) is liable to pay tax there on their worldwide income. Non-residents are taxed only on income earned in Cyprus.

- The terms 'alien' (foreigner) and 'citizen of the Republic' have been abolished as taxation terms and the distinction is now 'resident' and 'non-resident'.

- There are no longer exchange controls or restrictions on importing and exporting money. Financial and banking institutions are slowly being liberalised in line with EU regulations.

Cyprus tax law has now been harmonised with that of other EU countries, but its tax rates are still low. If you qualify or choose to be a tax resident in Cyprus, as opposed to your home country, you may save a considerable amount in taxes, depending on your circumstances and it's imperative to take expert professional advice (see below).

FINANCIAL ADVISERS

Residents

If you plan to retire or live permanently in Cyprus, it's wise to consult a reputable independent financial adviser **before** you make any irrevocable decisions. It's the best way to organise your affairs and make your move to Cyprus as tax efficient as possible for you and your family.

Information about local financial services firms can be obtained from the Central Bank of Cyprus, but many believe that there's no substitute for word of mouth recommendation. Before you appoint a financial adviser, make sure he's a member of the Cyprus Internation Financial Services Organisation (CIFSA) and therefore a bona fide professional. It's compulsory for all financial services companies to be registered with CIFSA, which ensures that members comply with the rules of the organisation and professional codes of conduct; you can complain to CIFSA if you feel you've been given bad advice. A list of CIFSA members can be found on its website (💻 www.cifsa.org).

Non-residents

It isn't necessary but is recommended for non-resident owners of a single property in Cyprus (even if they don't plan to make any other investments there) to have a financial adviser or at least an accountant, who will look after their financial affairs and declare and pay their taxes. You can employ a representative to deal with all the authorities and bill paying procedures in Cyprus. The Cypriot tax authorities will communicate with either your accountant or your representative and he can also receive your bank statements and ensure that your bank is paying your regular bills (such as electricity, water and telephone) by standing order and that you have sufficient funds in your account to pay them. A representative can be an individual or a company (such as a bank).

Professional financial representation usually costs from around CY£200 per year depending on the services provided. There may be additional charges for tax administration and completing tax returns. For the relatively small cost involved, most people (both residents and non-residents) are usually better off employing a professional representative to handle their Cypriot tax and other financial affairs than doing it themselves, particularly as the regulations are changing frequently at present; you can often save more than your adviser's fee in avoided tax.

INCOME TAX

Income tax in Cyprus is below the EU average and isn't supplemented by crippling social security rates as in some other EU countries. Paying Cypriot income tax can be advantageous, especially if you're a retiree. Foreign employees are treated in the same way as Cypriot employees and are subject to the same tax regime. If you can choose the country where you're taxed, you should obtain advice on your financial situation from an international tax expert.

Employees' income tax is deducted at source by employers, i.e. pay-as-you-earn, and employed individuals aren't reponsible for paying their own income tax. Self-employed people and companies must pay provisional amounts of income tax in advance three times a year on specified dates (see **Calculation & Tax Return** on page 177) and then make a full declaration at the end of the year. Non-residents who receive an income from a Cypriot source and non-resident property owners should instruct an accountant or financial adviser (see above) to file an income tax declaration on their behalf.

Liability

Your liability for income tax in Cyprus depends on whether you're officially resident there. You qualify as a Cyprus tax resident if you spend more than 183 days in the country during the tax year and will be taxed in Cyprus on your worldwide income. However, irrespective of the 183-day rule, if your spouse and dependent minor children normally reside in Cyprus and have residence permits, and you aren't legally separated, you're considered to be a fiscal resident in Cyprus (unless you can prove otherwise).

If you're a fiscal resident in two countries simultaneously, your 'tax home' may be resolved under the rules applied under international treaties. (Under such treaties you're considered to be resident in the country where you have a permanent home; if you have a permanent home in both countries, you're deemed to be resident in the country where your personal and economic ties are closer. If your residence cannot be determined under this rule, you're deemed to be resident in the country where you have a habitual abode. If you have a habitual abode in both or in neither country, you're deemed to be resident in the country of which you're a citizen. Finally, if you're a citizen of both or neither country, the authorities of the countries concerned will decide your tax residence between them!)

If you plan to live permanently in Cyprus, you should notify the tax authorities in your previous country of residence. You may be entitled to an income tax refund if you depart during the tax year, which usually requires the completion of a tax return. The authorities may require evidence that you're leaving the country, e.g. proof that you have a job in Cyprus. If you move to Cyprus to take up a job or start a business, you must register with the local tax authorities soon after your arrival.

Moving to Cyprus (or any new country) often provides opportunities for legal 'favourable tax planning'. To make the most of your situation, it's advisable to obtain income tax advice before moving the Cyprus, as there are usually a number of things you can do in advance to reduce your tax liability, both in Cyprus and your home country. Be sure to consult a tax adviser who's familiar with both the Cypriot system and that of your present country of residence.

Double Taxation

Cyprus has double-taxation treaties with Austria, Belarus, Belgium, Bulgaria, Canada, China, the Czech Republic, Denmark, Egypt, France, Germany, Greece, Hungary, India, Irealnd, Italy, Kuwait, Malta, Norway, Poland, Romania, Russia, Slovakia, South Africa, Sweden, Syria, the UK, the US and Yugoslavia.

Taxable Income

Income tax applies to both earned and unearned income. Your gross income includes earnings from employment as well as business profits, rental income, capital gains, overseas and cost of living allowances, bonuses (annual, performance, profit share, etc.), relocation allowances, payments in kind (such as free accommodation or meals, language lessons provided for a spouse, personal company car, and children's education), stock options and home leave or holidays paid by your employer. Not all your income is taxable, however, as certain exemptions apply.

Non-residents

Non-residents are liable for income tax only on income arising from within Cyprus, which includes the following:

● Income or benefits from any employment, trade, business or profession practised in Cyprus;

● Rental income from property in Cyprus (see page 176);

● A private pension from past employment in Cyprus.

Residents

Subject to the exemptions listed below, residents must pay income tax in Cyprus on both earned and unearned worldwide income. Employees' tax is deducted at source by employers on a monthly basis, but the self-employed must make advance payments that are offset when they make their annual declaration.

Exemptions

Certain types of income are exempt from income tax in Cyprus, including those listed below (which apply to both individuals and companies unless otherwise stated).

- A lump sum received on retirement or as compensation for the death of or injuries to a spouse;
- Profit from a permanent establishment outside Cyprus under certain circumstances;
- Dividends (see note below);
- Gains from trading in stocks and shares;
- Interest (50 per cent for companies, whole amount for individuals – see note below);
- 20 per cent (up to a maximum of CY£5,000 annually for up to three years) of any earnings in Cyprus if you weren't a resident previous to your employment;
- Earnings from salaried services given outside Cyprus for more than 90 days per year if your employer is resident in Cyprus;
- Profits from sale of securities (shares, bonds, etc.).

Tax Rates

Current personal income tax rates in Cyprus are as follows:

Taxable Income (CY£)	Tax Rate (%)	Cumulative Tax (CY£)
Up to 10,000	0	0
10,000 – 15,000	20	1,000
15,000 – 20,000	25	2,250
Over 20,000	30	

Foreign pensions and property income are taxed at different rates (see pages 176 and 176).

Deductions

Before you're liable for income tax, you can subtract certain deductions from your gross income, including the following:

● Contributions or premiums paid to widows' and orphans' pension funds or schemes;

● Donations to approved charitable funds;

● Membership fees for trade and professional organisations, if membership is mandatory;

● 40 per cent of amounts deposited with a Housing Finance Corporation;

● 20 per cent of any rental income from property in Cyprus;

● Interest on a loan taken out to purchase or improve a rental property.

● Depreciation on a rental property (3 per cent deduction);

● Social security contributions, provident fund, medical fund and pension fund contributions and life insurance contributions (the deduction is one-sixth of the chargeable income on all these payments);

● Expenditure incurred for the maintenance of a listed building where a Preservation Order applies (the deduction depends on the square footage of the building).

In order to claim deductions relating to personal expenditure or family circumstances, it's usually necessary to produce receipts.

Cash Grants

Under the 2003 tax reforms, tax allowances were either abolished or replaced by cash grants, as follows:

● **Child Grant** – All families resident in Cyprus are entitled to a basic child grant, plus a supplementary grant which varies according to the family's income, as follows (all amounts are in CY£):

No. of Children	Basic Grant	Supplementary Grant Income to 6,000	Income 6,000-12,000
1	200	50	25
2	400	200	150
3	1,200	450	375
More than 3	600 each	200 each	125 each

- **Higher Education Grant** – CY£1,500 per annum for each child receiving full-time higher education in Cyprus or at a foreign university;
- **Blind Grant** – CY£1,800 per annum for blind people.

Taxation of Foreign Pensions

If you're receiving a pension in Cyprus, you have a choice of two taxation systems: your pension can be taxed at standard income tax rates, i.e. with the first CY£10,000 tax-free (see above) or it can be taxed at 5 per cent after an initial CY£2,000 exemption. This means in effect that, if you earn less than around CY£12,760 per year from a pension, you're better off choosing the standard rate and that, if you earn more than this, the 5 per cent option is preferable.

If you're a pensioner planning to retire to Cyprus, you must obtain professional advice on your financial and tax position both in your home country and in Cyprus. In the UK, the Inland Revenue publishes several free leaflets which provide all the necessary information. They're part of the 'International Series' and have the following titles: *Residents and Non-residents. Liability to Tax in the UK* (IR20); *Living or Retiring Abroad? A Guide to UK tax on your UK income and pension* (IR138); and a *Help Sheet* (IR304), which explains tax relief under double-taxation agreeements. They can all be obtained from any UK tax office or the Inland Revenue's orderline (☎ UK 0845-900 0404) or website (🖳 www.inlandrevenue.gov.uk/leaflets).

Some countries, e.g. Canada and the UK, have an agreement with Cyprus that allows state pensions to remain index-linked when pensioners are resident in Cyprus. UK retirees should contact the Inland Revenue's International Centre for Non-Residents (☎ UK 0151-210 2222, 🖳 www.inlandrevenue.gov.uk) or the International Pensions Service (☎ UK 0191-218 7777, 🖳 www.dwp.gov.uk).

Taxation of Property Income

Residents and non-residents must pay tax on property income at standard income tax rates (see above), and property income must therefore be included in your annual income tax declaration. However, a 20 per cent deduction from letting income is allowed, as is any interest on a loan taken out to purchase or improve the property; there's a further 3 per cent deduction for depreciation (see below). Residents must pay an additional tax at 3 per cent (known as Special Contribution for Defence or SCD) on 75 per cent of their **total** rental income. For example, on letting income of CY£15,000, you would be taxed as follows:

	CY£
Income Tax	
Letting income	15,000
Exemption	(10,000)
Taxable income	5,000
Deductions (23%)	(1,150)
Net taxable income	3,850
Tax at 20%	**770**
SCD	
Taxable income	15,000
Allowance (25%)	(3,750)
Net taxable income	11,250
Tax at 3%	**337.50**
TOTAL TAX	**1,107.50**

Calculation & Tax Return

The tax year in Cyprus is from 1st January to 31st December. If you're an employee and have no sources of income other than your salary, you don't need to make an annual tax declaration. If you're self employed or a director of a limited company, you must make provisional tax payments by 1st August, 30th September and 31st December. For self-employed individuals, an annual tax return, detailing actual earned income must be made before 30th April the following year. Your liability is assessed and you either receive a refund or are charged for the shortfall. A limited company must have paid all tax due by 1st August the following year. Arrears for companies and individuals are charged at a rate of 5 per cent for up to six months from the due date or 9 per cent if arrears are more than six months late.

You should submit your returns and pay your tax to your nearest Inland Revenue Office, of which there are four, as follows:

● **Larnaca** – Griva Digheni 42, 6045 Larnaca (☎ 24-803 658);

● **Limasssol** – Gladstonos 3, 3002 Limassol (☎ 25-803 700);

● **Nicosia** – M. Paridi and Byzantiou, 2064 Strovolos, Nicosia (☎ 22-807 412);

- **Paphos** – Corner N. Nicolaidi and Digheni Akrita, 8010 Paphos (☎ 26-802 100).

You can submit returns yourself directly to the office or, if an accountant has prepared your tax return, he can do it on your behalf. The Director of the Inland Revenue department is in Nicosia (☎ 22-807 482) and can answer any general queries you have.

IMMOVABLE PROPERTY TAX

This is an annual tax payable by all property owners in Cyprus, irrespective of their residence status. It's imposed on the market value of the property as of 1st January 1980 (*sic*), and you're exempt from tax if this value is below CY£100,000, so there's often nothing to pay. Above that value the tax rates are as follows:

Value (CY£) on 1/1/1980	Tax Rate (%)	Cumulative Tax (CY£)
Up to 100,000	0	0
100,000 – 250,000	0.25	375
250,000 – 500,000	0.35	1,250
Over 500,000	0.4	

Buildings under a preservation order or belonging to a charitable organisation are exempt. Immovable property tax is payable annually on 30th September.

CAPITAL GAINS TAX

Capital gains tax is payable by both residents and non-residents at a rate of 20 per cent on gains from the disposal of immovable property in Cyprus. If the property is a principal residence, there's a lifetime (i.e. once only) exemption of CY£50,000. For any other kind of property (e.g. a holiday home), only CY£10,000 is exempt, and this exemption is per registered owner, not per property (see **Single or Joint Names** on page 147). (You cannot claim both of these exemptions!)

Other exemptions from capital gains tax include the following:

- Transfers due to death (see **Inheritance Tax** below);
- Gifts to close relatives such as spouses or children;
- Gift to the government or a charity;
- Exchanges or sale in accordance with Agricultural Land Laws;

- Exchanges of properties where the value is equal.

If you've made any improvements or additions to the property, this will be deducted from the assumed profit, thereby reducing your liability.

INHERITANCE TAX

Inheritance tax and estate duty were abolished in Cyprus on 1st January 2000, when the Deceased Persons Estate Law came into force. This requires the executor of an estate to submit a statement of the assets and liabilities of the deceased to the tax authorities within six months of the date of death. Where the deceased's estate includes property, this must be registered in the name of legitimate heirs, who aren't liable for inheritance tax. Therefore, provided you have a valid will (see below), if you're resident in Cyprus and you die, the inheritance of your worldwide estate is tax free.

Wills

It's imperative that both residents and non-residents have wills which account for their assets in Cyprus. Owners of holiday homes are advised to make a local will to deal with their property in Cyprus, so that the inheritance of your assets in Cyprus can be dealt with relatively quickly under Cypriot law. If you make a will in Cyprus, you should inform your lawyer(s) and ensure that it doesn't contradict or invalidate any other will you already have. An addendum, taking account of your will in Cyprus, can be attached to any will you may have in your home country. Wills can be drawn up by a lawyer and must be signed and witnessed.

SPECIAL CONTRIBUTION FOR DEFENCE

This tax is imposed on dividends and interest (except that arising from ordinary business activites) and on a proportion of rental income earned by residents. Rates are 15 per cent on dividend income, 10 per cent on interest and 3 per cent on rental income, subject to a 25 per cent deduction (see **Taxation of Property Income** on page 176).

VALUE ADDED TAX

There are three rates for value added tax (VAT): the standard rate of 15 per cent, which was introduced on 1st January 2003; the reduced rate of

5 per cent, which came into force on 1st January 2000; and zero rating for certain goods and services. Since 2002, VAT rating has changed on a number of goods, but below are the main items currently included in each category. **VAT regulations have still not been finalised since the country's EU accession, so always check the latest situation with your financial adviser or lawyer, especially when buying property.**

Since 1st May 2004, when Cyprus joined the European Union, VAT has applied to all new properties, except those where the application for planning permission was submitted to the Planning Department before 1st May 2004. (Previously all immovable property had been exempt from VAT.) First-time buyers qualify for VAT at the reduced rate (5 per cent); all other buyers must pay VAT at the standard rate (15 per cent).

Exemption from VAT

Certain goods and services are exempt from VAT, including rents, medical services and insurance and financial services. (The difference between exemption and zero rating is that businesses that supply only exempt products may not recover any VAT they've been charged.)

Zero Rate

Zero-rated good and services include supplies of goods to other EU member states, exports, certain foods, medicines, children's clothing, international air and sea transportation, and commissions received from abroad.

Reduced Rate

Reduced rate goods and services include new property (first-time buyers only – see above), animal feed, accommodation in hotels and tourist establishments, refuse collection, and books, newspapers and magazines.

Standard Rate

This is imposed on all goods and services, except those that are exempt or at the reduced rate, including new property (other than for first-time buyers – see above).

8.

INSURANCE

An important aspect of owning a home in Cyprus is insurance, not only for your home and its contents, but also health insurance for you and your family. If you live in Cyprus permanently, you will require additional insurance. It's unnecessary to spend half your income insuring yourself against every eventuality, although it's important to insure against any event that could precipitate a major financial disaster, such as a serious accident or your house being demolished by a storm. The cost of being uninsured or under-insured can be astronomical.

 It's vital to ensure that you have sufficient insurance when visiting your home abroad. This should include travel insurance, building and contents insurance, and health insurance (covered in this chapter) as well as car insurance (including breakdown insurance) if you have a car in Cyprus.

As with anything connected with finance, it's important to shop around when buying insurance. Collecting a few brochures from insurance agents or making a few calls can save you a lot of money. **In matters regarding insurance, you're responsible for ensuring that you and your family are legally insured in Cyprus.** Regrettably you cannot insure yourself against being uninsured or sue your insurance agent for giving you bad advice!

Bear in mind that if you wish to make a claim on an insurance policy, you may be required to report an incident to the police within 24 hours (this may also be a legal requirement). The law in Cyprus may differ considerably from that in your home country or your previous country of residence and you should **never** assume that it's the same. If you're uncertain of your rights, you're advised to obtain legal advice for anything other than a minor claim.

Under EU rules, an insurance company registered in an EU member country can sell its policies in any other EU country. There are a number of international insurance companies operating in Cyprus, and it's advisable to choose a well established name. Some smaller insurance companies will do almost anything to avoid paying claims and will use any available legal loophole, so it pays to deal with reputable companies, although this doesn't provide you with a guarantee.

SURVIVAL TIP

Not all insurance companies are equally reliable or have the same financial stability and it may be better to insure with a large international company with a good reputation rather than with a small company, even if this means paying higher premiums.

Always read insurance contracts carefully and make sure that you understand the terms and the cover provided before signing them.

HEALTH INSURANCE

Whether you're living or working in Cyprus or just visiting, it's extremely risky not to have health insurance for your family; if you're uninsured or under-insured you could be faced with some very high bills. You won't be covered under the Cypriot health system unless you pay social security contributions. However, all international visitors are offered free emergency assistance and treatment if they fall seriously ill or have a serious accident while visiting Cyprus.

When deciding on the type and extent of health insurance to buy, make sure that it covers **all** your family's present and future health requirements. A policy should cover you for **all** essential healthcare whatever the reason, including accidents and injuries, whether they occur in your home, at your place of work or while travelling. Don't take anything for granted, but check.

If you're planning to take up residence in Cyprus and will be contributing to social security there, you and your family will be entitled to subsidised or free medical and dental treatment, but not immediately. In the meantime, and if you aren't covered by Cypriot social security, it's important that you have private health insurance; indeed it's mandatory if you want to apply for residence. **Proof of health insurance must be provided when applying for a residence permit** (see **Temporary Residence Permits** on page 31).

```
SURVIVAL TIP
When travelling, you should always
have proof of your health insurance with you.
```

Visitors

Short-stay visitors to Cyprus (i.e. those spending less than 90 days on the island) should have travel insurance (see page 193). You may be covered by a reciprocal social security agreement between your home country and Cyprus (see page 186), but this may not provide adequate cover, and you should check. Citizens of certain countries should obtain a European Health Insurance Card (see below). **This is only for short stays such as holidays and business trips and covers you only for essential (and not routine) healthcare.** If your country doesn't have an agreement with

Cyprus and you aren't covered by Cypriot social insurance (see page 186), you **must** have private health insurance.

If you plan to spend up to six months in Cyprus, you should take out either a long-stay policy or an annual international health policy (see **Annual Policies** on page 194), which should cover you in your home country and when travelling in other countries.

European Health Insurance Card

If you're a citizen of an EEA country or of Switzerland, you should apply for a European Health Insurance Card (EHIC) from your local social security office at least three weeks before you plan to travel to Cyprus. This entitles you to free or reduced cost medical treatment in Cyprus for up to 90 days.

UK citizens should apply for a revised E111 form (i.e. one issued after 19th August 2004). This is valid until 31st December 2005, when it will be replaced by the EHIC itself. The new card (and, in the interim, the revised E111 form) should now be valid in all 25 EU countries, but local arrangements (especially in the new member states, including Cyprus) are taking a while to put into place, so check before you go. The EHIC will be open-ended and valid for life provided you continue to make social security contributions in the country where it was issued; **if you become a resident in another country (e.g. in Cyprus) it becomes invalid. An EHIC covers emergency hospital treatment but doesn't include prescribed medicines, special examinations, X-rays, laboratory tests, physiotherapy and dental treatment.**

Britons can obtain further information about the UK's reciprocal health agreement with Cyprus from the Department of Social Security, Pensions and Overseas Benefits Directorate, Newcastle-upon-Tyne, NE98 1BA, UK (☎ 0191-218 7777, 🖳 www.dwp.gov.uk).

Residents

If you're planning to work in Cyprus, you will be covered by Cyprus social insurance (see below). EU pensioners also qualify for Cyprus social insurance cover. **All other residents must have private health insurance (see page 188).**

Cyprus Social Insurance

The Cyprus social insurance scheme is compulsory for all those working in Cyprus. It provides pensions and benefits in all areas of social security and is financed by contributions from employees, employers and the state. Currently, social insurance contributions are 16.6 per cent of earings (6.3 per cent of your gross salary is paid by both employee and employer and the state pays the remaining 4 per cent). Self-employed people pay a total of 11.6 per cent of income and the state contributes 4 per cent.

If you contribute to Cypriot social insurance, you and your family are entitled to free or subsidised medical and dental treatment. Anyone who has paid regular social security contributions in another EU country for two full years prior to coming to Cyprus is entitled to similar cover for a limited period (see **EU Citizens** below).

Benefits (which are free or subsidised according to your status – see **Medical Cards** below), include general and specialist care, hospitalisation, laboratory services, discounted drugs and medicines, basic dental care, maternity care, appliances and transportation. Cyprus has an efficient network of government general hospitals and clinics in urban areas with health centres and dispensaries in more rural areas. Nevertheless, most Cypriots and foreign residents who can afford it take out private health insurance, which offers a wider choice of medical practitioners and hospitals, and more importantly, frees them from public health waiting lists.

Medical Cards: If you qualify for Cyprus social insurance benefits, you must obtain a health card. There are two cards, which are allocated according to your means, as follows:

● **Medical Card A** – This is issued to individuals without dependants and an annual income of under CY£9,000, couples with an annual income of under CY£18,000 (increased by CY£1,000 for each dependent child), and members of families with four or more children (irrespective of income). It entitles the holder to free healthcare.

● **Medical Card B** – This is issued to individuals without dependants and an annual income of between CY£9,000 and CY£12,000, and to members of families with up to three children and an annual income of between CY£18,000 and CY£22,000. It entitles the holder to half-price healthcare.

If you earn above these amounts, you must pay around CY£7 for a consultation with a doctor and around CY£50 per day for in-patient hospital care.

You should complete the appropriate application form (which you can obtain from any general hospital in Cyprus) and submit it, along with proof of income and evidence of payment of tax and social insurance contributions, to the Ministry of Health in Nicosia. You can normally do this via your local health centre or general hospital in Cyprus. You should receive your medical card within around three weeks. Medical cards are valid for two years, and you must apply for renewal a month before expiry.

Further information about entitlement to a health card can be found on the Ministry of Health website (🖳 www.moh.gov.cy).

EU Citizens

Anyone who has paid regular social security contributions in another EU country for two full years prior to coming to Cyprus is entitled to public health cover for a limited period from the date of their last contribution. Social security form E106 must be obtained from the social security authorities in your home country and presented to your local Social Insurance office in Cyprus.

Pensioners: Retirees living in Cyprus and receiving a state pension from another EU country are entitled to free or subsidised state healthcare on the same conditions as wage earners (see above). You will need to obtain the necessary forms from your home country and submit them with your application for a medical card in Cyprus (see **Medical Cards** on page 187). In the UK, you should contact the Department of Work and Pensions (DWP), Medical Benefits Section (☎ 0191-218 7547, 🖳 www.dwp.gov.uk). When you contact the DWP about getting your pension paid in Cyprus, they should automatically check that you have the required form, which is currently form E121.

Private Health Insurance

If you aren't covered by the Cyprus social security system, you **must** take out private health insurance. Even if you are, you should consider doing so; most Cypriots and foreign residents who can afford it take out private health insurance, which offers a wider choice of medical practitioners and hospitals, and more importantly, frees them from public health waiting lists. If you already have private health insurance in another country, you may be able to extend it to cover you in Cyprus.

When buying private health insurance, choose a company that will pay large medical bills directly. Most private health insurance policies don't pay family doctors' fees or pay for medication that isn't provided in a hospital, or charge an excess (deductible), which often exceeds the cost of treatment. Most will, however, pay for 100 per cent of specialist fees and hospital treatment. The insurance market in Cyprus is highly competitive and sophisticated and there's a huge range of both Cypriot and international insurance companies offering policies.

It's impossible to give reliable price information, as premiums and conditions are constantly changing in this highly competitive market. Due to the enormous diversity of cover, it's essential that you research the market thoroughly before you decide on a policy. Generally, the higher the premium, the more choice you have regarding doctors, specialists and hospitals. There may be an annual surcharge for those over 60, which increases with age, and supplements for certain services such as basic dental treatment or for pregnant women. You may be able to obtain a discount if you accept a larger excess value.

Changing Employers or Insurance Companies

When changing employers or leaving Cyprus, you should ensure that you have continuous health insurance. If you and your family are covered by a company health plan, your insurance will probably cease after your last official day of employment. If you're planning to change your health insurance company, you should ensure that important benefits aren't lost, e.g. existing medical conditions won't usually be covered by a new insurer. When changing health insurance companies, it's advisable to inform your old company if you have any outstanding bills for which they're liable.

HOUSEHOLD INSURANCE

Household insurance includes cover for the building, its contents and third party liability, all of which are contained in a multi-risk household insurance policy. If a policy doesn't include third party liability cover, you should obtain it separately, although it isn't compulsory, to safeguard yourself against claims by visitors (or tenants if you let), e.g. if they're bitten by your child or fall down the stairs.

Policies are offered by both Cypriot and foreign insurance companies and premiums are similar, although foreign companies may provide more comprehensive cover. Insurance companies are listed in the yellow pages and advertise in the local and expatriate press. Cyprus Net (🖥 www.cyprus-net.com) is a useful internet directory of Cyprus, which has an extensive insurance section. **Always read the small print of contracts.** Note that some insurance companies will do their utmost to find a loophole that makes you negligent and relieves them of liability.

Buildings

It's wise to take out property insurance that covers damage to a building due to fire, smoke, lightning, water, explosion, storm, freezing, snow, theft, vandalism, malicious damage, acts of terrorism, impact, broken windows and natural catastrophes (such as falling trees), although buildings insurance isn't compulsory in Cyprus. Insurance should include glass, external buildings, aerials and satellite dishes, gardens and garden ornaments.

Bear in mind that Cyprus is affected by earthquakes from time to time, so you should ensure that damage caused by earthquakes is included. Cover for earthquakes, lightning damage and subsidence usually aren't included in a standard policy, so check exactly what's excluded and what it will cost to include extra risks. Note that if a claim is the result of a defect in building or design, e.g. the roof is too heavy and collapses, the insurance company won't pay up (one of many reasons to have a survey before buying!).

Buildings insurance is based on the cost of rebuilding your home and should be increased each year in line with inflation. Make sure that you insure your property for the true cost of rebuilding.

Contents

Contents are usually insured for the same risks as a building (see above) and are insured for their replacement value (new for old), with a reduction for wear and tear for clothes and linen. Valuable objects are covered for their actual declared (and authenticated) value. Most policies include automatic indexation of the insured sum in line with inflation. Contents insurance may include accidental damage to sanitary installations, theft, money, replacement of locks following damage or loss of keys, frozen food, alternative accommodation cover, and property belonging to third parties stored in your home. Some items are usually optional, e.g. credit cards, frozen foods, emergency assistance (plumber, glazier, electrician, etc.), redecoration, garaged cars, replacement pipes, loss of rent, and the cost of travel to Cyprus for holiday homeowners. Many policies include personal third party liability, although this may be an option. All-risks policies offering a world-wide extension to a household policy covering jewellery, cameras and other items may be available.

Items of high value must usually be listed and documentation (e.g. a valuation) along with photographs provided. Some companies even recommend or insist on a video film of belongings. When claiming for contents, you should produce the original bills if possible (always keep bills for expensive items) and bear in mind that replacing imported items in Cyprus may be more expensive than buying them abroad.

Contents policies contain 'security clauses' and, if you don't adhere to them, a claim won't be considered. For example, if you're planning to let a property, you may be required to inform your insurer. A building must be secure, especially ground-floor windows and patio doors, shutters and locks. Most companies give a discount if properties have high security locks and alarms (particularly alarms connected to a monitoring station). Policies pay out for theft only when there are signs of forcible entry.

Community Developments

If you own a property that's part of a community development (see page 108), the building may be insured by the community (although you should ensure that it's comprehensively insured). You must, however, be insured for third party risks in the event that you cause damage to neighbouring properties, e.g. through a flood or fire.

Holiday Homes

Premiums are generally higher for holiday homes, as they're usually left unattended for long periods, which makes them vulnerable, particularly to burglaries. Premiums are usually based on the number of days a year a property is occupied and the interval between periods of occupancy. Cover for theft, storm, flood and malicious damage may be suspended when a property is left empty for an extended period. **Note that you're required to turn off the water supply at the mains when vacating a building for more than 72 hours.**

It's possible to negotiate cover for periods of absence for a hefty surcharge, although valuable items are usually excluded (unless you have a safe). If you're absent from your property for long periods, e.g. more than 30 days a year, you may be required to pay an excess on a claim arising from an occurrence that takes place during your absence (and theft may be excluded). Where applicable, it's important to ensure that a policy specifies a holiday home and not a principal home.

It's unwise to leave valuable or irreplaceable items in a holiday home or a property that will be vacant for long periods.

Rented Property

A rental contract normally requires you to insure against 'tenant's risks' (i.e. have third party liability insurance), including damage you may cause to the rental property and (if you live in an apartment) to adjoining properties, e.g. due to a flood, fire or explosion. You can choose your own insurance company and aren't required to use one recommended by your landlord.

Insuring Abroad

It's possible (and legal) to take out buildings and contents insurance in another country for a property in Cyprus (some foreign insurance companies offer special policies for holiday homeowners), although you must ensure that a policy is valid under Cypriot law. The advantage is that you will have a policy you can understand and you will be able to handle claims in your own language, although insurance agents and employees in Cyprus will usually speak good English. Insuring in your home country may seem like a good option for a holiday home in Cyprus, although it can be more expensive than insuring with a Cypriot company and can lead to conflicts if, for example, the building is insured with a Cypriot-registered company and the contents with a foreign based company. Most experts advise that you insure a Cypriot home and its contents with a Cypriot insurance company through a local agent.

Premiums

Household insurance premiums are usually calculated on the size (constructed area in square metres) of a property, its age, the value of the contents, and the security of the property, e.g. its location, window protection at ground level, the number of entrance doors and their construction. As a rough guide, buildings insurance for an average home costs around CY£30 to CY£100 per year, depending on the value of the property, and contents insurance around CY£5 per thousand of the sum insured. Detached, older and more remote properties often cost more to insure than apartments and new properties (especially if located in towns), and premiums are sometimes slightly higher in 'high-risk' areas, such as the major cities.

Take care that you don't under-insure your house contents and that you periodically reassess their value and adjust your insurance premium accordingly. You can arrange to have your insurance cover automatically increased annually by a fixed percentage or amount. If you make a claim and the assessor discovers that you're under-insured, the amount due will be reduced by the percentage by which you're under-insured.

Claims

If you wish to make a claim, you must usually inform your insurance company in writing (by registered letter) within two to seven days of an incident or 24 hours in the case of theft. Thefts should also be reported to the local police within 24 hours, as the police report (of which you receive a copy for your insurance company) constitutes irrefutable evidence of your claim. Check whether you're covered for damage or thefts that occur while you're away from your property and are therefore unable to inform the insurance company immediately.

HOLIDAY & TRAVEL INSURANCE

Holiday and travel insurance is recommended for those who don't wish to risk having their holiday or travel ruined by financial problems or to arrive home broke. As you probably know, anything can and often does go wrong with a holiday, sometimes before you even get started (particularly when you **don't** have insurance). The following information applies equally to residents and non-residents, whether you're travelling to or from Cyprus or within Cyprus.

Travel insurance is available from many sources, including travel agents, insurance companies and agents, banks, automobile clubs and transport companies. Package holiday companies and tour operators also offer insurance policies (some of which are compulsory and too expensive and don't provide adequate cover!). You can buy 24-hour accident and flight insurance at major airports, although it's expensive and doesn't offer the best cover.

Before taking out travel insurance, carefully consider the range and level of cover you require and compare policies. Short-term holiday and travel insurance policies should include cover for holiday cancellation or interruption; missed flights; departure delay at both the start **and** end of a holiday (a common occurrence); delayed, lost, stolen or damaged baggage, personal effects and money; medical expenses (including repatriation – see below); personal liability and legal expenses; flight insurance and default or bankruptcy insurance, e.g. against a tour operator or airline going bust.

Health Cover

Medical expenses are an important aspect of travel insurance and you shouldn't rely on insurance provided by reciprocal health arrangements (see page 186), charge and credit card companies, household policies or private medical insurance (unless it's an international policy), none of which usually provide adequate cover (although you should take advantage of what they offer). The minimum medical insurance recommended by experts is GB£500,000 in Cyprus and the rest of Europe, and the equivalent of around GB£2 million for the rest of the world (many policies cover for more). If applicable, check whether pregnancy-related claims are covered and whether there are any restrictions for those over a certain age, e.g. 65, as travel insurance is becoming increasingly expensive for those aged over 65.

Always check any exclusion clauses in contracts by obtaining a copy of the full policy document, as not all the relevant information is included in an insurance leaflet. High-risk sports and pursuits should be specifically covered and **listed** in a policy (there's usually an additional premium). Special winter sports policies are available and are more expensive than normal holiday insurance ('dangerous' sports are excluded from most standard policies).

Cost

The cost of travel insurance varies considerably according to where you buy it, how long it's required and your age. Generally, the longer the period covered, the cheaper the daily cost, although the maximum period covered is usually limited, e.g. six months. With some policies an excess must be paid for each claim. As a rough guide, travel insurance for Cyprus (and most other European countries) costs from around GB£50 for one week, GB£70 for two weeks and GB£130 for a month for a family of four (two adults and two children under 16). Premiums may be higher for those aged over 65.

Annual Policies

For people who travel abroad frequently, whether on business or pleasure, an annual travel policy usually provides the best value, but carefully check exactly what it includes. Most international insurance companies offer health policies for different areas, e.g. Europe, worldwide excluding North America, and worldwide including North America. Most companies also offer different levels of cover, e.g. basic, standard, comprehensive and 'prestige'. There's always a limit on the total annual medical costs, which is usually least CY£600,000 (although some prestige schemes offer cover of up to CY£3 million), and some companies also limit the charges for specific treatment or care such as specialists' fees, operations and hospital accommodation.

A medical examination isn't usually required for international health policies, although existing health problems are normally excluded for a period, e.g. one or two years. Most international health policies include repatriation or evacuation (although it may be optional), which may also include shipment by air of the body of a person who dies abroad to his home country for burial. Note that an international policy also allows you to choose to have non-urgent medical treatment in the country of your choice. When comparing policies, carefully check the extent of cover and exactly what's included and excluded (often indicated only in the **very** small print), in addition to premiums and excess charges.

Claims are usually settled in major currencies and large claims are usually settled directly by insurance companies (although your choice of hospitals may be limited). **Always check whether an insurance company will settle large medical bills directly – if you're required to pay bills and claim reimbursement it can take several months before you receive your money (some companies are slow to pay).** Most international health insurance companies provide emergency telephone assistance.

There's a a wide selection of health insurance companies in Cyprus, both local and international, so compare policies carefully and decide which is best suited to your needs. Policies offered by Cypriot and international companies may differ considerably in the extent of cover, limitations and restrictions, premiums, and the choice of doctors, specialists and hospitals.

The cost of international health insurance varies greatly according to your age and the extent of cover. Many insurance companies offer annual travel policies for a premium of around GB£200 for an individual (the equivalent of around two months' insurance with a standard travel insurance policy), which are excellent value for frequent travellers. Most policies must be taken out before you reach a certain age, e.g. 60, to be guaranteed continuous cover in your old age. Premiums can sometimes be paid monthly, quarterly or annually, although some companies insist on payment annually in advance. In some countries, premium increases are limited by law, although this may apply only to residents of the country where a company is registered and not to overseas policyholders. Although there may be significant differences in premiums, generally you get what you pay for and can tailor premiums to your requirements.

If you're in good health and are able to pay for your own outpatient treatment, such as visits to a family doctor and prescriptions, the best value is usually a policy covering specialist and hospital treatment only.

Some insurance companies offer an 'emergency travel policy' for holiday homeowners who need to travel abroad at short notice to inspect a property, e.g. after a severe storm. The cost of an annual policy may depend on the area covered, e.g. Europe, worldwide excluding North America, and worldwide including North America, although it doesn't usually cover travel within your country of residence. There's also a limit on the number of trips a year and the duration of each trip, e.g. 90 or 120 days.

9.

LETTING

The law relating to property letting in Cyprus is different from that in most other European countries in that there are severe restrictions on letting. Many foreigners let their properties illegally, whether through ignorance or in defiance of the law, and few are prosecuted. Nevertheless, there are ways you can let your property legally.

THE LAW

Cypriot law is clear on the subject of property letting: **non-residents aren't permitted to let property on a short-term basis to holidaymakers, although they can let long-term to Cypriot residents.** The restriction is connected to the fact that, non-resident foreigners (even EU citizens) must obtain permission to buy property in Cyprus. (Since the country's accession to the EU in May 2004, Cypriot law has distinguished between residents and non-residents, as opposed to Cypriots and foreigners.) Unless you're a Cypriot or an EU citizen resident in Cyprus, you must apply to the Council of Ministers for permission to buy a property (see page 150). Although this is almost always a formality, permission is granted on condition that the property won't be used for commercial purposes or will be let only on a long-term basis to residents of Cyprus.

Letting a property on a short-term basis to holidaymakers is illegal unless you apply to the Cyprus Tourism Organisation (CTO) to have the property certified for holiday letting. This is permitted only on detached properties, and certification can be a long and complicated procedure. There are many estate agents and developers who can help with this, but make sure you get independent legal advice before you commit yourself financially. The CTO will then inspect your property in the same way that it inspects any tourist accommodation and will charge you 3 per cent of the expected income from the property annually. **You must pay this charge even if you don't receive the estimated projected income (or any income at all!).**

If you're planning to let property on a community development, you must also check whether there are any community rules that prohibit or restrict letting, aside from the legal restrictions. You may also be required to notify your insurance company.

If you let a property in Cyprus, you're required by law to pay tax on your rental income in Cyprus even if the rental income is received in another country.

Many people illegally let their properties privately to families and friends on a short-term basis and many agents and developers offer a buy-to-let service to this purpose. Although the law is clear, it isn't policied vigorously, as the Cypriot government realises that the increased investment in the island and increased tourist revenue resulting from such lets are boosting the economy; they don't want to discourage property buyers or potential investors, who will be paying taxes, nor tourists, who will be spending money in Cyprus.

Since joining the EU in May 2004, Cyprus is going through a period of change and adaptation, and legal experts agree that the letting laws may change in the near future. **Nevertheless, if you plan to buy to let, you must obtain advice on your legal position from a qualified professional.**

Contracts

Most people who do holiday letting draw up a simple agreement that includes a description of the property, the names of the clients, and the dates of arrival and departure. However, if you do regular letting you may wish to check with a lawyer that your agreement is legal and contains all the necessary safeguards. If you use an agent, he will usually provide a standard contract.

FINANCIAL CONSIDERATIONS

If, after taking legal advice, you decide to go ahead and let your property in Cyprus, there are plenty of financial considerations to be made, according to your intentions and needs. For example, you may be looking for an income to cover the running costs and help with the mortgage payments and believe that letting a property for a few months in the summer can achieve this as well as paying for your holidays in Cyprus.

 If you're planning to let a property, it's important not to overestimate the income, particularly if you're relying on letting income to help pay the mortgage and running costs. Most experts recommend that you don't purchase a home in Cyprus if you need to rely on rental income to pay for it.

The letting season can be all year round in Cyprus, especially if you let long-term, although this naturally restricts your own use of the property. If you obtain permission for short-term lets, the mild winter weather in Cyprus may allow you to let almost all year round and you may be able to achieve occupancy of 25 or even 30 weeks per year. Apartments and townhouses tend to have year-round letting potential, whereby villas (especially large ones) are generally in demand from only from Easter to late autumn plus Christmas.

You must also take into account the 3 per cent letting income 'tax' that must be paid to the CTO (see above). **Buyers who over-stretch their financial resources often find themselves on the rental treadmill, constantly struggling to earn enough money to cover their running costs and mortgage payments.**

LOCATION

If income from a Cypriot home has a high priority, its location must be one of the main considerations when buying. When considering the location for a property you plan to let, you should bear in mind the following factors (see also **Location** on page 56).

Climate

Properties in areas with a pleasant year-round climate have greater rental potential, particularly outside high season. Cyprus is a small island and there are few climatic variations across the island (see page 24). However, the Troodos mountains are far cooler than the rest of the island in the summer (which is why so many Cypriots seek them out in the summer months), whereas Nicosia, because of its position in the centre of the island, is particularly hot and dusty in July and August.

Proximity to an Airport

A property should always be within easy reach of a major airport. Either Larnaca or Paphos international airport is usually within a half-hour drive of most places on the island. However, although Paphos is closer to most of the popular tourist resorts, flights outside the summer period are less frequent (see page 63) and visitors may have to use Larnaca airport. It's thought that more charter airlines and possibly some budget airlines may begin to fly to Cyprus in the near future, but you shouldn't rely on this – or indeed rely on any existing services, as airline routes are notoriously ephemeral.

Public Transport

It's an advantage if a property is served by public transport or is situated in a town where a car is unnecessary.

Attractions

The property should be close to attractions and/or a good beach, depending on the sort of clientele you wish to attract. If you want to let to families, a property should be within easy distance of leisure activities such as theme parks, water parks and sports facilities, and even nightlife. If you're planning to let a property in a rural area, it should be somewhere with good hiking and sightseeing possibilities, usually somewhere in the Troodos mountains. Proximity to one or more golf courses is also an advantage to many holidaymakers and is an added attraction outside the high season.

SWIMMING POOL

If you're planning to let your property, a swimming pool is obligatory in most areas, as properties with pools are much easier to let than those without, unless a property is situated on a beach, lake or river. It's usually necessary to have a private pool for a single-family home (e.g. a detached villa); a shared pool is adequate for an apartment or townhouse. If you plan to let mainly to families, it's advisable to choose an apartment or townhouse with a 'child-friendly' communal pool, e.g. with a shallow area or a separate paddling pool. You can charge a higher rent for a property with a private pool and it may be possible to extend the letting season even further by installing a heated or indoor pool, although the cost of heating a pool may be higher than the rental return.

A pool must be cleaned regularly (every other day in the summer) to avoid deterioration of the water quality, making the pool unsafe to use. Pool cleaning sometimes comes as part of a management package offered by agents or you can ask for recommendations about reliable local companies.

SURVIVAL TIP
You should have third party insurance covering accidents and injuries for guests (or anyone) using your pool (and your property in general).

LETTING RATES

Rates vary greatly according to the season, the region, and the size and quality of a property. An average apartment or townhouse sleeping four to six in an average area can be let for between CY£300 (low season) and CY£500 (high season) per week. A villa in a popular area can be let for around CY£700 per week in the summer. Most people who let year round have low, mid- and high season rates. The high season usually includes the months of July and August and possibly the first two weeks of September. Mid-season usually comprises June, late September and October, and the Easter and Christmas/New Year periods, when rents are around 25 per cent lower than the high season. The rest of the year is classed as the low season. During the low season, which may extend from October to May, rates are usually up to 50 per cent lower than the high season. Note that rates usually include linen, gas and electricity, although electricity and heating (e.g. gas bottles) are usually charged separately for long lets in winter.

To get an idea of the rent you can charge, simply ring a few letting agencies and ask them what it would cost to rent a property such as yours at the time of year you plan to let it. They're likely to quote the highest possible rent, so this should be adjusted as appropriate. You should also check advertisements.

Increasing Rental Income

Rental income can be increased outside high season by offering special interest or package holidays – which can be organised in conjunction with local businesses or tour operators – to broaden the appeal and cater for larger parties. These may include:

● Activity holidays, such as golf, tennis, cycling or hiking;

● Cooking, gastronomy and wine tours/tasting;

● Arts and crafts such as painting, sculpture, photography and writing courses.

You don't need to be an expert or conduct courses yourself, but can employ someone to do it for you.

FURNISHINGS

If you let a property, it isn't advisable to fill it with expensive furnishings or valuable belongings. While theft is rare, items will get damaged or broken over a period of time. When furnishing a property that you plan to let, you should choose hard-wearing, dark-coloured rugs, which won't show stains (most properties have tiled or marble floors rather than carpets) and buy durable furniture and furnishings. Simple, inexpensive furniture is best in a modest home, as it will need to stand up to hard wear.

Appliances should include a washing machine and microwave, and possibly a dishwasher and tumble dryer. Properties should be well equipped with cooking utensils, crockery and cutlery, and it's also usual to provide bed linen and towels (some agents provide a linen hire service). Make sure the bed linen and towels are of good quality, and replace them before they wear out. You can buy good quality, inexpensive household linen at department stores in Nicosia and Limassol, especially during the sales (see **Shopping** on page 224). Two-bedroom properties usually have a sofa bed in the living room. You may also need a cot and/or highchair.

Electricity is usually included in the rent, with the possible exception of long winter lets. Depending on the rent and quality of a property, your guests may also expect central heating, air-conditioning, covered parking, a barbecue and garden furniture (including loungers). Heating is essential if you want winter lets, while air-conditioning is an advantage when letting property in summer, although it's only considered mandatory when letting a luxury villa. (For information on utilities, heating and air-conditioning, see **Chapter 10**.) Some owners provide bicycles, and badminton and table tennis equipment. It isn't usual to have a telephone, although you could install a credit card telephone or one that just receives incoming calls.

KEYS

You will need several sets of spare keys, which are bound to get lost at some time. If you employ a management company or letting agent, their address should be on the key fob and not the address of the house. You should ensure that 'lost' keys are returned, or you may need to change the lock barrels (in any case it's sensible to change them at least annually). You don't need to provide guests with keys to all the external doors, only the front door (the others can be left in your home). If you arrange your own lets, you can send keys to guests in your home country or they can be collected in Cyprus. As an alternative to keys, it's possible to install a security key-pad entry system, the code of which can be changed after each let.

USING AN AGENT

Despite the fact that short-term letting is illegal in Cyprus, you will find many agents offering a letting service and even a buy-to-let service. If you're letting a second home and you don't have much spare time, you're better off using an agent, who will take care of everything and save you the time and expense of advertising and finding clients. Agents usually charge commission of between 10 and 20 per cent of rental income, although some of this can be recouped through higher rents. They can organise a range of services to suit your needs, including cleaning and maintenance, administration and advertising. If you want your property to appear in an agent's catalogue or website, you must usually contact him the summer before you wish to let it (the deadline for catalogues is usually September).

It's absolutely essential to employ a reliable and honest (preferably long-established) company. Always ask a management company to substantiate rental income claims and occupancy rates by showing you examples of actual income received from other properties. Ask for the names of satisfied customers and contact them. Other things to ask a letting agent include:

- When the letting income is paid;
- What additional charges are made and what they're for;
- Whether he provides detailed accounts of income and expenses (ask to see samples);
- Who he lets to (e.g. what nationalities and whether families, children or singles);
- How he markets properties (the larger companies market homes via newspapers, magazines, the internet, overseas agents and coloured brochures, and have representatives in a number of countries);
- Whether you're expected to contribute towards marketing costs;
- Whether you're free to let the property yourself and use it when you wish (many agents don't permit owners to use a property during July and August).

Management contracts usually run for a year and should include arranging emergency repairs, carrying out routine maintenance of house and garden, including lawn cutting and pool cleaning, arranging cleaning and linen changes between lets, advising guests on the use of equipment if necessary and providing them with information and assistance (24 hours a day in the case of emergencies). Agents may also provide someone to meet and greet guests, hand over the keys and check that everything is in order. The services provided usually depend on whether a property is a budget apartment or a luxury villa, for example. A letting agent's representative should also make periodic checks when a property is empty to ensure that it's secure and everything is in order.

DOING YOUR OWN LETTING

Some owners prefer to let a property to family, friends, colleagues and acquaintances, which allows them more control – and **hopefully** the property will also be better looked after – even though this is illegal in Cyprus without official certification. In fact, the best way to get a high volume of lets is usually to do it yourself, although many owners use a letting agency in addition to doing their own marketing in their home country.

You will need to decide whether you want to let to smokers or accept pets and young children – some people won't let to families with children under five due to the risk of bed-wetting. Some owners also prefer not to let to young, single groups. Note, however, that this reduces your letting prospects. Many people have a minimum two-week rental period in July and August.

Rates & Deposits

Set a realistic rent, as there's lots of competition (see **Letting Rates** on page 204) and bear in mind that, although you won't have to pay an agent's commission, you must allow for the cost of maintenance and the other services an agent normally provides. Add a returnable deposit (e.g. CY£150 to CY£500 depending on the rent) as security against loss (e.g. of keys) and breakages. This is returnable less any deductions. A booking deposit is usually refundable up to six weeks before a booking, after which it's forfeited.

Advertising

If you wish to let a property yourself, there's a wide range of newspapers and magazines in which you can advertise, e.g. *Dalton's Weekly* (☎ UK 020-8329 0222, 🖥 www.daltonsholidays.com) and the *Sunday Times* in the UK. Many of the English-language newspapers and magazines listed in **Appendix B** include advertisements from property owners. You will need to experiment to find the best publications and days of the week or months to advertise. Note, however, that most owners find it prohibitively expensive to advertise a single property in a national newspaper or magazine.

Cheaper and possibly more effective media are property directories such as *Private Villas* (☎UK 020-8329 0195, 💻 www.privatevillas. co.uk) and websites such as those of Holiday Rentals (☎ UK 020-8743 5577, 💻 www.holiday-rentals.co.uk) and Owners Direct (☎ UK 01372-722708, 💻 www.ownersdirect.co.uk), where you pay for the advertisement and handle the bookings yourself. **These need to be arranged the previous year.**

You can also advertise among friends and colleagues, in company and club magazines (which may even be free), and on notice boards in companies, shops and public places – but not in Cyprus! It also pays to work with other local people in the same business and send surplus guests to competitors (they will usually reciprocate). It isn't necessary to restrict your advertising to your local area or even your home country, as you can extend your marketing abroad (or advertise via the internet). However, it's usually necessary to have a telephone answering machine and possibly a fax machine. The more marketing you do, the more income you're likely to earn.

Website

A personalised website is an excellent advertisement and can include photographs, booking forms and maps, as well as comprehensive information about your property. You can also provide information about flights, car rental, local attractions, sports facilities and links to other websites. A good website should be easy to navigate (avoid complicated page links or indexes) and must include contact details, ideally email. It's wise to exchange links with as many other websites as possible, as this will increase the chance of your site's appearing via an internet search (e.g. with Google). It's possible (and cheap) to set up a site yourself but, unless you have expertise in this field, it's better to pay a professional, or your site may prove counter-productive!

Brochures & Leaflets

Even if you have a website containing photographs and information, you should ideally produce a coloured brochure or leaflet. This should contain external and internal pictures, and comprehensive details of the property, the exact location and local attractions (with a map included).

You should enclose a stamped addressed envelope when sending out details and follow up within a week if you don't hear anything. It's necessary to make a home look as attractive as possible in a brochure or leaflet without distorting the facts – advertise honestly and don't over-sell the property.

Handling Enquiries

If you plan to let a home yourself, you will need to decide how to handle enquiries about flights and car hire. It's easier to let clients book these themselves, but you should be able to offer advice and put them in touch with airlines, travel agents and car hire companies.

INFORMATION PACKS

Pre-arrival

After accepting a booking, whether through an agent or one you've generated yourself, you should provide guests with a pre-arrival information pack containing the following:

- A map of the local area and instructions how to find the property. If it's in a small village where signposts are all but non-existent, you may also need to erect signs. Holidaymakers who spend hours driving around trying to find a place are unlikely to return or recommend it! Maps are also helpful for taxi drivers, who may not know the area.
- Information about local attractions (available free from tourist offices);
- Emergency contact numbers in your home country (e.g. the UK) and Cyprus if guests have any problems or plan to arrive late;
- The keys or instructions about where to collect them on arrival.

It's ideal if someone can welcome your guests when they arrive, explain how things work, and deal with any special requests or problems.

Post-arrival

You should also provide an information pack in your home, explaining the following:

- How things work, such as kitchen appliances, television set and video or DVD player, heating and air-conditioning;
- Security measures (see page 218);
- What not to do and possible dangers (for example, if you allow young children and pets, you should make a point of emphasising dangers such as falling into the pool);
- Local emergency numbers and health services such as a doctor, dentist and hospital;
- Useful contacts such as a general repairman, plumber, electrician and pool maintenance person (or a local caretaker who can handle any problems – see below);
- Details of recommended shops, restaurants and attractions.

Many people provide a visitors' book for guests to write comments and suggestions, and some send out questionnaires. If you want to impress your guests, you can arrange for fresh flowers, fruit, a bottle of wine and a grocery pack to greet them on their arrival. It's personal touches that ensure repeat business and recommendations; you may even find after the first year or two that you rarely need to advertise. Many people return to the same property year after year. Simply do an annual mail-shot to previous clients. **Word-of-mouth advertising is the cheapest and always the best.**

MAINTENANCE

A property should always be spotlessly clean when guests arrive and you should provide basic cleaning equipment. If you're letting through an agent, he will usually arrange cleaning at your expense – currently at around CY£5 to CY£6 per hour in coastal resorts. If applicable, you will also need to arrange pool cleaning (around CY£20 per week throughout the summer) and a gardener, which should cost around CY£10 to CY£20 per week, depending on the amount of work required. Ideally you should have someone on call seven days a week.

Caretaker

If you own a second home in Cyprus, you will find it beneficial or even essential to employ a local caretaker, irrespective of whether you let it. You can have your caretaker prepare the house for your family and guests, as well as looking after it when it isn't in use. If it's a holiday home, have your caretaker check it periodically (e.g. weekly) and allow him to authorise minor repairs. If you let the property yourself, your caretaker can arrange for (or do) cleaning, linen changes, maintenance, repairs and gardening and pay bills. If you employ a caretaker, you should expect to pay around CY£5 per hour.

Closing a Property for the Winter

If you're going to close a property for the winter, you should turn off the water at the mains (required by insurance companies), remove fuses (except ones for a dehumidifier or air-conditioner if you leave them on), empty food cupboards and the fridge/freezer, disconnect gas cylinders and empty bins. You should leave interior doors and a few small windows (with grilles or secure shutters), as well as wardrobes, open to provide ventilation. Lock main doors, windows and shutters, and secure anything of value or leave it with a neighbour or friend. Check whether any work needs to be done before you leave and if necessary arrange for it to be done in your absence. Most importantly, leave a set of keys with a neighbour or friend and arrange for them (or a caretaker) to check your property periodically.

SECURITY

Most people aren't security conscious when in a property that doesn't belong to them, particularly when they're on holiday. You should therefore provide detailed instructions for guests regarding security measures and emphasise the need to secure the property when they're out. Ideally you should install a safe for your guests (and for yourself when you're there) and leave the key for it in the property. When you or your guests leave the property unattended, it's important to employ all security measures available, including the following:

- Storing valuables in a safe (if applicable);
- Closing and locking all doors and windows;
- Closing shutters and securing any bolts or locks;
- Setting the alarm (if you've installed one) and notifying the alarm company when absent for an extended period;
- Making it appear as if a property is occupied by the use of timers and leaving lights and a TV/radio on;

Bear in mind that prevention is always better than cure, as stolen possessions are rarely recovered. If you have a robbery, you should report it to your local police station, where you must make a statement. You will receive a copy, which is required by your insurance company if you make a claim. See also **Home Security** on page 218.

10.

MISCELLANEOUS MATTERS

This chapter contains miscellaneous – but nevertheless important – information for homeowners in Cyprus, including a list of public holidays, a chart of time differences, and details of postal, telephone and internet services, television and radio broadcasting, shopping, heating and air-conditioning, utilities, crime and home security.

CRIME

The crime rate in Cyprus is remarkably low – around one-sixth of the European average. Visitors are invariably surprised and reassured by this aspect of life on the island, where serious crime is virtually unheard of and theft is relatively rare. Thefts from hotels were previously uncommon and most vehicles could be safely left unlocked, although the incidence of theft from both cars and hotels has increased in recent years and you should always lock property and vehicles. The low incidence of crime is one reason for the country's popularity with foreign homebuyers, for whom security is a key element. There's a relatively small amount of petty crime, crimes against the person are very rare and respect for children, women and the elderly is high. Cypriot police speak English and are unarmed, with the exception of those who guard the airports.

HEATING & AIR-CONDITIONING

If you're used to central heating and like a warm house in winter, you will probably want central heating in your Cyprus home. Winters are usually a lot shorter than those in northern Europe and far milder, although there's a significant drop in temperature at night. Central heating systems may be powered by oil, gas, electricity, solid fuel (usually wood) or solar power (see below). For a holiday home, however, it isn't usually necessary to have central heating, and individual heaters are adequate for most people.

Whatever form of heating you use, it's important to have good insulation, without which around half of the heat generated is lost through the walls and roof. Note that many homes, particularly older and cheaper properties but also new ones, don't have good insulation and builders don't always adhere to current regulations. Apartment blocks may have a communal central heating system which provides heating for all apartments, the cost of which is divided among the tenants.

Heating

Electric

Electric heating isn't particularly common, as it's expensive and requires good insulation and a permanent system of ventilation. Night storage heaters can be economical, as the EAC has special pricing plans for the use of these. Some stand-alone electric heaters are expensive to run and are best suited to holiday homes. An electric air-conditioning system (see below) with a heat pump provides economical heating in winter.

Gas

This is the cheapest and most popular method of heating a home in Cyprus, even though Cyprus has no natural gas. You can use gas bottles or a tank (see **Gas** on page 241). Modern gas heaters are efficient and the gas is odour free. Nevertheless, gas heaters must be used only in rooms with adequate ventilation and it can be dangerous to have too large a difference between indoor and outdoor temperatures. For this reason, gas heaters aren't recommended for bedrooms or bathrooms. **Gas poisoning due to faulty ventilation ducts for heaters isn't uncommon.**

Oil & Solid Fuel

Oil-fired central heating isn't as commonly used as gas because of the high cost of oil and the difficulty of storage. Oil can be bought by the tank or half tank and can usually be delivered the same day. The price of heating oil fluctuates with the price of oil; at present it's around CY£0.38 per litre.

In rural areas, many houses have wood-burning fireplaces and stoves, which may be combined with a central heating system.

Solar Energy

The use of solar energy to provide hot water and heating (via hot-air 'radiators') is popular in Cyprus (see page 244). The amount of energy provided each year by a square metre of solar panels is equivalent to that generated by eleven gas bottles – the sun provides around 8,000 times the world's present energy requirements annually! A solar power system can be used to supply all your energy needs, although it's usually combined with an electric or gas heating system, as it cannot usually be relied upon for year-round heating and hot water. Solar power can also be used to provide electricity in a remote rural home, where the cost of extending mains electricity is prohibitive, or to heat a swimming pool.

The main drawback is the high cost of installation, which varies considerably according to how much energy you require. A 400-litre hot-water system costs around CY£2,500 (it must be installed by an expert). The advantages are no running costs, silent and maintenance-free operation, and no (or very small) electricity bills. A system should last 30 years (it's usually guaranteed for ten years) and can be uprated to provide additional power in the future. Advances in solar cell and battery technology are expected to dramatically increase the efficiency and reduce the cost of solar power, which is expected to become the main source of energy worldwide in the next century.

Air-conditioning

In summer, the temperature can reach over 40°C (104°F) in Cyprus. Properties are built to withstand the heat, but you may wish to install air-conditioning. Note, however, that there can be negative effects if you suffer from asthma or respiratory problems, as the air from an air-conditioning unit is very dry. You can choose from a huge variety of air-conditioners: fixed or moveable; indoor or outdoor installation; high or low power. Expect to pay around CY£1,500 for a unit sufficient to cool an average size room. An air-conditioning system with a heat pump and outside compressor provides cooling in summer and economical heating in winter. Many people fit ceiling fans (costing from around CY£25) for cooling in summer; these are standard fixtures in some new homes.

Humidifiers & De-humidifiers

Central heating dries the air and may cause your family to develop coughs and other ailments. Those who find dry air unpleasant can install humidifiers. These range from simple water containers hung from radiators to electric or battery-operated devices. Humidifiers that don't generate steam should be disinfected occasionally with a special liquid available from chemists.

If you're going to be using a holiday home only occasionally, it's worthwhile installing de-humidifiers, especially in the bedrooms, to prevent clothes and linen going mouldy.

HOME SECURITY

Although the crime rate is very low in Cyprus (see above), you cannot afford to be complacent about home security, particularly if your property will be left empty for long periods. Obtain advice from local security companies and neighbours who know the area. There are specialist home security companies who will inspect your home and offer free advice on security, although you should always shop around and obtain at least two quotations before having any work done.

When moving into a new home it's often wise to replace the locks (or lock barrels) as soon as possible, as you have no idea how many keys are in circulation for the existing locks. This is true even for new homes. In any case, it's advisable to change the external lock barrels regularly, e.g. annually, particularly if you let a home. If they aren't already fitted, it's advisable to fit high security (double cylinder or dead bolt) locks. Although crime rates are relatively low, petty crime does exist in some city and tourist areas and it may be advisable to take extra security measures such as two locks on external doors, internal locking shutters, and security bars or metal grilles on windows and patio doors on ground and lower floors. An insurance policy may specify that all forms of protection on doors must be employed when a property is unoccupied. Check with your insurance company.

You may wish to have a security alarm fitted, which is a good way to deter thieves and may also reduce your insurance. It should include all external doors and windows and may also include a coded entry keypad and 24-hour monitoring (with some systems, it's possible to monitor properties remotely, e.g. from another country, via a computer). With a monitored system, when a sensor detects smoke or forced entry or a panic button is pushed, a signal is sent automatically to a 24-hour monitoring station. The person on duty will telephone to check whether it's a genuine alarm (a password must be given) and, if he cannot contact you, will send someone to investigate.

You can also deter thieves by ensuring that your home is lit at night and not conspicuously unoccupied. You can fit external security 'motion detector' lights (that switch on automatically when someone approaches) and random timed switches for internal lights, and radios and televisions. You can fit UPVC (toughened clear plastic) security windows and doors, which can survive an attack with a sledge-hammer without damage, and external steel security blinds (which can be electrically operated), although these are expensive. You should have the front door of an apartment fitted with a spy-hole and chain so that you can check the identity of visitors before opening the door. **Remember, prevention is better than cure, as stolen possessions are rarely recovered.**

Holiday homes are particularly vulnerable and, if you have a holiday home in Cyprus, it's inadvisable to leave anything of value (monetary or sentimental) there and to have full insurance for your belongings (see **Household Insurance** on page 189).

No matter how good your security, a property is rarely impregnable, so you should never leave valuables in an unattended home unless they're kept in a safe.

One way to protect a home when you're away is to employ a house-sitter. This can be done for short or long periods. It isn't usually necessary to pay someone to house-sit for a period of six months or more, when you can usually find someone to do so in return for free accommodation. However, take care whom you engage and obtain references.

An important aspect of home security is ensuring you have early warning of a fire, which is easily accomplished by installing smoke detectors. Battery-operated smoke detectors can be purchased cheaply and should be tested periodically to ensure that the batteries aren't exhausted. You can also fit an electric-powered gas detector that activates an alarm when a gas leak is detected.

When closing up a property for an extended period, e.g. over the winter, you should ensure that everything is switched off. If you vacate your home for an extended period, you may also be obliged to notify a caretaker, landlord or insurance company, and to leave a key with a caretaker or landlord in case of emergencies.

If you have a robbery, you should report it immediately to your local police station where you must make a statement. You will receive a copy, which is required by your insurance company if you make a claim.

NEWSPAPERS & MAGAZINES

For a small island, Cyprus has an amazing number of newspapers and magazines. Most foreign newspapers and magazines are available, usually around 24 hours after publication in their home country, alongside a variety of indigenous publications in Greek and in English. Many international newspapers and magazines are, of course, available online.

Newspapers

There's a wide range of national and local newspapers in Greek; newspaper reading is a popular pastime for Greek Cypriots. Freedom of the press is part of the constitution in Cyprus, although several of the Greek-language newspapers are affiliated to different political parties and most of them are, not surprisingly, anti-Turkish.

The two main English-language newspapers are *The Cyprus Mail* and *The Cyprus Weekly* and there's a weekly English-language business newspaper called *The Financial Mirror* (see **Appendix B**). *The Cyprus Mail* is the oldest newspaper in Cyprus (it was first published in 1945) and offers national and international news and sport along with details of local events and television schedules. It's published daily (except Mondays). *The Cyprus Weekly* is published every Friday and has a large readership. It provides a good overview of events on the island over the past week, with details of forthcoming events and a good classified advertisements section. Both newspapers can be read online. As its name suggests, *The Financial Mirror* covers economic, financial and investment news about Cyprus and its readers are mainly business people. It's published weekly in English with a Greek supplement and is also available online.

Magazines

There are several free English-language magazines available in Limassol and Paphos, usually distributed from news kiosks and selected supermarkets. The *Limassol Focus* is published quarterly, while the *Grapevine* magazine (Limassol and Paphos) and *The Express* (Paphos) are both published at the beginning of every month. *Time Out (Cyprus)* is a popular monthly magazine in Greek and it's published twice a year in English. It contains useful information about where to go and what to do as well as a comprehensive restaurant guide.

POSTAL SERVICES

Cyprus has a good postal service, operated by the government-owned Cyprus Postal Services, although it isn't as efficient as the service in some other European countries. The four district post offices provide a full range of services. These are in Larnaca, Limassol, Nicosia and Paphos (addresses and telephone numbers can be found on Ministry of Communications and Works website, 🖥 www.mcw.gov.cy – click on 'Organisational Chart' and then 'Department of Postal Services'). These include letter and parcel post (within Cyprus and abroad), Electronic Mail Service (EMS) and Datapost to almost any other country, postal orders and money orders. EMS and Datapost are a very fast and reliable service, operated separately from the normal postal service, as items are usually cleared immediately by customs. EMS post is usually delivered by messenger within 48 hours of arrival in the destination country. Ordinary airmail services from Cyprus usually take around three or four days to reach European destinations and approximately a week to reach destinations outside Europe.

Most villages and the smaller towns have a postal agency, much like a sub-post office, but services vary considerably. Some agencies sell a limited range of stamps only, while others can deal with registered post. If you will be relying on a village postal agency, it's advisable to check what services are available.

All district post offices and most postal agencies have post office boxes (POBs, also called private POBs) for rental, but these are much in demand, so you may find availability limited. In some villages, POBs are free of charge.

Opening Hours

Post offices are usually open Mondays to Fridays from 7.30am to 1.30pm and (except on Wednesdays) from 3 to 6pm; they open and close later in the afternoon in July and August. District post offices are also open on Saturday mornings, from 8.30 to 10.30am.

Collection & Delivery

There are yellow post boxes in towns, but it may take a while for post to reach a main sorting office and urgent post should be taken directly to a district post office (see above). Similarly, there are usually post boxes close to village postal agencies but these may not be emptied every day.

House-to-house deliveries are made in the main towns on weekdays but not at weekends. The reason for the popularity of POBs in the main post offices is that delivery to them is continuous during office hours. A few of the villages operate house-to-house deliveries, but you may have to collect your post from the postal agency or your POB.

Incoming packages and parcels may be examined by customs officials and, if necessary, import duty and VAT may be charged. You will usually be sent a note to say that a package has arrived; take this to the relevant post office to collect it.

Courier Services

Courier services are available from all district post offices and also from private companies in Cyprus, including those listed below. Couriers can offer next-day delivery to most European and Middle East destinations.

There are DHL, Federal Express, Skynet, TNT and UPS courier services in all the main towns in Cyprus. Addresses and telephone numbers for their main offices in Nicosia are listed below:

- **DHL** (Cyprus) Ltd, 13 Acropolis Avenue, PO Box 22002, Nicosia (☎ 22-799 000);
- **Federal Express** (Fedex), represented in Cyprus by Gap Express (☎ 22-710 100);
- **Skynet**, PO Box 26829, Michalakopoulou 14, Nicosia (☎ 22-762 062);
- **TNT** Customer Service Centre, PO Box 1071, Nicosia (☎ 22-817 060);
- **UPS**, represented by Airtrans Express Services Ltd, 1 Stasinou Street, 2404 Engomi, Nicosia (☎ 22-453 311).

PUBLIC HOLIDAYS

Public holidays are familiar to most visitors and residents from Western countries and follow, more or less, the Christian calendar, with some exceptions and additions due to the Greek Orthodox religion, which is observed by many Greek Cypriots.

Date	Holiday
1st January	New Year's Day
6th January	Epiphany
Feb/March	Green (Lent) Monday (50 days before Greek Orthodox Easter)
March/April	Good Friday
March/April	Easter Sunday
25th March	Greek National Day
1st April	Greek Cypriot National Day
1st May	Labour Day/Orthodox Easter
2nd/3rd May	Orthodox Monday/Tuesday
June	Whit Monday
15th August	Feast of the Assumption
1st October	Cyprus Independence Day
28th October	Ochi Day – Greek National Day
25th December	Christmas Day
26th December	St Stephen's Day

In coastal towns and sometimes elsewhere, Easter celebrations go on for a week or more. In addition to the above, each town has feast days, which are taken as holidays. Further information about holidays and festivals can be obtained for the Cyprus Tourism Organisation (⬛ www. cyprustourism.org).

SHOPPING

Cyprus isn't one of Europe's great shopping countries, although it offers a wide choice of reasonably priced, locally produced, handmade arts and crafts, and clothes and shoes are good value. As far as shopping is concerned, Cyprus is a relatively inexpensive country, although the recent addition of VAT to the price of many items has increased the cost of living. Most Cypriot retail enterprises are family-run and, consequently, shopping is a pleasant social experience, often punctuated with endless cups of Cypriot coffee.

In recent years, the more traditional shopping scene has been joined by shopping centres, although these are mainly limited to Nicosia and Limassol. In these towns there are several British department stores, such as Woolworths (the first department store to open on the island), BHS, Marks & Spencer, and the US coffee chain, Starbucks. There are a few large supermarkets, some cash-and-carry supermarkets and a profusion of small supermarkets and corner grocery shops. With the exception of some souvenir shops, where haggling over the price is part of the enjoyment, retail prices are fixed in Cyprus and prices shown include VAT.

Among the best buys in Cyprus are the diverse handicrafts, which include hand-woven textiles, ceramics, leather goods, handmade lace, copper, silverware, handmade baskets, wines and spirits, and perhaps rather surprisingly, spectacles (including sunglasses). These are considerably cheaper in Cyprus than in the rest of Europe and opticians offer a free eye test and can usually supply glasses to you within 24 hours. In some areas, there's even a special tourist service! Handicrafts from throughout the country are available at most souvenir shops, but are usually cheaper when purchased in the area where they're made or from the government-run Cyprus Handicraft Service, which has shops in major towns.

Prices of many consumer goods, such as TVs and stereo systems, computers, cameras, electrical apparatus and household appliances, have fallen considerably in recent years and many familiar brands are available. Prices are still generally higher than in many other European countries, where there's more competition. The best time to buy is during the sales, which usually last for the whole of February and August.

Cypriots prefer to pay cash when shopping, although credit cards are widely accepted in major stores and those frequented by tourists.

However, in remote areas you may find that only cash is accepted. Although crime rates are low on the island, in major towns and tourist areas you should be wary of pickpockets and bag-snatchers, particularly in markets and other crowded places. Don't tempt fate with an exposed wallet or purse.

Opening Hours

Shop opening hours in Cyprus depend largely on the heat. From June to September, when it's often too hot to do anything in the afternoon, shops open early (8am) and close in the afternoons from 2 to 5pm, when they re-open until around 8.30pm. In the winter months, they're usually open from 8am to 1pm and from 2.30 to 5.30pm (later in the large towns). Shops are generally closed on Wednesday and Saturday afternoons and on Sundays all year round, although those in tourist areas are open on most days, including Sundays, and are usually open until later in the evening. It's important to shop around and compare prices in Cyprus, which can vary considerably, even between shops in the same town. Note, however, that price differences often reflect different quality, so ensure that you're comparing similar products.

Markets

The main towns in Cyprus (except Larnaca) all have central covered markets which sell mainly foodstuffs and fruit and vegetables. Food markets are highly popular, despite the presence of supermarkets and hypermarkets. Food is invariably beautifully presented and includes fruit and vegetables (including many exotic varieties), meat, herbs, olives and olive oil. Food is usually cheaper and fresher in markets than in supermarkets, particularly if you buy what's in season and grown locally. You should arrive early in the morning for the best choice, although bargains can often be found when stall holders are packing up for the day. Markets usually operate from around 7am to 2pm. Queues at a particular stall are usually a good sign.

Vendors may object your handling fruit and vegetables, although you needn't be shy about asking to taste a piece of fruit. **Make sure that the quality of produce you're given is the same as on display, which isn't always the case.** It's sensible to take a bag, as carrier bags aren't usually provided. Another good place to buy fresh fruit and vegetables is from roadside stalls set up in rural areas. Here the produce couldn't be fresher and is often grown by the seller himself.

Furniture & Furnishings

The kind of furniture you buy for your Cypriot home will depend on a number of factors, including its style and size, whether it's a permanent or holiday home, your budget, the local climate, and not least, your personal taste. If you plan to furnish a holiday home with antiques or expensive modern furniture, bear in mind that you will need adequate security and insurance (see **Home Security** on page 218 and **Household Insurance** on page 189).

Holiday homes are sometimes sold furnished, particularly apartments. Buying a furnished property can represent a bargain, as the cost of the furnishings often isn't reflected in the price. However, you may find that the furniture is of poor quality and not to your taste. It may be worthwhile shipping surplus items of furniture you have in your main home to your holiday home in Cyprus. If you intend to live permanently in Cyprus in the future and already have a house full of good furniture, there's little point in buying expensive furniture in Cyprus. However, many foreigners who decide to live permanently in Cyprus find that it's better to sell their furniture than to bring it with them, as the furniture often isn't suitable for the climate and the style of home. It's good to have a fresh start in your new home and it saves paying substantial amounts to ship furniture only to discover it looks out of place in your Cypriot home.

There are few innovative furniture makers in Cyprus, where furniture tends to be made by in traditional styles (i.e. heavy and dark) by craftsmen using high quality materials. The demand for modern furniture, e.g. made of chrome, glass, pine and bamboo, has meant that new furniture shops have begun to open on the outskirts of the main towns, mostly importing furniture from well known companies in France, Italy and Scandinavia. There's Habitat and Debenhams in Nicosia, and IKEA plans to open a shop in Nicosia by 2007. The French companies Gautier and Rochebobois also have outlets on the island. Only a few local companies have started producing modern furniture, e.g. Andreotti (Agios Athanasios Industrial Estate, PO Box 54352, 3723 Limassol, ☎ 25-721 128, 🖳 www.andreotti.cy.com), which has branches in Limassol and Nicosia, and V& S Bamboo Furniture (42 Ioannion Street, PO Box 57248, 3314 Limassol, ☎ 25-578 106). The Cyprus Furniture website (🖳 www.cyprusfurniture.com) lists the major furniture manufacturers, importers and stores on the island and has details of office furniture as well as furniture for the home.

If you're buying a large quantity of furniture, don't be reluctant to ask for a reduction, as many stores will give you a discount. Many furniture stores offer special deals on complete furniture packages. If you're looking for antique furniture, at affordable prices, you may find a few bargains at auction houses on the island. Check the yellow pages for details. You can buy, sell or rent antique, restoration and reproduction furniture. There's a reasonable market for second-hand furniture in Cyprus and many sellers and dealers advertise in the expatriate press.

The DIY culture hasn't gripped Cyprus as it has some northern European countries, so you won't find many DIY superstores on the island. However, the Woolworths stores (in Larnaca, Limassol, Nicosia and Paphos) include substantial DIY departments.

Household Goods

Household goods in Cyprus are generally of high quality and, although the choice isn't as wide as in some other European countries, it has improved considerably in recent years. Electrical items have traditionally been more expensive in Cyprus, but the gap has narrowed and prices are now comparable (particularly in hypermarkets). A wide range of imported and familiar brands is available.

Bear in mind when importing household goods that aren't sold in Cyprus that it may be difficult or impossible to get them repaired or serviced locally. Note also that the standard size of kitchen appliances and cupboard units in Cyprus may not be the same as in other countries and it may be difficult to fit an imported dishwasher or washing machine into a Cypriot kitchen. If you import appliances, don't forget to bring a supply of spares and consumables such as bulbs for a refrigerator or sewing machine, and spare bags for a vacuum cleaner. Check the size **and** the latest safety regulations before shipping these items to Cyprus or buying them in your home country, as they may need expensive modifications.

If you already own small 2220–240V household appliances, it's worthwhile bringing them to Cyprus, where UK-style three-pin plugs are used (see page 239). However, if you're coming from a country with a 110–115V electricity supply, such as the US, you will need a lot of expensive transformers (see page 239) so it's usually better to buy new appliances. Don't bring a TV or video recorder without checking its compatibility first, as TVs made for other countries often don't work in Cyprus without modification (see page 234). If your need is only temporary, many electrical and other household items (such as TVs, beds, cots/highchairs, electric fans, refrigerators, heaters and air-conditioners), can be rented by the day, week or month.

Duty-free Allowances

If you travel between Cyprus and another EU country, you're entitled to import or export goods of an unlimited value provided they're for personal use. If you import or export cigarettes or alcohol above the limits shown below, you must be able to 'prove' that they're for your personal use; if you cannot, they may be confiscated by customs officials. These limits are subject to change, and you should check with an official source before buying large amounts:

- 800 cigarettes;
- 400 cigarillos;
- 20 cigars;
- 1kg of smoking tobacco;
- 90 litres of wine (of which no more than 60 should be sparkling);
- 10 litres of spirits;
- 20 litres of fortified wine;
- 110 litres of beer.

If you're coming to Cyprus from a non-EU country you're entitled to import the following goods duty-free:

- One litre of spirits (over 22 degrees proof) **or** two litres of fortified wine, sparkling wine or other liqueurs (under 22 degrees proof);
- Two litres of still table wine;
- 200 cigarettes **or** 100 cigarillos **or** 50 cigars **or** 250g of tobacco;
- 50g of perfume;
- 250ml of toilet water;
- Other goods, including gifts and souvenirs to the value of CY£175 (CY£90 for under 15s).

Duty-free allowances apply on both outward and return journeys, even if both are made on the same day, and the combined total (i.e. double the above limits) can be imported into your 'home' country.

If you reside outside the EU, you can reclaim VAT on single purchases over CY£100. Retailers provide an export sales invoice, which must be validated by a customs officer when leaving Cyprus, so make sure any purchases you've made are in your hand luggage. Your refund will be sent to you later or paid to a credit card account. With certain purchases, particularly large items, it's better to have them sent directly abroad, when VAT won't be added.

TELEPHONE SERVICES

Telecommunications in Cyprus are generally excellent. They are principally via satellite links and fibre optic cables. Currently services are provided only by the Cyprus Telecommunications Authority (CYTA), a semi-government organisation, but the market was liberalised in 2003 to allow competition and some licences have been granted to other telecommunications organisations, although it still isn't clear what alternative services will be available. The CYTA provides a complete service, including the installation of telephone lines, mobile telephones, data transmission, television transmission and reception, ADSL, ISDN, and internet services. Detailed information about services provided by the CYTA and its charges can be found in the front of any telephone directory. Directories are available at CYTA shops and customer service centres, which are in all the main towns. You can check their location on the CYTA's website (💻 www.cyta.com.cy). The website also offers a number of online services, including bill-paying facilities.

Installation

When moving to a new home in Cyprus with a telephone line, you should have the account transferred to your name. If you're planning to move into a property without an existing telephone line, you may want to get one installed. Installation of a new or additional line cost CY£30, but this is only to provide the connection to the wall of the premises. You must then hire an electrician to install the internal wiring and sockets; the wire and equipment can be bought from an electrical shop or provided by the electrician, and handsets can be bought from electricians or CYTA offices.

To have a line installed (externally), you should visit your local CYTA office (see above) or contact the CYTA Call Centre (☎ 132 during office hours or ☎ 08000-8080 at other times), where information is available in English. Any application for an installation is subject to its being technically possible (all lines must run underground), and applications are processed in order of submission. Take along some identification, such as your passport, your residence card (if you have one) and proof of address such as a rental contract or a copy of your deed or sale contract. Temporary residents must pay a deposit of CY£100, which is refundable when you give up the service. It usually takes around three to four weeks from application to connection, but this depends on the area. **Delays may be up to six months and even longer if you live in a remote village.**

> **SURVIVAL TIP**
> If a property doesn't have a telephone line, ensure that you will be able to get one installed within a reasonable time if it's important to you. You may also wish to check whether it's possible to have a broadband internet connection installed (see page 233).

Using the Telephone

Dialling codes within the Republic of Cyprus are as follows:

Area	Code
Agia Napa	23
Larnaca	24
Limassol	25
Nicosia	22
Paphos & Polis	26
Paralimni/Protaras	23
Platres	25

Most telephone numbers have eight digits (including the above codes), all of which must be dialled irrespective of where you're calling from. Mobile telephone numbers start with the prefix 99.

Dial ☎ 192 for a 24-hour national directory enquiries service and ☎ 194 for international enquiries.

International Calls

Most other countries can be dialled directly from Cyprus, using International Direct Dialling (IDD) from both private and public telephones. A full list of country codes is available in telephone directories and yellow pages. To make an international call, you need to first dial 00 to obtain an international line, then the country code, e.g. 44 for the UK. Then dial the area code **without** the first zero and the subscriber's number. The off-peak period for international calls (see **Costs** below) is 9pm to 8am during weekdays and all day on Saturdays, Sundays and public holidays. The CYTA also offers a service called Call Direct, which allows you to make reverse charge calls both nationally and internationally, offering reduced rates nationally between 8pm and 7am and international calls between 10pm and 8am every day and all day Sunday.

Costs

Line rental and call charges are low compared with those in other European countries. Installation is CY£30 and monthly rental is CY£5, although there's an alternative charging system whereby you pay only CY£1.50 per month, but have a 2 per cent surcharge on every call (worth it unless you spend more than CY£175 per month on calls). The Republic became a single charge zone in 2001. National call rates are approximately 2 cents for two minutes, and international calls from a fixed line cost around 3 cents per minute to European destinations, although in February 2005 the CYTA announced that it would cut international call rates by up to 80 per cent. Calls from fixed lines to mobile phones cost almost four times as much and mobile-to-mobile calls five times, but calls from a mobile phone to a fixed line in the UK, for example, can cost as little as 5 cents per minute. The CYTA offers off-peak rates for both national and international calls, although off-peak rates aren't significantly cheaper. The off-peak period for national calls is 8pm to 7am on weekdays and all day on Saturdays, Sundays and public holidays; for international calls, it's 9pm to 8am on weekdays and all day Saturdays, Sundays and public holidays. VAT at 15 per cent is levied on all charges.

Bills

The CYTA sends out itemised bills monthly for all services. Bills can be paid at any CYTA office (see above), at a bank, by direct debit or online via the CYTA's e-bill service (🖥 www.ebill.cyta.com.cy). This service also allows you to check your monthly charges and billing history and pay online.

Emergency Numbers

To summon any of the three main emergency services – police, fire or ambulance – anywhere on the island call ☎ 199 or ☎ 112. For air-sea rescue, call ☎ 1441; forest fire, call ☎ 1407. You can find out about night pharmacies by calling ☎ 192 (directory enquiries) or listen to an automatic recording on ☎ 1404 (Larnaca), ☎ 1405 (Limassol), ☎ 1402 (Nicosia), ☎ 1406 (Paphos). Dial ☎ 197 to report a fault on your telephone. Emergency and service numbers are listed at the front of telephone directories.

Fax

If you're planning to take a fax machine to Cyprus, check that it will work there or can be modified. Most fax machines made for other European countries will operate in Cyprus, although getting them repaired locally may be impossible due to lack of availability of parts, unless the same machine is sold there. Fax machines can be purchased from CYTA offices and purchased or rented from telephone and business equipment retailers. Public fax services are provided at district post offices.

Public Telephones

There are public telephones in central locations all over the island. They're in all towns and villages as well as at Larnaca and Paphos international airports and harbours. They can be used for both national and international calls and full dialling instructions and charges are available inside the booths. There are 'Coinphones', which accept 2, 5, 10 and 20 cent coins and card-operated telephones, which work with CY£3, CY£5 and CY£10 'Telecards'. These can be bought from banks, post offices, souvenir shops and any CYTA office.

Mobile Telephones

Mobile phones are widely used throughout Cyprus and there's excellent reception in most areas on the island, although in some remote areas it can be poor. The CYTA has a partnership agreement with Vodafone and uses the GSM 900 system. You can use your mobile from your home country in Cyprus provided there's a roaming agreement between your mobile service provider and Cytamobile Vodafone. Roaming agreements have been set up between the CYTA and service providers in 103 countries; you can check whether your country is included by dialling the customer service number (☎ 132) or checking on the Ctytamobile website (🖥 www.cyta.mobile-vodafone.com.cy). However, roaming charges can be exorbitant, and it's better to have your telephone adapted to use a Cypriot SIM card, which you can use while you're there. You can sign a contract and pay a fixed monthly fee or 'pay as you talk'. Details of all the services available can be found in the front of telephone directories.

Internet

During the last few years, Cyprus has seen a substantial increase in private computer ownership and internet access. However, the provision of broadband services and faster internet access is still relatively limited compared to other European countries and many customers use dial-up internet connections. Internet service providers in Cyprus are Avakom, Cytanet, Globalsoft, Logosnet, Planitis, Spidernet and Thunderworx, all of which provide a dial-up service. Dial-up charges are fairly low – only CY£5 for connection and a monthly charge of CY£11 – but you must add call charges to this, which are currently 2 cents per six minutes' internet use. For occasional internet users, such as visitors and business travellers, the CYTA offers an internet service called 'Cytanet for All'. You need a computer with a modem and a telephone line and you can use the service without access codes or monthly charges. To access the service, dial ☎ 90-902 626 from anywhere in Cyprus.

Broadband

Broadband or ADSL has been available in Cyprus since 2001 but is offered only by the CYTA, under the brand name I-Choice. The service covers only urban areas, which account for around 65 per cent of the population. Charges for the fastest ADSL service are CY£40 for connection and around CY£20 for monthly rental.

TELEVISION & RADIO

Cypriot television isn't renowned for its quality, although it has improved considerably in recent years. Both terrestrial and satellite TV reception are excellent in most areas. **There's no longer a charge for operating television or radio receivers in Cyprus.**

The Cyprus Broadcasting Corporation (CyBC), which is government-controlled, has two channels, CyBC ONE and CyBC TWO (still referred to by some Cypriots as RIK1 and RIK2 after *Radiofoniko Idryma Kyprou*, the original name of the CyBC), both of which broadcast 24 hours a day. There are six news bulletins in Greek and one in Turkish. CyBC TWO caters for the international viewer and, as well as two news bulletins in Greek, broadcasts daily bulletins in English at 8pm daily (around 7.20pm at weekends). This channel links with Euronews, which is transmitted from 1.30am to 1.30pm on weekdays and 1.30am to 8am at weekends. CyBC also links into Eurovision for the live transmission of major sporting events.

There are four main commercial channels: the Cypriot Channel SIGMA and the Greek channels ANT 1, ERT SAT and MEGA. Most of them broadcast programmes and films in English with Greek subtitles or in Greek with English subtitles. There are also several independent channels, such as Lumiere TV and Alpha, to which you must subscribe and which transmit mainly films.

TV programmes are listed in most Cypriot newspapers and in TV guides. Some Cypriot programmes are also listed in English-language newspapers and magazines, along with a selection of satellite TV programmes. CyBC's website (⌨ www.cybc.com.cy) has programming information, along with many other useful links.

Television Standards

The standards for TV reception in Cyprus aren't the same as in all other countries. Local TVs and video recorders operate on the continental PAL system. If you want a TV that will work in Cyprus and other European countries, and a video cassette recorder (VCR) that will play back videos, you must buy a multi-standard TV and VCR. These are widely available and contain automatic circuitry that can switch from PAL-I (Britain) and SECAM-L (France) to PAL-B/G (rest of Europe). Some multi-standard TVs also handle the North American NTSC standard and have an NTSC-in jack plug connection allowing you to play American videos. Electrical goods are reasonably priced in Cyprus and many familiar brands are available, so it may be preferable to buy a television and video recorder once you arrive. Some people opt for two TVs, one to receive local TV programmes and another (e.g. PAL-I or NTSC) to play their favourite videos. A British or US video recorder won't work with Cypriot TV unless it's dual-standard. Foreign DVD machines don't need re-tuning.

Satellite Television

Cyprus is well served by satellite TV. There are a number of satellites positioned over Europe carrying over 200 stations and broadcasting in a variety of languages. TV addicts are offered a huge choice of English- and foreign-language stations, which can be received throughout Cyprus with a 1.9m dish. A bonus is the availability of radio stations via satellite, including the major BBC stations (see page 236).

A satellite receiver should have a built-in Videocrypt decoder (and others such as Eurocrypt, SECAM or Syster if required) and be capable of receiving satellite stereo radio. A 1.9m dish (and receiver) is required to received signals from the Astra station in Cyprus, which is on the edge of the satellite's signal footprint. Shop around, as prices vary; you usually pay for a package of services, so check what's included in a package. You can also install a motorised 1.2m or 1.5m dish and receive hundreds of stations in a multitude of languages from around the world. If you wish to receive satellite TV on two or more TVs, you can buy a system with two or more receivers. To receive stations from two or more satellites simultaneously, you need a motorised dish or a dish with a double feed (dual LNBs) antenna. When buying a system, ensure that it can receive programmes from all existing and planned satellites.

Satellite programme listings are provided in a number of British publications such as *What Satellite*, *Satellite Times* and *Satellite TV*, available on subscription and from some news kiosks in Cyprus. Satellite TV programmes are also listed in some expatriate newspapers and magazines.

Satellite Dishes

To receive programmes from any satellite, there must be no obstacles between the satellite and your dish, i.e. no trees, buildings or mountains must obstruct the signal, so check before renting or buying a home. Before buying or erecting a satellite dish, you must check whether permission is required. Some towns, buildings and new developments have strict laws and regulations regarding the positioning of dishes, although generally owners can mount one almost anywhere without receiving complaints. Dishes can usually be mounted in a variety of unobtrusive positions and can also be painted.

When an apartment or townhouse is advertised as having satellite TV, it often means that it's linked to a communal system and doesn't have its own satellite dish, which means that your choice of programmes may be limited, although you can sometimes pay to receive more programmes. If this is important to you, check carefully before you commit yourself to a purchase.

Digital Satellite TV

Digital TV was launched on 1st October 1998 by Sky Television (⌨ www.sky.co.uk) in the UK. To watch digital TV you require a receiver and a digital dish. Cyprus receives its digital services via the Astra satellite. In addition to the usual analogue channels (see above), Sky digital TV offers BBC and ITV channels, plus many other digital channels. In theory, you aren't allowed to receive BBC and ITV programmes outside the UK because of copyright issues, although many people do. If you want to receive the service, you need to have a

UK address. Despite this, local satellite installation companies offer installation services.

BBC

The BBC's commercial subsidiary, BBC Worldwide Television, broadcasts two 24-hour channels: BBC Prime (general entertainment) and BBC World (24-hour news and information). BBC World is free-to-air and is transmitted via the Eutelsat Hot Bird satellite, while BBC Prime is encrypted and transmitted via the Intelsat satellite. BBC Prime requires a D2-MAC decoder and a smartcard costing around GB£25 and an annual GB£75 subscription fee (plus VAT). Smartcards are available from TV Extra, PO Box 304, 59124 Motala, Sweden (☎ +46-141-56060). For more information and a programming guide contact BBC Worldwide Television, Woodlands, 80 Wood Lane, London W12 0TT, UK (☎ 020-8576 2555). The BBC publishes a monthly magazine, *BBC On Air*, giving comprehensive information about BBC Worldwide Television programmes. A programme guide is also listed on the internet (🖳 www.bbc.co.uk/worldservice/onair) and both BBC World and BBC Prime have their own websites (🖳 www.bbcworld.com and www.bbcprime.com). When accessing them, you need to enter the name of the country, e.g. Cyprus, so that schedules appear in local time.

Video & DVD

There's no shortage of video and DVD rental shops in all the large towns. Films are available in Greek, English and some other languages. Beware of the multitude of pirate copies that you find in many of the markets and tourist shops on the island. If you aren't a permanent resident and want to hire a film, you will usually need to show proof of identity and pay a deposit which covers the cost of replacing the film. If you want to bring a video or DVD player with you to Cyprus, make sure it's a multi-standard machine (see **Television Standards** on page 234).

Radio

Radio in Cyprus comes under the auspices of the Cyprus Broadcasting Corporation (CyBC), which has three stations: Channel 1 (in Greek only), Channel 2 (in English, Turkish and Armenian), and Channel 3 (in Greek only). English-language programmes are broadcast on Channel 2 from 6pm to midnight on 91.1 MHz, 92.4 MHz (in Larnaca), 94.2 MHz and 96.5MHz (in Paphos) on FM; they include 'Round and About', between

6 and 8pm, providing information for visitors and foreign residents. There are news bulletins in English at 1.30, 6 and 10pm.

There are numerous private radio stations, including two English music stations, Kiss FM (89.0) and Mix FM (102.3), which transmit in the Nicosia area. There's a local radio station in Agia Napa (Radio Napa), and Paphos Radio offers a mix of Greek and English programmes. The British Forces Broadcasting Service (BFBS) has two radio stations, primarily aimed at British forces. You will need a UHF aerial and tune your radio to 92.1MHz (BFBS 1) or 89.9MHz (BFBS 2). If you're able to receive BFBS stations, you will also be able to tune in to BBC Radio 4 and 5 as well as many other English-language stations.

The BBC World Service can be received on 1323kHz for most of the day. BBC radio stations, including the World Service, are also available via the Astra satellites. The BBC publishes a monthly magazine, *BBC On Air*, containing comprehensive information about BBC world service radio and television programmes. For a free copy and frequency information write to BBC On Air, Room 227 NW, Bush House, Strand, London WC2B 4PH, UK.

If you have satellite TV, you can receive many radio stations via your satellite receiver. For example, BBC Radio 1, 2, 3, 4 and 5, the BBC World Service, Sky Radio, Virgin 1215 and many non-English stations are broadcast via the Astra satellites. Satellite radio stations are listed in British satellite TV magazines such as the *Satellite Times*.

TIME DIFFERENCE

Cyprus is two hours ahead of Greenwich Mean Time in winter and one hour ahead of Central European Time. Clocks go forward one hour on the last Sunday in March and back one hour on the last Sunday in October, so Cyprus is always two hours ahead of the UK and one hour ahead of Western Europe. The time in some major cities when it's 12 noon in Cyprus (in winter) is shown below.

LONDON	NEW YORK	LOS ANGELES	SYDNEY	JO'BURG
10am	5am	2am	7pm	11am

UTILITIES

Immediately after buying or renting a property (unless utilities are included in the rent), you should arrange for the meter (if applicable) to be read, the contract (e.g. electricity or water) to be registered in your name and the service switched on. If you're buying a new property, you must arrange for a contract to be set up for your electricity and water supply. See also **Heating & Air-Conditioning** on page 216.

Electricity

Electricity in Cyprus is provided by the Electricity Authority of Cyprus (EAC) which is a semi-governmental, non-profit-making body with the monopoly on electricity supply. To arrange connection, the fitting of a meter, or the transfer of an account, you must go in person to an EAC customer service centre or authorise someone to do so on your behalf. There are EAC offices are in all the main towns and some smaller villages (listed on the EAC website, ⌨ www.eac.com.cy, which also offers instructions for connection and disconnection can be found on the website). You or your representative must take some identification, e.g. your passport and a rental agreement or contract of sale. If you're buying through an estate agent, he may arrange for the utilities to be transferred to your name or go with you to the electricity company's office (no charge should be made for this service). If you're a non-resident owner, you should also give your foreign address in case there are any problems requiring your attention, such as a bank failing to pay the bills.

When registering, make sure all that previous bills have been paid and that the contract is put into your name from the day you take over, or you may be liable for debts left by the previous owner. The cost of electricity connection and the installation of a meter is usually between CY£75 and CY£100, but charges vary considerably with the area, power supply and the type of meter installed.

Power Supply

The electricity supply in Cyprus is 220–240 volts AC with a frequency of 50 Hertz (cycles). Sockets are 13 amp. Power cuts can be frequent and unannounced in some areas (especially during bad weather). If you use a computer, it's sensible to fit an uninterrupted power supply (UPS) with a battery back-up, which allows you time to save your work and shut down your computer after a power failure. **Even more important than a battery back-up is a power surge protector for appliances such as TVs, computers and fax machines, without which you risk having equipment damaged or destroyed.** If you live in an area where cuts are frequent and rely on electricity for your livelihood, you may need to install a back-up generator.

Wiring Standards

Most modern properties, e.g. less than 20 years old, have good electrical installations. If you buy an old home, or one that hasn't had an electricity supply for more than 12 months, you must have it checked by a representative of the EAC. You should ensure that the electricity installations are in good condition well in advance of moving house, as it can take some time to get a new meter installed or to be reconnected.

Plugs & Fuses

UK-style, flat three-pin plugs with an earth pin are used in Cyprus, so imported British appliances can be used without adapters or new plugs. If you're bringing non-British appliances, you can buy plug adapters in Cyprus, although it's wise to bring some adapters with you, plus extension cords and multi-plug extensions that can be fitted with local plugs. There's often a shortage of electric sockets in homes, with perhaps just one per room (including the kitchen), so multi-plug adapters may be essential, but take care not to overload a circuit. Small low-wattage electrical appliances such as table lamps, small TVs and computers, don't require an earth. However, plugs with an earth must always be used for high-wattage appliances such as fires, kettles, washing machines and refrigerators. Electrical appliances that are earthed have a three-core wire must never be used with a two-pin plug without an earth socket. **Always make sure that a plug is correctly and securely wired, as bad wiring can be fatal.**

In modern properties, fuses are of the circuit breaker type. When there's a short circuit or the system has been overloaded, a circuit breaker is tripped and the power supply is cut. If your electricity fails, you should first suspect a fuse of tripping off, particularly if you've just switched on an electrical appliance. Before reconnecting the fuse, however, switch off any high-power appliances such as a stove, washing machine or dishwasher. Make sure you know where the trip switches are located and keep a torch handy so that you can find them in the dark.

Converters & Transformers

If you have electrical equipment rated at 110–115 volts AC (for example, from the US), you will require a converter or a step-down transformer to convert the 220–240 volt supply. However, some electrical appliances are fitted with a 110/220-volt switch. Check for the switch, which may be inside the casing, and make sure it's switched to 220 volts **before** connecting it to the power supply. Converters can be used for heating appliances, but transformers are required for motorised appliances. Total the wattage of the devices you intend to connect to a transformer and make sure that its power rating **exceeds** this sum. Generally, small, high-wattage, electrical appliances, such as kettles, toasters, heaters, and irons need large transformers. Motors in large appliances such as cookers, refrigerators, washing machines, dryers and dishwashers will need replacing or fitting with a large transformer.

An additional problem with some electrical equipment is the frequency rating, which, in some countries, e.g. the US, is designed to run at 60 Hertz (Hz) and not Europe's 50Hz. Electrical equipment without a motor is generally unaffected by the drop in frequency to 50Hz (except televisions). Equipment with a motor may run with a 20 per cent drop in speed, but automatic washing machines, cookers, electric clocks, record players and tape recorders must be converted from 60Hz to 50Hz. To find out, look at the label on the back of the equipment. If it says 50/60Hz, there shouldn't be a problem; if it says 60Hz, you can try it, **but first ensure that the voltage is correct as outlined above.** Bear in mind that the transformers and motors of electrical devices designed to run at 60Hz will run hotter at 50Hz, so make sure that apparatus has sufficient space around it for cooling.

In most cases it's simpler to buy new appliances locally, which are of good quality and reasonably priced. Note also that the dimensions of cookers, microwave ovens, refrigerators, washing machines, dryers and dishwashers purchased abroad may differ from those in Cyprus, so they may not fit into a local kitchen.

Tariffs

Electricity in Cyprus is relatively cheap, the price for domestic users being well below average European prices. However, it's still the most expensive form of energy on the island and many people prefer to use bottled gas (see below). Electricity charges are around CY£35 per month for an average family house, although this naturally depends on consumption.

There are four pricing structures for domestic users, depending on day/night-time usage; all have a small fixed charge (less than CY£2) and then a per kilowatt charge, which averages around 4 cents. The EAC's website (💻 www.eac.com.cy) has a detailed explanation of each pricing structure.

Meters: Detached homes usually have their own electricity meters. There are two types of meter: a single rate meter and a two-rate meter, which logs your daytime and night time (lower rate) electricity use. Meters for apartment blocks may be installed in a basement or in a meter 'cupboard' under the stairs or outside a group of properties. You should have free access to your meter and should be able read it.

Bills: Electricity is billed every two months, usually after meters have been read. The EAC encourages your to read your own meter (instructions can be found on its website). You should learn to read your electricity bill and check it against the consumption on your meter. You can pay your bills at an EAC customer service centre, by post or by direct debit. Paying by direct debit from a Cypriot bank account is advisable if you own a holiday home in Cyprus. Bills should then be paid automatically on presentation to your bank.

Gas

There's no mains gas in Cyprus although, at the beginning of 2005, the Cypriot government was in discussion with Qatar about the possible supply of liquefied natural gas. If this materialises, it won't be until around 2009, so at least until then, users will be restricted to bottled gas. The price of bottled gas is controlled by the government and is currently around CY£4.50 for a 10kg bottle, which will last an average family around a month when used just for cooking. The initial price of a gas container is around CY£15, and these can be bought from petrol stations, grocery shops and supermarkets. Bear in mind that gas bottles are heavy and have a habit of running out at the most inconvenient times, so keep a spare bottle handy and make sure you know how to change them (get the previous owner or a neighbour to show you).

In rural areas, many people use as many gas appliances as possible, e.g. for cooking, hot water and heating, although for a central heating system you will need a gas tank (e.g. 500 litres). You can have a combined gas hot water and heating system (providing background heat) installed, which is relatively inexpensive as well as being cheap to run.

Water

Water, or rather the lack of it, is a major concern in Cyprus and the price paid for all those sunny days. **As in all hot countries, water is a precious resource and not something simply to pour down the drain! Use of hosepipes in Cyprus is illegal.** The government's Water Development Department (WDD) is responsible for implementing the water policy of the Ministry of Agriculture, Natural Resources and Environment – the body charged with making the most of Cyprus' meagre annual rainfall, which has been decreasing over the last 30 years and is now around 460mm. The WDD is responsible for dams, irrigation, water works, sewage schemes, water treatment and desalination plants.

The natural shortage of water is exacerbated in some areas by poor infrastructure (much is lost from leaking pipes), wastage due to poor irrigation methods, and the huge influx of visitors to resort areas where the local population swells five to tenfold during the summer (the hottest and driest period of the year). In some areas, water shortages can create low water pressure, resulting in insufficient water to take a bath or shower and sometimes no water at all on the upper floors of apartment buildings.

Supply

One of the most important tasks before renting or buying a home in Cyprus is to investigate the reliability of the local water supply and the cost. Ask your prospective neighbours and other local residents for information. In most towns and cities, supplies are adequate, but in rural areas there are often severe shortages in summer unless you have your own well.

Water supply is often suspended for lengthy periods as a conservation measure during periods of high demand and drought. If a water company needs to cut off your supply, e.g. to carry out maintenance work on pipes or installations, it will usually notify you in advance so that you can store water.

Note that in some developments, water is provided by electric pump and therefore if your electricity is cut off, so is your water supply. In communal developments, the tap to turn water on or off is usually located outside properties, so if your water goes off suddenly you should check that someone hasn't switched it off by mistake.

If your property is supplied by a well, remember that a well containing water in winter may be bone dry in summer.

Quality

Water pollution is very low in Cyprus and all water supplied to households by District Water Boards is safe to drink. The Boards regularly test water samples in all areas of consumption around the island, although if your property is in a remote, rural area, it's advisable to get the water supply checked by the local Water Board to ensure that it meets the required standards for drinking water. Despite being **safe** to drink, tap water may taste unpleasant and many people prefer to drink bottled water. Tap water in many areas is very hard and heavy lime deposits occur. You can install filtering, cleansing and softening equipment to improve its quality or a water purification unit to provide drinking water. However some purification systems that operate on the reverse osmosis system waste three times as much water as they produce. Obtain expert advice before installing a system, as not all are effective.

Springs & Wells: Be sure to check the water quality if you're drawing water from a well or a spring. Water from mountain springs may be contaminated by fertilisers and nitrates used in farming, although the Ministry of Agriculture is taking measures to reduce and modify the application of these to avoid contamination. In many areas, septic tanks are used for the disposal of domestic sewage and this can affect water from a well. Your local water board will always test wells for you and tell you whether the water is safe to drink. **Although boiling water will kill any bacteria, it won't remove any toxic substances contained in it.**

Storage

Most modern properties have storage tanks, which are usually large enough to last a family of four for around a week or even longer with careful use. Tanks are usually roof-mounted. Check whether a property has a water storage tank or whether you can install one. If you have a detached house or villa, you can reduce your water costs by collecting and storing rainwater. To save water (and cost), it's possible to use water from baths, showers, kitchens and apparatus such as washing machines and dishwashers to flush toilets or water a garden.

Hot Water

Hot water in apartments may be provided by a central heating source for the whole building, or apartments may have their own water heaters. If you install your own water heater, it should have a capacity of at least 75 litres. Many holiday homes have quite small water boilers, which are inadequate for more than two people.

If you need to install a water heater (or fit a larger one), you should consider the merits of both electric and bottled gas heaters. An electric water boiler with a capacity of 75 litres (sufficient for two people) usually takes between 60 and 90 minutes to heat water to 40 degrees in winter. A gas flow-through water heater is more expensive to purchase and install than an electric water boiler, but you get unlimited hot water immediately whenever you want it. Make sure that a gas heater has a capacity of 10 to 16 litres per minute if you want it for a shower. A gas water heater with a permanent flame may use up to 50 per cent more gas than one without one. A resident family with a constant consumption is better off with an electric heater operating on the night-tariff, while non-residents using a property for short periods will find a self-igniting gas heater more economical.

Costs

The Urban Water Boards in Cyprus, which are administered by the Ministry of the Interior, have no competition, but the service is reasonably priced, and all water is metered. There have been no price rises on the island for more than ten years, although that's set to change as experts have recommended that prices double by 2007. Current prices average 33.5 cents per cubic metre but it's recommended this should increase to 75 cents. There's an initial connection fee of around CY£20 and a standing charge which depends on the area you live in (e.g. CY£24 in Limassol). The cost per cubic metre depends on your consumption. Unlike most consumables, water costs **more** the more you use: e.g. in Limassol, you pay 10 cents per cubic metre if you use less than 40 cubic metres per quarter, but a whopping CY£2 per metre if you use more than three times as much. An average water bill for a family of four is around CY£30 per quarter in most urban areas – usually higher in rural areas.

If your water is supplied from a well, you will have to negotiate the price with the owner of the well; **always check the price before you commit yourself to such a water supply.**

Bills: Bills are sent out quarterly and you can pay them either by going to the offices of your local Urban Water Board, which are listed in the yellow pages, or by direct debit at your bank. It's advisable to arrange direct debit payment if you aren't living permanently in Cyprus. Your estate agent may arrange this on your behalf along with other utilities services. If you don't pay your bill, you will be sent a reminder; if you still fail to pay, you will be charged a CY£10 administrative fee. If you then fail to pay promptly, legal action will be taken and your supply disconnected.

Solar Energy

Cyprus is committed to renewable energy sources, as the country is almost entirely dependent on imported energy products. The one energy source that Cyprus has in abundance is sun and harnessing this energy has proved very successful. More than 90 per cent of households and hotels on the island use solar energy to produce hot water. Even in the winter, most days are sunny enough to provide warm water, although it's advisable to have an immersion heater as a back-up. There are around ten major manufacturers of solar water-heating systems in Cyprus, listed in the yellow pages. The cost of installing a system in an average house is around CY£1,400, which can be recouped in savings on electricity in around four years. See also **Solar Energy** on page 217.

Sewerage

In 1992, the construction of a central sewerage system began and all the main towns and tourist areas now have an efficient mains sewerage system. Nevertheless, in many parts of Cyprus, especially rural areas, septic tanks are used for the disposal of domestic sewage. If your property has a septic tank, bear in mind that this can create unpleasant smells and even become blocked in summer, especially if the property is fully occupied. If you have a septic tank, you should use enzyme bio-digesters and employ bleach and drain unblockers sparingly, as they kill the friendly bacteria that break down the waste and prevent nasty smells.

Mains sewerage charges are reasonable and depend on the assessed value of your property as of 1st January 1980, as determined by the Lands Office. Average annual charges are around CY£50 and bills can be a paid at the office of your local water board, through a bank or by direct debit.

11.

NORTHERN CYPRUS

Many people, especially the British, are tempted by the comparatively low property prices and beautiful unspoiled landscape of northern Cyprus. A report by the *Guardian* newspaper in February 2005 suggested that around 6,000 British citizens have invested in northern Cyprus, buying off plan and even via the internet. If you're considering buying property in this part of Cyprus, it's important to know a little about the island's recent history and the current political climate and **essential** to know their implications for property ownership (see **The Cyprus Problem** below).

You cannot afford to ignore the political situation in northern Cyprus, as it may affect your rights to legal property ownership.

If you do decide to buy a property in northern Cyprus, the remainder of this chapter looks at the most popular areas for homebuyers (including average prices), an overview of the buying process, and various practical considerations, such as the language and currency, how to get there and how to get around once you're there.

THE CYPRUS PROBLEM

Cyprus is effectively two countries: the Republic of Cyprus and what's known as the Turkish Republic of Northern Cyprus (TRNC). The Republic of Cyprus is what the majority of people mean when they refer to Cyprus. It's administered by a Greek Cypriot government, is internationally recognised and encompasses the southern two-thirds of the island. The TRNC, recognised internationally only by Turkey, is administered by a Turkish Cypriot government and covers the remaining northern third of the island. The Republic of Cyprus, joined the European Union on 1st May 2004, but the TRNC did not. Cyprus is a divided island and its capital, Nicosia, is the last divided city in Europe. This chapter explains why the country is divided, with a brief history and background to the current situation. It also looks at the effects this division may have on homebuyers and examines the practicalities and the potential problems associated with buying property in the TRNC, which is referred to in this book as northern Cyprus.

History

Cyprus has long been a magnet for a succession of invading armies, settlers and immigrants, thanks to its strategic position between Europe,

Asia and Africa. Although never invaded or ruled by the Greeks, the island has for 1,500 years been under their cultural influence; but the two most recent ruling powers, the Ottoman Turks and the British, also left a lasting mark on the island, so that modern Cyprus is a mixture of Greek, Turkish and British influences. These influences have combined, directly or indirectly, to create the political situation in modern Cyprus.

Britain took control of Cyprus in 1878 from the Turks, who had ruled the island since 1571, although Turkey retained sovereignty until 1914, when Britain annexed Cyprus, and continued to rule the island until 1960, when the independent Republic of Cyprus was created. Although Cyprus undoubtedly prospered under British rule, it was also a period of growing political conflict between Cypriots of Greek and Turkish origin. The Greek and Turkish communities lived side by side, but politically there were serious differences about the division of power between the two. This underlying conflict continued after independence, culminating in the Turkish invasion of the island in 1974.

On 15th July 1974, extremist National Guard officers from mainland Greece staged a military coup in Cyprus with the intention of overthrowing and assassinating the Cypriot president, Archbishop Makarios. The coup was backed by the military junta which governed Greece at the time. The extremists wanted Cyprus to establish what was called *enosis* (political union with Greece). Archbishop Makarios survived the coup and escaped to the UK. Nikos Sampson, a Greek Cypriot guerrilla leader, whose stated goal was *enosis*, was proclaimed the new president of Cyprus. Sampson's antipathy towards Turkish Cypriots was well known and, concerned by the possibility of a unified Greece and Cyprus, Turkish troops invaded the northern part of the island on 20th July 1974. They overturned the new government and, after fierce fighting, eventually took control of 38 per cent of the island. Some 200,000 Greek Cypriots were evacuated or fled to southern Cyprus and 100,000 Turkish Cypriots fled to the north. An enormous number of refugees were created and the economic cost to Cyprus was huge. Cyprus remains divided, more than 30 years later, and while the Republic of Cyprus in the south has performed an impressive economic recovery, the Turkish Republic of Northern Cyprus remains politically isolated and relatively poor.

Following the invasion, a United Nations peacekeeping force was established on the island, maintaining a buffer zone between the two parts of the island. The Green Line, as it's called, is patrolled by Greek Cypriot soldiers on the southern side and Turkish soldiers from the mainland on the northern side, with UN soldiers in between.

After partition, neither Greek nor Turkish Cypriots were allowed to move freely between the north and the south of the island. When the

Turkish Cypriot government relaxed border restrictions in April 2003, many Cypriots had their first chance to see the other side of the Green Line for 29 years. Thousands of Cypriots from both sides of the border returned to their old homes and there were emotional meetings with old friends and neighbours. Nevertheless, many Cypriots still cannot move freely between the two parts of the island.

Now that the Republic of Cyprus has joined the European Union, EU citizens (including Greek Cypriots) should be able to move freely from one side to the other. In theory, any restriction of free movement is in contravention of EU legislation, but some restrictions remain (see below).

Cyprus & the European Union

It was hoped that EU accession would contribute to a solution for Cyprus. When the European Commission began accession negotiations with Cyprus in 1998, it made it clear that it wanted Cyprus to join the EU as a united country on 1st May 2004. As a result, there were renewed efforts to find a solution to the division of the country and United Nations Secretary General, Kofi Annan, was called on to help. He drew up comprehensive proposals for reunification of the island, which would allow both the Greek and Turkish Cypriot administrations considerable autonomy, the right of return to their homes for Greek Cypriots and an alternating Greek/Turkish presidency. During the spring and summer of 2002, frequent talks were held between the leaders of the two sides, but they ended in stalemate. Negotiations were restarted in 2003, but agreement still couldn't be reached.

In 2004, with Cyprus' EU entry approaching, Kofi Annan put a revised agreement to both communities that allowed a referendum on both sides of the Green Line. On 24th April 2004, the peace plan was put to the vote and although 65 per cent of Turkish Cypriots accepted it, it was rejected by 76 per cent of Greek Cypriots. Greek Cypriots were unhappy about three main aspects of the plan:

- Turkey would be allowed to keep large numbers of troops on the island;

- An alternating presidency would be allowed despite Turkish Cypriots being in a minority;

- A limit had been put on the number of refugees who would get their homes back.

The Annan Plan had failed and the Republic of Cyprus joined the EU without the TRNC in May 2004.

The Future

Although the Annan Plan is still on the table, no one expects a solution in the near future and political stalemate remains between the two sides. The key to reunification may lie with Turkey's aspirations to become an EU member. Accession negotiations begin in October 2005 and Turkey knows that the Republic of Cyprus can veto its membership. There's renewed hope that an agreement may be reached during Turkey's accession negotiations. Increased movement between the two sides is encouraging a new atmosphere, and in May 2005 Turkish Cypriots elected the moderate Mehmet Ali Talat as their leader, ending decades of hawkish rule by Rauf Denktash and raising hopes of reunification. Although it may be a long time coming, an agreement will be eventually be reached and Cyprus will become a united island once more.

Relevance for Property Buyers

A political agreement could have far-reaching effects for people who buy what was, before the invasion of 1974, Greek Cypriot land or property in northern Cyprus, although it's almost impossible to know what these might be.

 If you're considering buying a home in northern Cyprus, it's important to understand that feelings run high on both sides of the Green Line.

Turkish Cypriots and those selling property there (many of them British) will welcome you and often play down the potential problems. Property sales to foreigners benefit the ailing Turkish Cypriot economy and increase international acceptance of Turkish controlled northern Cyprus. On the other hand, Greek Cypriots, perhaps understandably, point out the illegality and immorality of buying property or land that's rightfully owned by Greek Cypriots. There are many Greek Cypriots living in the Republic of Cyprus who are refugees from the north and who believe that even visiting the north while it's still under Turkish control is morally wrong.

 Morals aside, if you decide to buy property in northern Cyprus, you must ensure that you will have legal ownership of the land and property that's being sold to you, even if Cyprus is reunited.

Title

It's essential to check the title deed of a property before buying it. When Greek Cypriots were forced to leave their homes in the north, their properties and land were taken over by the Turkish authorities, who used them to house Turkish settlers from the mainland and Turkish Cypriot refugees who had moved to the northern Cyprus after the invasion of 1974.

SURVIVAL TIP
It's vital that you make absolutely
sure you aren't buying property or land that was
appropriated from a Greek Cypriot. If you do so and
Cyprus is reunited, the original owner could
reclaim the property or land and you could
be left with nothing.

The European Court of Human Rights has ruled that Greek Cypriots are the 'only true and lawful owners' of their appropriated land and will never lose their legal title. In a highly publicised case, a British couple has been ordered to knock down the house they built on land owned by a Greek Cypriot before 1974. According to EU law, the owners of the land could have the judgement enforced in the UK and the couple could lose their home there too.

As well as having the status of the title deed confirmed by an independent lawyer before you agree to purchase, you should do so yourself by asking to see the deed at the Lands Office in North Nicosia. There are three possibilities: the property has no title deed; it has a deed with a number prefaced by the letters 'TRNC'; or it has a deed with only a number, i.e. the deed dates from before the 1974 invasion and ownership hasn't changed since then (known as a 'clean' title deed). The status of each of these types of property is explained below.

'Clean' Title Deed: The only type of totally secure title deed (known as a clean freehold title deed) is one issued before the Turkish invasion, which won't be prefaced by the letters 'TRNC'. These are internationally recognised deeds (and can be checked at the Lands Office in the Republic). Clean title deeds are usually listed first by agents, but unfortunately they're virtually impossible to find.

TRNC Title Deed: A TRNC (referring to the Turkish Republic of Northern Cyprus) title deed (called in Turkish a *kesin tasarruf* or 'absolute possession' title deed) is the one most commonly found in northern Cyprus. It relates to property or land which was in Greek Cypriot ownership before 1974. When Turkish Cypriot refugees came to the north after the invasion, the authorities assessed the value of what they had lost in the south and awarded them a certain number of points. These points often allowed them to take possession of a Greek Cypriot house as a form of compensation. In return for the points, they had to sign over their properties in the south to the TRNC government, who held them pending a negotiated settlement between the two sides. Properties may have also been 'given' to settlers from the Turkish mainland and it's also believed TRNC properties were issued to military servicemen as a reward for their services on Cyprus.

If the number on the deed has TRNC in front of it, you should be very wary of proceeding with a purchase.

 The authorities and many estate agents may advise you that properties with a TRNC title deed are safe to purchase. However, these title deeds are recognised only by Turkey and by the government of northern Cyprus, and their purchase is considered illegal by all other authorities.

No Title Deed: If there are no title deeds for the land or property that you intend to buy, it could have been Turkish- or Greek Cypriot-owned before 1974. However, the absence of title deeds mean that its ownership is questionable. Properties without title deeds are often available at 'bargain' prices, but a bargain could turn out to be an expensive disaster if the real owner returns to claim after Cyprus' reunification!

 Purchasing a property without title deeds is illegal and is considered *very* unsafe, even by those estate agents who consider TRNC titles safe.

GETTING THERE

The main airport in northern Cyprus is Ercan (*Tymbou*, ☎ 231-4806), around 18km (11mi) south-east of Nicosia, which handles the majority of flights. However, because of an IATA boycott of the airport, **you cannot fly directly to Ercan from any country other than Turkey.** This means that there's an obligatory stopover in mainland Turkey (at Istanbul, Izmir, Dalaman or Antalya), where you may have to change planes. This naturally extends travel times considerably. **Don't believe any airline that offers 'direct' flights to northern Cyprus.** 'Direct' simply means you stay on the plane, but you must still stop in Turkey. Stopovers and changes of planes are usually handled efficiently, but it still means a journey time from the UK of six or seven hours, which is a major consideration if you're thinking of buying a holiday home in northern Cyprus.

It's possible to fly to Larnaca or Paphos (see page 63) and cross the border, subject to current restrictions, which may make it difficult to cross back into the Republic to catch your flight home (see **Moving Between North & South** on page 256).

Airlines that fly into Ercan are Cyprus Turkish Airlines (CTA), the official state airline, Turkish Airlines and an independent airline, Onur Air. CTA offers flights from many European airports, including London Heathrow and Gatwick (three times per week), Stansted (daily), Belfast and Glasgow (once a week) and Manchester (twice a week). Turkish Airlines flies from major cities worldwide, including London Heathrow and Manchester. As stated above, all international flights are via Turkey. The Heathrow flight stops in Istanbul and many people make a virtue of necessity by taking a break in the Turkish capital. Onur Air offers flights from Stansted (three times per week) and Manchester (once a week), stopping in Istanbul.

Visas & Entry Requirements

All nationals of the EU, Switzerland, Iceland, Liechtenstein, Norway, the US and Canada, Australia, New Zealand and Singapore can enter northern Cyprus with a valid passport and stay for up to 90 days without a visa.

 If you have a northern Cyprus stamp in your passport, you will be refused entry to the Republic of Cyprus and possibly Greece too. When entering northern Cyprus, you should ask customs officials to stamp a separate piece of paper, rather than your passport. This is a commonly accepted procedure.

If you wish to stay in northern Cyprus longer than 90 days, you must obtain a temporary residence permit, which is issued at your local police station. Temporary residence permits are valid for a year and can be obtained by completing an application form and supplying four passport photographs. You must also have a medical to prove you're free of TB and AIDS. Permits are usually automatically renewed annually and you may apply for permanent residence after five years of residence in the TRNC. Further information is available from the Migration Department of the Ministry of the Interior in north Nicosia (☎ 228-3344, ✉ info@trnc.gov com).

GETTING AROUND

Road

During the last few years, roads in northern Cyprus have been improved considerably thanks to financial aid from Turkey. There's a good dual-carriageway between Ercan airport and Nicosia and the main roads between Nicosia and Famagusta and Nicosia and Güzelyurt have recently been upgraded. Driving is on the left as it is in the Republic of Cyprus.

Car Hire

You may not hire a car and drive it over the Green Line in either direction. To hire a car in northern Cyprus, you must be at least 25 and have a full driving licence from your home country. As in the Republic of Cyprus, the condition of rental cars often leaves much to be desired. If possible, test a car before you rent it and in particular check the efficiency of the brakes! Rates start at around UK£15 per day. Hire cars are fitted with distinctive red plates with numbers prefixed by a 'Z'.

Public Transport

There are no rail services in northern Cyprus, where buses and taxis vary in terms of reliability and standard of service.

Buses

If you arrive at Ercan airport, there's no public bus service from the airport (even into Nicosia city), so you must take a taxi from the airport to your destination (see below), unless you're staying at one of the larger hotels or arrive as part of a package holiday, in which case you will usually be met at the airport. You can get a bus **back** to Ercan airport from the Cyprus Turkish Airlines Office in the new town, Bedrettin Demirel Caddesi (☎ 227-1240). Buses depart two hours before flights leave Ercan airport.

Buses serve central and suburban Nicosia city and operate between all the main towns, but these are less frequent after 5pm and at weekends.

Taxis

Taxis are widely available throughout northern Cyprus, although they aren't metered. Ask the driver to quote you the fare before getting into the taxi. You can pay in either Turkish liras or pounds sterling (but change will be given in liras). Fares from the airport are approximately UK£5 into Nicosia, UK£20 to Kyrenia and UK£25 to Famagusta.

There's also a shared taxi system, using minibuses (*dolmuslies*), between Nicosia, Kyrenia and Famagusta.

Moving Between North & South

Movement between northern Cyprus and the Republic has become increasingly easy since 2003, when the Turkish Cypriot government relaxed restrictions, and particularly since May 2004, when the Republic of Cyprus became part of the EU – especially for EU citizens. Nevertheless, **you may not drive a hired car over the Green Line in either direction**.

Before Cyprus' EU accession, tourists were denied entry to the Republic of Cyprus if they had entered via a port or airport in the north, in accordance with the Republic's Aliens and Immigration Law. They could even be arrested or deported. (Until 2003, tourists in the south weren't allowed to stay overnight in the north.) However, this law is now at odds with the EU's policy of free movement and specifically with the Green Line regulation (that the Green Line isn't an external border of the EU), which the government of the Republic agreed to implement on accession. So, in theory, the Cypriot authorities may now only hand out information leaflets about the situation in northern Cyprus. Nevertheless, just after EU accession in May 2004, the Cypriot justice minister warned that those who enter the Republic through what's considered an illegal port or airport (i.e. any port or airport in northern Cyprus) could face on-the-spot fines of between CY£20 and CY£500.

In practice, freedom of movement between north and south depends largely on the point at which you cross the Green Line. Until recently, the only recognised crossing points were Ledra Palace and Agios Dhometis in the old city of Nicosia, but in 18th April 2005 the EU announced two new crossing points: Ledra Street, in Nicosia city, and Zodhia, just south of Morfou. However, you should check that these new points are operational before attempting to use them. **Note that parts of the 'buffer zone' between north and south are mined and that there are no recognised crossing points inside the British base areas in the south-east of the island.** The EU is pressing for amendments to the Green Line regulation, including freer movement of people and goods, the opening of more crossing points and an EU-sponsored de-mining programme for the buffer zone.

LANGUAGE

Although Turkish is the official language in northern Cyprus, English is widely used and understood. Many hotels employ German-, French- and Arabic-speaking staff. However, in more remote areas, few Turkish Cypriots speak English.

CURRENCY

The currency in northern Cyprus changed on 1st January 2005 and is now the new Turkish lira (*Yeni Türk Lirasi*/YTL), which is roughly equivalent to CY£0.35 or GB£0.40 – in other words, there are approximately three liras to the Cyprus pound and two-and-a-half to the British pound. The lira is divided into 100 New Kurus (*Yeni Kurus*/YKr). Coins are minted in denominations of YKr5, 10, 25 and 50 and YTL1, and there are notes of YTL1, 5, 10, 20, 50 and 100.

Unfortunately (for foreigners), the old currency is still in circulation and will continue to be valid until 31st December 2005 (old notes can be exchanged for new ones until 31st December 2016!), so you may need to familiarise yourself with it. There's no risk of confusion, however, as an old Turkish lira (TL) is worth one-millionth of a new Turkish lira, so a glass of Turkish tea that now costs YTL1 previously cost TL1 million!

There are no restrictions on the import and export of foreign currency. Most foreign currencies and travellers' cheques are accepted in banks, exchange bureaux and hotels, and major credit cards are accepted in the main towns.

GEOGRAPHY & POPULAR LOCATIONS

Northern Cyprus is dominated by the Kyrenia mountain range, which runs along most of the northern coastline. As it extends east, it loses height along to the Karpas Peninsula, where long stretches of deserted beach can be found. To the south of the Kyrenia range is Nicosia (*Lefkosa*), the northern part of whose capital city (of the same name) is the capital of northern Cyprus. The most popular locations with tourists and homebuyers are the towns of Famagusta (*Gazimagusa* or *Magusa*) and Kyrenia (*Girne*) and the city of Nicosia and their surrounding areas.

 If you're thinking of buying land or property anywhere in northern Cyprus, check its ownership beforehand (see page 252). Your new home may be being built on a legal and political minefield.

Famagusta Town (*Magusa*)

The district of Famagusta (*Ammochostos*) incorporates the Karpas Peninsula on the far eastern coast of the island. Its capital, Famagusta town, which is south of the peninsula, on the east coast of the island, enjoyed a booming tourist industry during the '60s and '70s, but after the Turkish invasion of 1974, the area was 'closed down'. It remains that way to this day, and part of it resembles a ghost town with abandoned high-rise hotels. However, the people of Famagusta town still extend a warm welcome to visitors and there has recently been a concerted effort to turn the town around and make it a more inviting place.

There are many historic buildings and monuments in Famagusta town. Like Nicosia's, the old town area is enclosed by 16th century Venetian walls, which some say were Shakespeare's inspiration for *Othello*. There's the remains of a Venetian Palace and the magnificent Gothic Cathedral of St. Nicholas, which was converted into a mosque by the Ottomans.

Famagusta town isn't as popular as Kyrenia town with foreign homebuyers, although there are several developments under construction in surrounding areas, such as the hilltop village of Bogaz and the villages of Iskele and Vrysoullies. Average prices are under GB£50,000 for a two- or three-bedroom apartment, under GB£100,000 for a three-bedroom semi-detached house and around GB£130,000 for a detached villa.

Kyrenia (*Girne*)

The district of Kyrenia, on the north coast of Cyprus, is considered one of the most beautiful parts of Cyprus and it's the most popular area in the north for both visitors and homebuyers. Most of those who buy in northern Cyprus settle in the foothills of the Kyrenia mountains. The coast of Turkey is around 90km (55mi) away. Kyrenia town is also beautiful. The harbour, a favourite spot for tourists, is dominated by an enormous Byzantine castle with a backdrop of tall Gothic-looking mountains overlooking the sea. Although the town is being increasingly developed, there are as yet only a few shops and restaurants. For many foreign buyers this is part of its attraction.

Although some buyers are keen to restore old houses, most prefer modern properties, and developers and estate agents (mainly British) are moving in to take advantage of a burgeoning market. Developers are busy building new developments, almost all for British clients.

Older properties to restore can be found in the peaceful hillside village of Bellapais, which is just ten minutes from Kyrenia. Bellapais is famous for its abbey and the fact that the author Laurence Durrell was the first foreigner to buy and restore a home there, in the '50s. You can buy a 'ruin' for as little as GB£15,000 and a restored three-bedroom restored village house for less than GB£70,000. Luxurious modern properties are less of a bargain, however, and a large four-bedroom villa can cost GB£300,000.

Modern developments can be found in and around Çatalköy, Edremit, Esentepe and the village of Lapta. One-bedroom apartments cost around GB£50,000 and three-bedroom bungalows from GB£65,000 to GB£150,000, depending on the area. Larger villas cost around GB£200,000.

Nicosia City (*Lefkosa*)

The northern half of Nicosia city is rather overshadowed by its southern half (see page 53). It's far quieter and has rather lost out to Kyrenia town, which takes the lion's share of tourism and, more recently, property development. North Nicosia city has changed little since 1974, but it does its best to welcome the visitors that come from the south to experience a little of life on the other side of the Green Line. Like the southern part of the city, it isn't as popular with foreign buyers as some other areas, although there are plenty of beautiful old stone houses that have been restored.

PURCHASE PROCEDURE

Once the price of a property has been agreed, a lawyer will draw up a sale contract detailing the terms of the purchase and any conditions, and both parties must sign it. It's likely that the contract will be in Turkish so (unless your Turkish is fluent) you will need to get it translated so that you understand exactly what you're signing. If you're using one of the many British estate agents in northern Cyprus, he will usually arrange this for you.

You will be asked to pay a 10 per cent deposit on signing, and your lawyer will then apply to the Ministry of the Interior for permission for you to buy the property. This can take several months but, once permission has been granted, the balance is payable and the transfer of the title can take place.

Normally a buyer pays 6 per cent of the purchase price in tax and the seller pays 3 per cent (on a first sale) or 6 per cent (on subsequent sales). Generally, the purchase price is under-declared to reduce tax liability although this is illegal. VAT isn't charged on house building as it is in the Republic of Cyprus, although in February 2005 there was a report in a local newspaper that the government was planning to charge foreign buyers VAT at 15 per cent on new properties. Check this carefully before you commit to purchase a property.

ESTATE AGENTS

If you decide to buy in northern Cyprus, it's advisable (although no guarantee) to use an agent who has long-standing experience of the property market in the Turkish Republic of Northern Cyprus and knows the possible pitfalls facing foreign buyers. There's no shortage of estate agents and more and more have been setting up business in the north as the property market has shown increasing signs of potential growth, but estate agents in northern Cyprus aren't licensed by law as they are in the Republic of Cyprus. **Exercise extreme caution and check the credentials of any estate agent you use.** Talk to other expatriate house buyers and get their recommendations.

BANKS & FINANCE

Banks in northern Cyprus aren't as reliable as those in the Republic of Cyprus and many of them folded in 2001, along with banks on the Turkish mainland. You can open an account (in either Turkish liras or sterling) with a local bank, but it's preferable to use one that has branches in your home country. The Turkish Bank has branches in London, and the British bank HSBC has branches in Kyrenia and north Nicosia city. You can change money at foreign exchange offices, which are usually open from 8.30am to 1pm and from 2 to 5pm. **It's impossible to get a mortgage in northern Cyprus, although developers may offer an instalment payment plan.**

POSTAL SERVICES

Postal services are efficient from northern Cyprus and costs are similar to those in the Republic (see page 221). Post offices are open from 7.30am to 2pm and from 4 to 6pm Mondays to Fridays and from 8.30am to 12.30pm on Saturdays. All northern Cyprus addresses must finish with 'Mersin 10, Turkey' and not 'northern Cyprus' or 'the Turkish Republic of Northern Cyprus' or simply 'Cyprus'.

TELEPHONE SERVICES

Netas, the northern Cyprus telephone company, isn't noted for its efficiency. It can take up to a month to get a line installed in an urban property and **much** longer (up to two years) in a more remote area with no telegraph poles. Telephone lines cost around GB£25 to install.

When dialling a number in northern Cyprus, you must first dial the international code for Turkey (90) and then the northern Cyprus code (392), followed by the number. Even if you're dialling from one side of the Green Line to the other, you must use the full code and will be charged for an international call. It's advisable to use a mobile telephone with roaming facilities instead, but make sure it's one that you can use in both parts of Cyprus. Mobile phone companies in the north are Telsim and Türkcell.

UTILITIES

Power cuts and water shortages are commonplace in northern Cyprus. Most people have rechargeable lights and surge protectors on their computers to prevent damage during dangerous power surges. The worst water shortages are inland from the Kyrenia Mountains. Your solicitor can help you open water and electricity accounts.

APPENDICES

APPENDIX A: USEFUL ADDRESSES

This appendix is divided into three sections: Republic of Cyprus, northern Cyprus, and other countries.

REPUBLIC OF CYPRUS

Embassies & High Commissions

All embassies and high commissions are located in the capital, Nicosia (*Lefkosa*). Before writing or calling in person you should telephone to confirm that you have the correct office. The area code for Nicosia is 22 (not shown below).

Australia: Gonia Leoforou Stasinou & Annis Komninis 4, 2nd Floor, 1060 Nicosia (☎ 753 001/756 002).

Belgium: 6 Idis Street, 2066 Nicosia, PO Box 22023, 1516 Nicosia (☎ 444 533).

Bulgaria: Konstantinou Palaiologou 13, 2406 Egkomi, Nicosia (☎ 672 486).

China: Archimidous 28, Egkomi, PO Box 24531,1300 Nicosia (☎ 352 182).

Cuba: 1 Androcleous Street (corner Thoukididou), Nicosia (☎ 769 743).

Czech Republic: Arsinois 48, Akropolis, PO Box 25202, 1307 Nicosia (☎ 421 118).

Egypt: Leoforos Aigyptou 3, PO Box 21752, 1097 Nicosia (☎ 680 650).

France: Ploutarchou 6, 2406 Egkomi, PO Box 21671, 1512 Nicosia (☎ 779 910).

Germany: Nikitara 10, 1080 Nicosia, PO Box 21795, 1513 Nicosia (☎ 451 145).

Greece: Leoforos Vyronos 8-10, PO Box 21799, 1513 Nicosia (☎ 445 111).

Hungary: Pringipos Karolou 2, 2373, Agios Dometios, Nicosia (☎ 459 130).

India: Indira Gkandi 3, Montparnasse Hill, Egkomi, PO Box 25544, 2413 Nicosia (☎ 351 741/351 170).

Iran: Armenias 42, Akropolis, PO Box 28908, 2084 Nicosia (☎ 314 459/315 896).

Ireland: Aiantas 7, Agioi Omologites, 1082 Nicosia, PO Box 23848 1686 Nicosia (☎ 818 183).

Israel: I. Grypari 4, PO Box 25159, 1307 Nicosia (☎ 369 500).

Italy: 25 Martiou 11, 2408 Egkomi, Nicosia (☎ 357 635–6/358 258).

Lebanon: Chiou 6, 1101, Agios Dometios, PO Box 21924, 1515 Nicosia (☎ 878 282–3)

Libya: Leoforos Stassinou 7, PO Box 22487, 1522 Nicosia (☎ 460 055).

Netherlands: 34 Dimosthenis Severis Ave, 1080 Nicosia, PO Box 23835, 1686 Nicosia (☎ 873 666/872 393-4).

Poland: Leoforos Tzon Kennedy 12–14, 1087 Nicosia, PO Box 22743, 1523 Nicosia (☎ 753 517/753 784).

Romania: Pireos 27 Strovolos, 2023 Nicosia, PO Box 22210, 1518 Nicosia (☎ 495 333).

Russia: Gonia Agiou Prokopiou & Arch. Makariou III, Egkomi, PO Box 21845, 1514 Nicosia (☎ 774 622/772 141).

Serbia & Montenegro: Vasillissis Olgas 2, Egkomi, 1101 Nicosia (☎ 777 511).

Slovakia: Kalamatas 4, 2002 Strovolos, PO Box 21165, 1503 Nicosia (☎ 879 681).

Spain: Leoforos Strovolou 32, 2018 Strovolos, PO Box 28349, 2093 Strovolos, Nicosia (☎ 450 410).

Switzerland: Themistokli Dervi 46, MEDCON Bldg., 6th floor, PO Box 20729, 1663 Nicosia (☎ 466 800).

Syria: Nikodimou Mylona 24, 1071 Nicosia, PO Box 21891 1514 Nicosia (☎ 817 333).

Ukraine: Miaouli 10, Makedonitissa, Egkomi, Nicosia (☎ 464 380).

United Kingdom: Alexander Pallis Street, PO Box 21978, 1587 Nicosia (☎ 861 100/861 369 (visa enquiries), 🖥 www.britain. org.cy).

United States of America: Gonia Metochiou & Ploutarchou, Egkomi, 2406 Nicosia (☎ 776 400).

Delegation of the European Union in Cyprus: Leof. Archiepiskopou Makariou III & Agapinoros 2, Irish Tower, 1076 Nicosia, PO Box 23480, 1683 Nicosia (☎ 817 770).

Government Departments

Director of Customs, Corner Michalaki Karaoli & Gregori Afxentiou, 1096 Nicosia (☎ 22-601 657, ✉ headquarters@ customs.mof.gov.cy).

Migration Department (Ministry of the Interior), 1457 Nicosia (☎ 22-804 502, ✉ migrations@crmd.moi.gov.cy). General enquiries and applications to Immigration Offices in relevant area (see below).

Ministry for Commerce, Industry and Tourism, 6 Andreas Araouzos St.,1421 Nicosia (☎ 22-867 100, 🖥 www.mcit.gov.cy). Trade, export and consumer information.

Ministry of Education and Culture, Corner Thoucydides & Kimon, 1434 Nicosia (☎ 22-800 600/700/938, 🖥 www.moec. gov.cy).

Ministry of Finance, Corner M. Karaolis & G. Afxentiou Streets, 1439 Nicosia (☎ 22-601 149, 🖥 www.mof.gov.cy). Customs and excise, VAT and inland revenue information.

Ministry of Foreign Affairs, Dem. Severis Ave., 1447 Nicosia (☎ 22-300 713, 🖥 www.mfa.gov.cy). Consular and diplomatic information.

Ministry of the Interior, Dem. Severis Ave., 1453 Nicosia (☎ 22-867 625, 🖥 www.moi.gov.cy). Immigration and visa information, and Town Planning, District Administation, Lands and Surveys departments.

Ministry of Labour & Social Insurance, 7 Byron Avenue, 1463 Nicosia (☎ 22-401 600, 🖥 www.mlsi.gov.cy). Social security and health and safety at work information. The website contains a full list of District Labour Offices.

Road Transport Department, Archeon 28, 1424 Nicosia (☎ 22-807 139, 💻 www.mcw.gov.cy).

District Inland Revenue Offices

Larnaca: Griva Digheni 42, 6045 Larnaca (☎ 24-803 658).

Limasssol: Gladstonos 3, 3002 Limassol (☎ 25-803 700).

Nicosia: M. Paridi & Byzantiou, 2064 Strovolos, Nicosia (☎ 22-807 412).

Paphos: Corner N. Nicolaidi & Digheni Akrita, 8010 Paphos (☎ 26-802 100).

District Immigration Offices

Larnaca: Larnaca Police Station, Piale Pasia, Larnaca (☎ 24-804 242).

Limassol: Limassol Police Station, Kyrillou Loukareos, Kakos Center, Limassol (☎ 25-805 200).

Nicosia: Nicosia Police Station, Parodos Leoforou, RIC, Nicosia (general information ☎ 22-802 334; registration ☎ 22-802 348).

Paphos: Pafos Police Station,Ypolohagou N.Papageorgiou, Polykatikia, PA.SY.DI, 1st floor, 8011 Pafos (☎ 26-806 200).

Miscellaneous

Areti Charidemou & Associates, 21 Vasili Michailidi Street, 3026 Limassol/PO Box 54708, 3727 Limassol (☎ 25-746 103, ✉ info@aretilawyers.com). Lawyer.

Association of Cyprus Commercial Banks, 1E Menendrou Street, 1st floor, PO Box 23363, 1682 Nicosia (☎ 22-664 293, 💻 www.accb.com.cy).

Central Bank of Cyprus, 80 Kennedy Avenue, PO Box 25529, 1395 Nicosia (☎ 22-714 100, 💻 www.central bank.gov.cy).

Chr. Calogirou Ltd, 6e-6f, 6th floor, Roussos Centre Point, Pentadromos Square, Limassol/PO Box 50077, 3600 Limassol (☎ 25-362 798, 💻 www.bestcyprusproperties.com). Registered estate agent and member of CREAA.

Cyprus Automobile Association (CAA), 12 Chrysanthou Mylona Street, 2014 Nicosia (☎ 22 313233, 💻 www.cyprusaa. org). Maps of Cyprus, information on importing a car, 24-hour recovery assistance for members.

Cyprus Bar Association, 23 Loukis Akritas St., Ayios Dhometios, CY-1508 Nicosia (☎ 22-779 156, 💻 www.cyprus-barassociation.org).

Cyprus Broadcasting Corporation, CyBC Street, Nicosia 2120 (☎ 22-862 000, 💻 www.cybc.com.cy).

Cyprus Chamber of Commerce and Industry, Chamber Building, PO Box 21455, 1509 Nicosia (☎ 22-889 840, 💻 www. cci.org.cy).

Cyprus Consumers' Association, Head Office, 5 Acropolis Avenue, 2000 Strovolos, PO Box 24874 1304 Nicosia (☎ 22-516 112-4, 💻 www.cyprusconsumers.org.cy).

Cyprus International Business Association, 47 Athalassas Avenue, 4th floor No. 402, 2012 Strovolos Nicosia/PO Box 23933, 1687 Nicosia (☎ 22-512 722, 💻 www.ciba-cy.org). Promotes the interests of the international business community in Cyprus.

Cyprus International Financial Services Association (CIFSA), PO Box 23403, Suite 402, 47 Athalassa Avenue, Nicosia 1683 (☎ 22-496 179, 💻 www.cifsa.org).

Cyprus News Agency, Kastorias Street 7, Strovolos, PO Box 23947, 1687 Nicosia (☎ 22-499 662, 💻 www.cna.org.cy).

Cyprus Real Estate Agents Association (CREAA), 17 Hadjiloizi Michaelides Street, PO Box 50563, 3041 Limassol (☎ 25-367 467, ✉ solo@cytanet.com.cy).

Cyprus Scientific and Technical Chamber (ETEK, ☎ 22-877 644).

Cyprus Stock Exchange, Kampou St, IMC Strovolos, PO Box 25427, 1309 Nicosia (☎ 22-712 300, 💻 www.cse.com.cy).

Cyprus Telecommunications Authority (CYTA), Head Office, Telecommunications Str., Strovolos, Ô.Ê.24929, 1396, Nicosia (☎ 22-701 000, 💻 www.cyta.com.cy). The website gives details of CYTA Customer Service offices throughout the island.

Cyprus Tourism Organisation, Head Office, Leoforos Lemesou 19, PO Box 24535, 1390 Nicosia (☎ 22-691 100, 💻 www.cyprustourism.org). There are CTO offices in all main towns.

Electricity Authority of Cyprus (EAC), 11 Amphipoleos Street, 2025 Strovolos, 1399 Nicosia (☎ 22-201 000, 💻 www.eac.com.cy). The website has addresses of regional customer service centres and a detailed explanation of each pricing structure.

Employers' and Industrialists' Federation, 30 Grivas Dhigenis Ave., PO Box 1657, 1511 Nicosia (☎ 22-44 5102, 💻 www.oeb-eif.org).

Living Cyprus, JAF Marketing Ltd (☎ UK 0845-095 3486, 💻 www.livingcyprus.com/www.cypruspropertydreams.com). Works with an estate agent in Cyprus and can provide excellent, detailed information about all aspects of buying a property and living in Cyprus. The website is comprehensive and has good links.

UK Citizens' Association (☎ 25-344 578, 💻 www.ukca.com.cy). Branches in Larnaca, Limassol and Paphos.

NORTHERN CYPRUS

Cyprus Turkish Airlines, Bedreddin Demirel Avenue, Yenisehr, Lefkosa, Mersin 10, Turkey (☎ 228-3901, ✉ info@kthy.aero).

Ministry of the Interior, Lefkosa, Mersin 10, Turkey (☎ 228-3344, ✉ info@trnc.gov com).

Most other government department addresses are as above; these and some telephone numbers are listed on the TRNC government website (💻 www.trncgov.com).

OTHER COUNTRIES

Canada

Consulate General of the Republic of Cyprus, 365 Bloor Street East, Suite 1010, PO Box 43, Toronto, Ontario M4W 3L4 (☎ 416-944 0998, ✉ consulcy@ rogers.com).

United Kingdom

Cyprus Tourist Office, 17 Hanover Street, London W1R 0AA (☎ 020-7569 8800/8808, ✉ informationcto@btconnect.com).

Cyprus Trade Centre, 29 Princes Street, London W1R 7RG (☎ 020-7629 6288).

High Commission of the Republic of Cyprus, 93 Park Street, London W1K 7ET (☎ 020-7499 8272–4, 020-7629 5350 (consular section), ✉ cyphclondon@dial.pipex.com).

Inland Revenue International Centre for Non-Residents (☎ 0151-210 2222, 🖥 www.inlandrevenue.gov.uk).

International Pensions Service (☎ 0191-218 7777, 🖥 www.dwp.gov.uk). Useful information for UK retirees considering a move abroad.

North Cyprus Tourist Office Representative, 29 Bedford Square, London WC1B 3EG (☎ 020-7631 1920).

United States

Consulate General of the Republic of Cyprus, 13 East, 40th Street, New York, NY 10016 (☎ 212-686 6016–7).

Cyprus Tourism Organization, 13 East 40th Street, New York, NY 10016 (☎ 212-683-5280, ✉ gocyprus@aol.com).

Cyprus Trade Center, 13 East 40th Street, New York, NY 10016 (☎ 212-213 9100).

Embassy of the Republic of Cyprus, 2211 R Street NW, Washington DC 20008 (☎ 202-462 5772, 202-232 8993 (press office), 🖥 www.cyprusembassy.net).

APPENDIX B: FURTHER INFORMATION

English-language Newspapers & Magazines

General News

Cyprus Mail, PO Box 21144, 1502 Nicosia, Cyprus (☎ 22-818 585, 💻 www.cyprus-mail.com). Offices in Nicosia, Limassol, Larnaca and Paphos. Daily newspaper which includes a property supplement. Internet edition available.

Cyprus Weekly, PO Box 24977, 1306 Nicosia, Cyprus (☎ 22-666 047, 💻 www.cyprusweekly.com.cy). Published every Friday with a property supplement.

Financial Mirror (☎ 22-768 666, 💻 www.financialmirror.com). Cyprus' leading business newspaper, published weekly; also available online.

Property News

BuySell Magazine, BuySell Enterprises Ltd, Shops D23-D25, Coral Bay Plaza, Paphos (☎ 26-812 345, 💻 www.BuySell Cyprus.com). Weekly property magazine, with comprehensive listings, covering all areas of Cyprus. Linked to BuySell Real Estate.

Homes Overseas, Blendon Communications Ltd, 1st Floor, 1 East Poultry Avenue, London EC1A 9PT, UK (☎ 020-7002 8300, 💻 www.homesoverseas.co.uk). Bimonthly property magazine.

International Homes, 3 St John's Court, Moulsham Street, Chelmsford, Essex CM2 0JD, UK (☎ 01245-358877, 💻 www. international-homes.com). Bimonthly magazine.

Property & Home Cyprus, Catalan Ltd, 4 Petrou Tsirou St., CY-3021 Limassol (☎ 27-730 203, 💻 www.cypah.com). Monthly colour property magazine with associated articles. Available in Cyprus and the UK.

World of Property, 1 Commercial Road, Eastbourne, East Sussex BN21 3XQ, UK (☎ 01323-726040, ✉ outbounduk@ aol.com). Bimonthly property magazine.

Books

The books listed below are just a small selection of the many written for visitors to Cyprus. Note that some titles may be out of print, but may still be obtainable from book shops and libraries. Books prefixed with an asterisk are recommended by the author.

General Tourist Guides

*AA Baedeker Cyprus (AA Publishing)

AA Essential Cyprus, Robert Blumer (AA Publishing)

AA Explorer Cyprus, George McDonald (AA Publishing)

Berlitz Pocket Guide to Cyprus (Berlitz)

*Blue Guide: Cyprus, Bernard McDonagh & Ian Robertson (A&C Black)

Cyprus, Barnaby Rogerson (Cadogan)

Cyprus (Nelles Guides)

*Cyprus: The Rough Guide, Marc Dubin (Rough Guides)

Globetrotter Travel Guide to Cyprus, Paul Harcourt Davies (New Holland)

*Insight Guide Cyprus (APA Publications)

Landmark Visitors Guide: Northern Cyprus, K. Gursoy & L. Smith (Landmark)

*Lonely Planet: Cyprus, Paul Hellander (Lonely Planet)

*North Cyprus, Diana Darke (Bradt)

*Northern Cyprus, John & Margaret Goulding (Windrush Press)

Thomas Cook Traveller Cyprus (AA Publishing)

Visitors Guide to Cyprus, Fiona Bulmer (Moorland)

Miscellaneous

*Bitter Lemons of Cyprus, Lawrence Durrell (Faber)

Cyprus in Colour, Georges Kyriakou (KP Kyraikou)

The Cyprus Conspiracy, Brendan O'Malley & Ian Craig (IB Tauris)

Cyprus: Divided Island (World in Conflict), Tom & Thomas Streissguth (Lerner)

*Cyprus: Ethnic Conflict and International Politics, Joseph S. Joseph (Macmillan)

Cyprus: A Modern History, William Malllinson (IB Tauris)

Cyprus and its People, Vangelis Calotychos (Westview Press)

*The Cyprus Revolt, Nancy Cranshaw

Cyprus: the Search for a Solution, David Hannay (IB Tauris)

Echoes from the Dead Zone: Across the Cyprus Divide, Yiannis Papadakis (IB Tauris)

The European Union and Cyprus, Christopher Brewin (Eothen Press)

The Flora of Cyprus, R.D. Meikle (Bentham-Moxon Trust)

The Floral Charm of Cyprus, Sinclair (Interworld)

Footprints in Cyprus, Sir David Hunt (Trigraph)

*Journey into Cyprus, Colin Thubron (Penguin)

Nature of Cyprus, Christos Georgiades

Plant Checklist for Cyprus, Lance Chilton (Merengo)

The Republic of Cyprus, Kypros Chrysostomides (Martus Nijhoff)

Taste of Cyprus, G. Davies (Interworld)

Traditional Greek Cooking from Cyprus and Beyond, Julia & Xenia Chrysanthou (Olivetree)

*Walking in Cyprus, Donald Brown (Cicerone)

Walks in Western Cyprus, Lance Chilton (Marengo)

*Wines of Cyprus, Giovanni Mariti (Nicolas Books)

Major Property Exhibitions

Property exhibitions are common in the UK and Ireland and are popular with prospective property buyers, who can get a good idea of what's available in a particular area and make contact with estate agents and developers. Property exhibitions tend to have a smaller choice of properties in Cyprus than in some other countries and often only the main resort areas are represented. Below is a list of the main exhibitions in the UK and Ireland (all telephone numbers are in the UK). Note that you may be charged an admission fee.

Home Buyer (☎ 020-7069 5000, 💻 www.homebuyer.co.uk). Annual exhibition held in London.

Homes Overseas (☎ 020-7002 8300, 💻 www.homesoverseas. co.uk). Homes Overseas are the largest organisers of international property exhibitions and stage over 30 exhibitions annually throughout Britain and Ireland (plus a few abroad).

International Homes (☎ 01245-358877, 💻 www.international-homes.com). Exhibitions are held twice yearly, one in the north of England and one in the south.

International Property Show (☎ 01962-736712, 💻 www.inter-nationalpropertyshow.com). The International Property Show is held several times a year in Dublin, London and Manchester.

A Place in the Sun Live! (☎ 0870-272 8800, 💻 www.aplacein thesunlive.com). 'A Place in the Sun Live!' exhibitions are currently held twice a year in London.

World Class Homes (☎ 0800-731 4713 (UK only), 💻 www. worldclasshomes.co.uk). Exhibitions organised by World Class Homes are held in small venues around Britain and feature mainly UK property developers.

World of Property (☎ 01323-726040, 💻 www.outbound publishing.com). The World of Property magazine publishers (see Appendix B) also organise three large property exhibitions a year, two in the south of England and one in the north.

Appendix C: USEFUL WEBSITES

Republic of Cyprus

Cypria.com (🖥 www.cypria.com). Cyprus portal for news, sport and business and weather. Links to other European sites.

Cyprus (🖥 www.cyprus.gov.cy). Government site.

Cyprus Airways (🖥 www.cyprusairways.com). Booking and flight information.

Cyprus Net (🖥 www. cyprus-net.com). An internet directory for Cyprus and a portal to all kinds of websites, such as education, insurance, business and economy, news and media.

Kypros-Net: The World of Cyprus (🖥 www.kypros.org). Lots of varied information, including news in Greek and English, sport, weather, tourism, political information and details of a Greek language course (with CyBC).

Republic of Cyprus Public Information Office (🖥 www.poi. gov.cy). Official mouthpiece of the government of the Republic of Cyprus. Good for statistics, press information and background to the Cyprus political situation.

Welcome to Cyprus (🖥 www.welcometocyprus.com). Excellent guide to Cyprus, including comprehensive business directory, history, news, sport and entertainment.

Northern Cyprus

Cyprus Turkish Airlines (🖥 www.kthy.net).

The Republic of Northern Cyprus (🖥 www.trncgov.com). TRNC government website.

Super Cyprus (🖥 www.super-cyprus.com). Northern Cyprus portal.

TRNC Ministry of Tourism and Environment (🖥 www. tourism.trnc.net).

General Websites

ExpatBoards (🖥 www.expatboards.com). The mega website for expatriates, with popular discussion boards and special areas for Britons, Americans, expatriate taxes, and other important issues.

Escape Artist (💻 www.escapeartist.com). An excellent website and probably the most comprehensive, packed with resources, links and directories covering most expatriate destinations. You can also subscribe to the free monthly online expatriate magazine, Escape from America.

Expat Exchange (💻 www.expatexchange.com). Reportedly the largest online community for English-speaking expatriates, provides a series of articles on relocation and also a question and answer facility through its expatriate network.

Expat Forum (💻 www.expatforum.com): Provides interesting cost of living comparisons as well as seven European Union country-specific forums and chats (Belgium, the Czech Republic, France, Germany, the Netherlands, Spain and the UK).

Expat World (💻 www.expatworld.net). Newsletter containing a wealth of information for American and British expatriates, including a subscription newsletter.

Expatriate Experts (💻 www.expatexpert.com). Provides invaluable advice and support.

Expats International (💻 www.expats2000.com). The international job centre for expats and their recruiters.

Real Post Reports (💻 www.realpostreports.com). Relocation services, recommended reading lists and plenty of interesting 'real-life' stories containing anecdotes and impressions written by expatriates in just about every city in the world.

Travel Documents (💻 www.traveldocs.com). Useful information about travel, specific countries and the documents needed to travel.

World Travel Guide (💻 www.wtgonline.com). A general website for world travellers and expatriates.

American Websites

Americans Abroad (💻 www.aca.ch). This website offers advice, information and services to Americans abroad.

US Government Trade (💻 www.usatrade.gov). A huge website providing a wealth of information principally for Americans planning to trade and invest abroad, but useful for anyone planning a move abroad.

Australian & New Zealand Websites

Australians Abroad (💻 www.australiansabroad.com). Information for Australians concerning relocating, plus a forum to exchange information and advice.

Southern Cross Group (💻 www.southern-cross-group.org). A website for Australians and New Zealanders providing information and the exchange of tips.

British Websites

British Expatriates (💻 www.britishexpat.com). This website keeps British expatriates in touch with events and information about the UK.

Trade Partners (💻 www.tradepartners.gov.uk). A government-sponsored website whose main aim is to provide trade and investment information on just about every country in the world. Even if you aren't planning to do business abroad, the information is comprehensive and up to date.

UK Inland Revenue (💻 www.inlandrevenue.gov.uk/leaflets). Useful information about taxation issues and living and working abroad.

Worldwise Directory (💻 www.suzylamplugh.org/worldwise). This website is run by the Suzy Lamplugh charity for personal safety and provides a useful directory of countries with practical information and special emphasis on safety, particularly for women.

Websites for Women

Family Life Abroad (💻 www.familylifeabroad.com). A wealth of information and articles on coping with family life abroad.

Foreign Wives Club (⌨ www.foreignwivesclub.com). An online community for women in bicultural marriages.

Third Culture Kids (⌨ www.tckworld.com). A website designed for expatriate children living abroad.

Travel For Kids (⌨ www.travelforkids.com). Advice on travelling with children around the world.

Women of the World (⌨ www.wow-net.org). A website designed for female expats anywhere in the world.

Travel Information & Warnings

The websites listed below provide daily updated information about the political situation and natural disasters around the world, plus general travel and health advice and embassy addresses.

Australian Department of Foreign Affairs and Trade (⌨ www. dfat.gov.au/travel).

British Foreign and Commonwealth Office (⌨ www.fco. gov.uk).

Canadian Department of Foreign Affairs (⌨ www.dfait-maeci.gc.ca). They also publish a useful series of free booklets for Canadians moving abroad.

New Zealand Ministry of Foreign Affairs and Trade (⌨ www. mft.govt.nz).

SaveWealth Travel (⌨ www.save wealth.com/travel/warnings).

The Travel Doctor (⌨ www.tmvc.com.au). Contains a country by country vaccination guide.

US State Government (⌨ www.state.gov/travel). US government website.

World Health Organization (⌨ www.who.int).

APPENDIX D: WEIGHTS & MEASURES

Cyprus uses the metric system of measurement. Nationals of countries who are more familiar with the imperial system of measurement will find the tables on the following pages useful. Some comparisons shown are only approximate, but are close enough for most everyday uses. The following websites allow you to make instant conversions between different measurement systems: 🖳 www.omnis.demon.co.uk and 🖳 www.unit-conversion.info.

Women's Clothes

Continental	34 36 38 40 42 44 46 48 50 52
UK	8 10 12 14 16 18 20 22 24 26
US	6 8 10 12 14 16 18 20 22 24

Pullovers

	Women's	Men's
Continental	40 42 44 46 48 50	44 46 48 50 52 54
UK	34 36 38 40 42 44	34 36 38 40 42 44
US	34 36 38 40 42 44	sm med lar xl

Men's Shirts

Continental	36 37 38 39 40 41 42 43 44 46
UK/US	14 14 15 15 16 16 17 17 18 -

Men's Underwear

Continental	5	6	7	8	9	10
UK	34	36	38	40	42	44
US	sm	med		lar	xl	

Note: sm = small, med = medium, lar = large, xl = extra large

Children's Clothes

Continental	92	104	116	128	140	152
UK	16/18	20/22	24/26	28/30	32/34	36/38
US	2	4	6	8	10	12

Children's Shoes

Continental	18	19	20	21	22	23	24	25	26	27	28	29	30	31	32
UK/US	2	3	4	4	5	6	7	7	8	9	10	11	11	12	13
Continental	33	34	35	36	37	38
UK/US	1	2	2	3	4	5

Shoes (Women's and Men's)

Continental	35	36	37	37	38	39	40	41	42	42	43	44
UK	2	3	3	4	4	5	6	7	7	8	9	9
US	4	5	5	6	6	7	8	9	9	10	10	11

Weight

Imperial	Metric	Metric	Imperial
1oz	28.35g	1g	0.035oz
1lb*	454g	100g	3.5oz
1cwt	50.8kg	250g	9oz
1 ton	1,016kg	500g	18oz
2,205lb	1 tonne	1kg	2.2lb

Length

Imperial	Metric	Metric	Imperial
1in	2.54cm	1cm	0.39in
1ft	30.48cm	1m	3ft 3.25in
1yd	91.44cm	1km	0.62mi
1mi	1.6km	8km	5mi

Capacity

Imperial	Metric	Metric	Imperial
1 UK pint	0.57 litre	1 litre	1.75 UK pints
1 US pint	0.47 litre	1 litre	2.13 US pints
1 UK gallon	4.54 litres	1 litre	0.22 UK gallon
1 US gallon	3.78 litres	1 litre	0.26 US gallon

Note: An American 'cup' = around 250ml or 0.25 litre.

Area

Imperial	Metric	Metric	Imperial
1 sq. in	0.45 sq. cm	1 sq. cm	0.15 sq. in
1 sq. ft	0.09 sq. m	1 sq. m	10.76 sq. ft
1 sq. yd	0.84 sq. m	1 sq. m	1.2 sq. yds
1 acre	0.4 hectares	1 hectare	2.47 acres
1 sq. mile	2.56 sq. km	1 sq. km	0.39 sq. mile

Temperature

°Celsius	°Fahrenheit	
0	32	(freezing point of water)
5	41	
10	50	
15	59	
20	68	
25	77	
30	86	
35	95	
40	104	
50	122	

Notes: The boiling point of water is 100°C / 212°F.

Normal body temperature (if you're alive and well) is 37°C / 98.6°F.

Temperature Conversion

Celsius to Fahrenheit: multiply by 9, divide by 5 and add 32. (For a quick and approximate conversion, double the Celsius temperature and add 30.)

Fahrenheit to Celsius: subtract 32, multiply by 5 and divide by 9. (For a quick and approximate conversion, subtract 30 from the Fahrenheit temperature and divide by 2.)

Oven Temperatures

Gas	Electric	
	°F	°C
-	225–250	110–120
1	275	140
2	300	150
3	325	160
4	350	180
5	375	190
6	400	200
7	425	220
8	450	230
9	475	240

Air Pressure

PSI	Bar
10	0.5
20	1.4
30	2
40	2.8

Power

Kilowatts	Horsepower	Horsepower	Kilowatts
1	1.34	1	0.75

APPENDIX E: MAPS

The map of Cyprus opposite shows the six administrative districts of Cyprus and the district capitals (listed below, with Greek/Turkish names in brackets). The map on the following page shows the cities and main towns, villages of interest, airports and major geographical features. A map of the eastern Mediterranean is shown on page 6.

District/Capital

Famagusta (*Ammochostos*)

Kyrenia (*Girne*)

Larnaca (*Larnaka*)

Limassol (*Lemesos*)

Nicosia (*Lefkosa/Lefkosia*)

Paphos (*Pafos*)

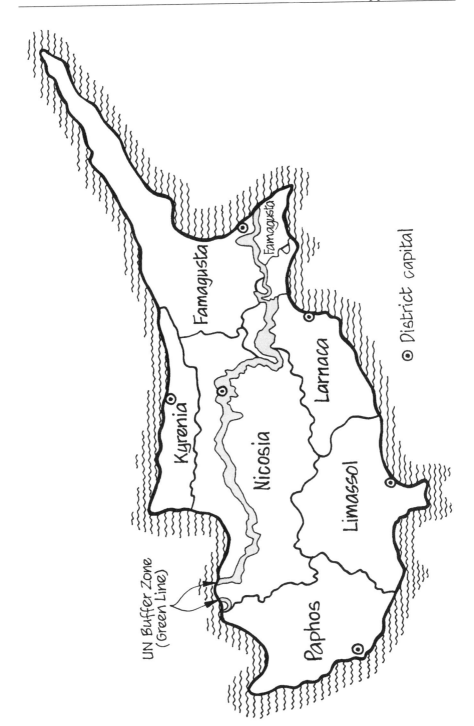

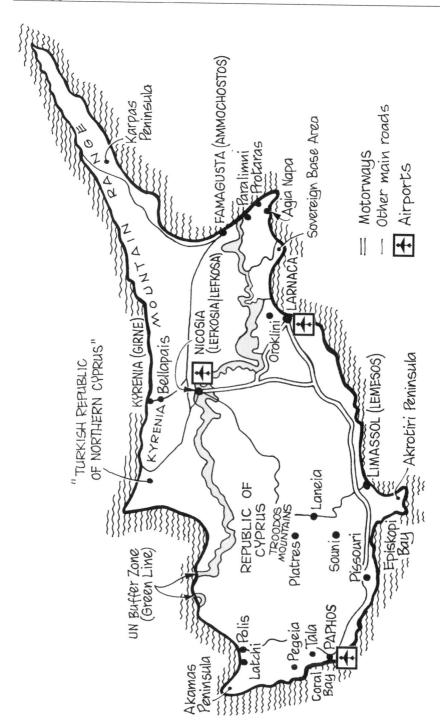

INDEX

Y

LIVING AND WORKING SERIES

Living and Working books are essential reading for anyone planning to spend time abroad, including holiday-home owners, retirees, visitors, business people, migrants, students and even extra-terrestrials! They're packed with important and useful information designed to help you **avoid costly mistakes and save both time and money.** Topics covered include how to:

- Find a job with a good salary & conditions
- Obtain a residence permit
- Avoid and overcome problems
- Find your dream home
- Get the best education for your family
- Make the best use of public transport
- Endure local motoring habits
- Obtain the best health treatment
- Stretch your money further
- Make the most of your leisure time
- Enjoy the local sporting life
- Find the best shopping bargains
- Insure yourself against most eventualities
- Use post office and telephone services
- Do numerous other things not listed above

Living and Working books are the most comprehensive and up-to-date source of practical information available about everyday life abroad. They aren't, however, boring text books, but interesting and entertaining guides written in a highly readable style.

Discover what it's *really* like to live and work abroad!

Order your copies today by phone, fax, post or email from: Survival Books, PO Box 3780, YEOVIL, BA21 5WX, United Kingdom (☎/🖷 +44 (0)1935-700060, ✉ sales@survivalbooks.net, 🖥 www.survivalbooks.net).

BUYING A HOME SERIES

Buying a Home books, including *Buying, Selling & Letting Property*, are essential reading for anyone planning to purchase property abroad. They're packed with vital information to guide you through the property purchase jungle and help you **avoid the sort of disasters that can turn your dream home into a nightmare!** Topics covered include:

- Avoiding problems
- Choosing the region
- Finding the right home and location
- Estate agents
- Finance, mortgages and taxes
- Home security
- Utilities, heating and air-conditioning
- Moving house and settling in
- Renting and letting
- Permits and visas
- Travelling and communications
- Health and insurance
- Renting a car and driving
- Retirement and starting a business
- And much, much more!

Buying a Home books are the most comprehensive and up-to-date source of information available about buying property abroad. Whether you want a detached house, townhouse or apartment, a holiday or a permanent home, these books will help make your dreams come true.

Save yourself time, trouble and money!

Order your copies today by phone, fax, post or email from: Survival Books, PO Box 3780, YEOVIL, BA21 5WX, United Kingdom (☎/▤ +44 (0)1935-700060, ✉ sales@survivalbooks.net, 🖥 www.survivalbooks.net).

OTHER SURVIVAL BOOKS

The Alien's Guides: *The Alien's Guides to Britain and France provide an 'alternative' look at life in these popular countries and will help you to appreciate the peculiarities (in both senses) of the British and French.*

The Best Places to Buy a Home in France/Spain: The most comprehensive homebuying guides to France or Spain, containing detailed profiles of the most popular regions, with guides to property prices, amenities and services, employment and planned developments.

Buying, Selling and Letting Property: The most comprehensive and up-to-date source of information available for those intending to buy, sell or let a property in the UK.

Foreigners in France/Spain: Triumphs & Disasters: Real-life experiences of people who have emigrated to France and Spain, recounted in their own words – warts and all!

Lifelines: Essential guides to specific regions of France and Spain, containing everything you need to know about local life. Titles in the series currently include the Costa Blanca, Costa del Sol, Dordogne/Lot, Normandy and Poitou-Charentes; Brittany Lifeline is to be published in summer 2005.

Making a Living: Essential guides to self-employment and starting a business in France and Spain.

Renovating & Maintaining Your French Home: The ultimate guide to renovating and maintaining your dream home in France: what to do and what not to do, how to do it and, most importantly, how much it will cost.

Retiring Abroad: The most comprehensive and up-to-date source of practical information available about retiring to a foreign country, containing profiles of the 20 most popular retirement destinations.

Broaden your horizons with Survival Books!

Order your copies today by phone, fax, post or email from: Survival Books, PO Box 3780, YEOVIL, BA21 5WX, United Kingdom (☎/🖨 +44 (0)1935-700060, ✉ sales@survivalbooks.net, 🖥 www.survivalbooks.net).

Qty.	Title	Price (incl. p&p)			Total
		UK	Europe	World	
	The Alien's Guide to Britain	£6.95	£8.95	£12.45	
	The Alien's Guide to France	£6.95	£8.95	£12.45	
	The Best Places to Buy a Home in France	£13.95	£15.95	£19.45	
	The Best Places to Buy a Home in Spain	£13.95	£15.95	£19.45	
	Buying a Home Abroad	£13.95	£15.95	£19.45	
	Buying a Home in Cyprus	£13.95	£15.95	£19.45	
	Buying a Home in Florida	£13.95	£15.95	£19.45	
	Buying a Home in France	£13.95	£15.95	£19.45	
	Buying a Home in Greece	£13.95	£15.95	£19.45	
	Buying a Home in Ireland	£11.95	£13.95	£17.45	
	Buying a Home in Italy	£13.95	£15.95	£19.45	
	Buying a Home in Portugal	£13.95	£15.95	£19.45	
	Buying a Home in South Africa	£13.95	£15.95	£19.45	
	Buying a Home in Spain	£13.95	£15.95	£19.45	
	Buying, Letting & Selling Property	£11.95	£13.95	£17.45	
	Foreigners in France: Triumphs & Disasters	£11.95	£13.95	£17.45	
	Foreigners in Spain: Triumphs & Disasters	£11.95	£13.95	£17.45	
	Costa Blanca Lifeline	£11.95	£13.95	£17.45	
	Costa del Sol Lifeline	£11.95	£13.95	£17.45	
	Dordogne/Lot Lifeline	£11.95	£13.95	£17.45	
	Poitou-Charentes Lifeline	£11.95	£13.95	£17.45	
	Living & Working Abroad	£14.95	£16.95	£20.45	
	Living & Working in America	£14.95	£16.95	£20.45	
	Living & Working in Australia	£14.95	£16.95	£20.45	
	Living & Working in Britain	£14.95	£16.95	£20.45	
	Living & Working in Canada	£16.95	£18.95	£22.45	
	Living & Working in the European Union	£16.95	£18.95	£22.45	
	Living & Working in the Far East	£16.95	£18.95	£22.45	
	Living & Working in France	£14.95	£16.95	£20.45	
Total carried forward (see over)					

ORDER FORM

Qty.	Title	Price (incl. p&p) UK	Europe	World	Total
			Total brought forward		
	Living & Working in Germany	£16.95	£18.95	£22.45	
	L&W in the Gulf States & Saudi Arabia	£16.95	£18.95	£22.45	
	L&W in Holland, Belgium & Luxembourg	£14.95	£16.95	£20.45	
	Living & Working in Ireland	£14.95	£16.95	£20.45	
	Living & Working in Italy	£16.95	£18.95	£22.45	
	Living & Working in London	£13.95	£15.95	£19.45	
	Living & Working in New Zealand	£14.95	£16.95	£20.45	
	Living & Working in Spain	£14.95	£16.95	£20.45	
	Living & Working in Switzerland	£16.95	£18.95	£22.45	
	Making a Living in Spain	£13.95	£15.95	£19.45	
	Normandy Lifeline	£11.95	£13.95	£17.45	
	Renovating & Maintaining Your French Home	£16.95	£18.95	£22.45	
	Retiring Abroad	£14.95	£16.95	£20.45	
				Grand Total	

Order your copies today by phone, fax, post or email from: Survival Books, PO Box 3780, YEOVIL, BA21 5WX, United Kingdom (☎/▤ +44 (0)1935-700060, ✉ sales@survivalbooks.net, 🖥 www.survivalbooks.net). If you aren't entirely satisfied, simply return them to us within 14 days for a full and unconditional refund.

I enclose a cheque for the grand total/Please charge my Amex/Delta/Maestro (Switch)/MasterCard/Visa card as follows. (delete as applicable)

Card No. _ _ _ _   _ _ _ _   _ _ _ _   _ _ _ _   Security Code* _ _ _

Expiry date _____   Issue number (Maestro/Switch only) _____

Signature _____   Tel. No. _____

NAME _____

ADDRESS _____

_____

_____

* The security code is the last three digits on the signature strip.

NOTES

NOTES

NOTES

NOTES

NOTES

NOTES

NOTES

NOTES